DAN SICKLES

GENERAL DANIEL E. SICKLES

DAN SICKLES

HERO OF GETTYSBURG AND
"YANKEE KING OF SPAIN"

———◆———

By *EDGCUMB PINCHON*

Doubleday, Doran and Company, Inc.

Garden City, New York
1945

To

DANIEL EDGAR SICKLES

who shares my view that his grandsire
belongs to history—and so
to history's probing, impartial light.

What is this Man, thy darling kissed and cuffed,
Thou lustingly engender'st,
To sweat, and make his brag, and rot,
Crowned with all honour and all shamefulness?
                                                   —FRANCIS THOMPSON

My thanks to Claribel Castle who,
with quick insight for the problem,
sensitive criticism for the page,
played no small part in bringing
this book to birth.

Contents

―――――◆―――――

Illustrations

DAN SICKLES

PART ONE: MANHATTAN OVERTURE

CHAPTER I

Instead of a Foreword

———◆◆———

WHEN HE FIRST OPENED HIS EYES in a modest New York home October 20, 1819, the skyscape beyond the Battery was fretted with the spars of hundreds of tall sailing ships. President Monroe was in the White House, Queen Victoria-to-be still in the nursery. . . .

When, May 3, 1914, those eyes—keen, gray, recalcitrant—closed for the last time, a stupendous one-hundred-year cycle almost had run its course. Woodrow Wilson was busying himself with the New Freedom at home, the Familyhood of Nations abroad. George V and Wilhelm Hohenzollern were exchanging cousinly notes. British dreadnaughts nosed unobtrusively toward Scapa Flow. German cruisers clotted at Kiel. . . .

Ninety-four years of America's turgid adolescence! And some fifty of them spent in the thick of national affairs. . . .

Down the roaring decades that blent a score of polyglot peoples to a new breed, thrust Mexico across the Rio Grande and Colorado, Canada beyond the Columbia, the West out to mid-Pacific, his was a stormy, dramatic figure in Congress, on the battlefield, at the courts of Madrid and St. James's, in the *palacios nacionales* of Colombia, Panama, Peru. . . .

And yet, on the crowded shelf of American biography, his niche stands vacant.

The fact is curious, and needs some explanation.

While, in odd paragraphs scattered through hundreds of old

volumes and newspaper files, his official record stands fairly complete, these sources give almost no glimpse of the man himself. And, in this instance, the personal archives—letters, diaries, the intimate memorabilia—so essential to the biographer's task, were almost entirely lacking. Some of this material had been lost; part of it had been left in forgotten caches here and abroad; the great bulk of it had been stolen—and, for a long time, was thought destroyed. Also, unfortunately, there could be small recourse to personal recollections. He outlived all the friends of his prime. His family, for the last thirty-five years of his life, had held no contact with him.

But, during the past two years, elaborate and persistent research has succeeded in retrieving a great many missing documents. Some of the most important of these—recaptured amid wartime complications in France and Spain, dispatched by boat and impounded by the British at Bermuda—were dictated from memory pending their release.

And so, at last, amid delays and difficulties—the present portrait: an attempt to paint "the man himself" in something of his complex human actuality, in something of the crimson and the black, the dun and the gold of his dauntless, brilliant, beclouded career.

Ambition drove him, patriotism inspired him, a tremendous vitality supported him; courage, eloquence, intellectual vigor, executive capacity lent their aid; ill chance thwarted him; undisciplined passions betrayed him; self-assurance, decisiveness, impetuosity gave a dramatic flair to his actions. But, first and last, the central fact of him abides in something profoundly characteristic of his era and his breed—his deep-rooted indomitability. . . .

Success, tragedy, crime, battle and mutilation, obloquy, neglect —he knew them all. But nothing could defeat him—not even himself!

A study in the contradictions of human personality, the dissonant tonalities of fate! With a genius for friendship, few men made more bitter enemies. His amours, fleeting as fierce, were innumerable, and recall—at other levels—the erotic record of a Liszt, a Goethe, a Pancho Villa. But he failed to create a single lasting, or significant, relationship.

A brilliant pleader at the bar, a politician and acknowledged leader of Tammany in his twenties, a diplomat in the early thirties, lover of the arts and conversant with the major languages of Europe, his education was heterodox, broken, self-chosen.

Notorious as he was for his affairs with women, he yet, in a mad moment, shot to death the son of Francis Scott Key who had engaged the affections of his young wife; and, in the most sensational trial in the history of American jurisprudence, was pronounced "not guilty." But immediately thereafter, to the astonished scandal of all Washington society, he reinstated his beloved "Terry" in her former position; and in a challenging letter to the press—"I am not aware of any code of morals which makes it infamous to forgive"—defended his action against the gossips.

At the outbreak of the Civil War he raised and equipped the Excelsior Brigade; and, with no more than an amateur's knowledge of military matters, rapidly rose to the rank of major general, came close to salvaging—and but for the gross neglect of his pleas for ammunition almost certainly would have salvaged—the disgraceful Union defeat at Chancellorsville; and, at Gettysburg, left to his own devices and boldly advancing his troops to a dangerous salient, won fame and blame, and lost a leg.

His political enemies were acrid; an inimical press missed few opportunities to belittle and deride him. But Lincoln dispatched him as his secret emissary to the Latin-American republics. Grant sent him as minister to Spain in the midst of the Cuban turmoil. Both men prized him dearly, as did Buchanan, Pierce, Stanton. Longstreet, his immediate opponent at Gettysburg, frankly adored him. . . .

Adolphe Thiers made him "Grand Croix de la Légion d'Honneur"; Bismarck gave him his confidence, Queen Isabella her couch. Europe knew him as the "Yankee King of Spain."

In old age, virile, crusty, benignant, he still remained a menace to his enemies and the secret terror of society matrons with venturesome daughters. Beloved more than any other by the men of the Grand Army, he served them to the end.

An American, then—"one of the turbulent breed," spanning a century of America's coming of age, and summing up in himself —after a dynamic fashion of his own—the major motivations of his time, here General Dan Sickles rides by.

AUTHOR'S NOTE: *In his last days Dan Sickles gave the year 1825 as the date of his birth. Whether in vanity or as a result of failing memory, he thus lopped six years from his actual age. The date here given, however, is sustained by the family archives, and is indubitably correct.*

CHAPTER II

America Emergent

———◆———

THE HUSTLING THIRTIES . . . America-to-be emerging. The Louisiana Purchase had stretched her borders from Mississippi to the Rockies, from Canada to the Gulf. By mule-drawn barge along the new Erie Canal, by cart and coach over the still newer Cumberland Road, by great rafts—equipped with cabins and bearing entire families with stock and tools—drifting adown the Ohio, native America streamed westward. *On to the Promised Land!*

At the same time, as though to fill the void thus left, great hordes of eager, sturdy peasants—Irish, English, German, Italian, Dutch, Scandinavian, even the Greek, Turk, Arab, Armenian—came swarming through the port of New York. *Behold the Promised Land!*

What if to many of these newcomers the Promised Land soon lost its dream-painted tints? For the most part they held on to their faith and went to work with a will. . . .

Were there not jobs to be had at the factories—even if at the pittance dictated by greed and the glut of hands? Was there not "political freedom"—or, at least, the vote, and a chance to swap it now and again for a pot of beer? And out West—if one could dodge the red scalper and the white speculator—was not good government land to be had for a dollar an acre? Best of all: there were no class distinctions, no arrogant lords and ladies, only the Rich and the Poor; no monarch—even if certain Wall Street gentlemen were said to have holdings larger than a dozen European duchies. But what if the picture were not so bright as it had been painted? One thing was sure: opportunity was open to all; the prizes beyond belief. Wasn't Andrew Jackson born in a shanty? See him now—in the White House! And look at John Jacob Astor—yesterday a penniless shagpate unable to sign his name—with his palaces and coaches, his twenty million dollars, still peddling the Indians cheap rotgut for priceless pelts, and thumbing his nose at the government! That shows what can be done! All one has to do is to be smart, get busy, go West. . . .

Such was the arising spirit of the time—breeding like a contagion.

With every ship that belched bundle-clutching humanity at the Battery, New York real estate boomed, stocks rose, western land prices stiffened. Soon even the stay-at-homes caught the excitement spread by this explosion of repressed peoples loosed on the wharves. They, too, waked, looked about, fell to.

In the thirties, in truth, the young Republic, hitherto a bit confused as to its destiny—what with the British invasion, humiliating struggles with the Seminoles, open treason in New England, incipient rebellion in the South, bitter feuding between shipmasters and millowners—suddenly began to achieve selfhood, began to sense its own vast potentialities and to realize that its strength, and the future of the democratic tradition, lay no longer with the Seaboard but with the new states being builded by "the men of the western waters." Instinctively it turned its back squarely upon Europe and set its face toward the Rockies. At the same time a great wave of hope swept the country. Scarcely a man, native or foreign born, but felt its impetus, gained a new sense of his own possibilities, or failed to quicken his pace under the exciting illusion that El Dorado lurked just around the corner. . . .

The Decade of Dream! And the birth of the American spirit of optimism! No ephemeral phenomenon, that spirit, but a force destined to endure, find cosmic voice in an Emerson, a Walt Whitman, and, in one hundred years, forge, amid froth and folly and fire, a civilization mechanistic, speed-mad, drab, corrupt, but, materially, the most powerful and enterprising known to man.

And with optimism came the spirit of venture. These shores, from the first, were peopled by those who had "taken a chance"—usually a tremendous chance. Now the new day, the ever expanding frontier, called for fresh gambles with fortune. And there emerged, especially in the "western waters," the American saluted by Kipling nearly a century later, who—

> *. . . greets th' embarrassed Gods, nor fears*
> *To shake the iron hand of Fate*
> *Or match with Destiny for beers.*

But optimism and readiness to bet on the board must be backed by action. If one is to forge ahead of the other fellow, one must get busy. And get busy every man did. "Even the carts proceed at a gallop," said one foreign critic of the time. Said another, "One has the sense that everyone of this people is afraid of being late somewhere." The spirit of hustle!

Optimism, take a chance, hustle—all good things in a raw people at grips with a raw empire. But in a competitive economy based on the right of the individual to appropriate the public resources, these inevitably gave rise to something less admirable: the spirit of "each for himself and devil take the hindmost!"

And westward lay a vast territory for the looting. Ahead of the settler sped the speculator. Terms of purchase pre-empted crops for years to come. The Free West became an ever receding mirage; and, usually, with the first furrow the adventurous farmer plowed, he sealed himself and all his family serfs for life to the new but invisible lords of mortgage bank and grain pit.

Still the optimistic flame could not be quenched. If there were those who wondered why a democracy on paper was not also a democracy on earth, they were few and unheard. An odd success, a stroke of luck here and there served to keep the illusion alive; and, as an ironic corollary to frontier conditions, the man who profited most by the scheme of things—the gentleman who never hitched a trace nor turned a sod—soon came to be looked upon as a new kind of titular deity to be envied, respected, copied. Naturally, if insidiously, there arose, as a permanent American attitude, the conviction that money is the man, and the making of money—no matter how brutal or shabby the means—the greatest of all private and civic virtues. The Calf donned a Puritan collar!

At the same time the unprecedented growth of population tended to throw the political machinery in reverse—especially in the larger cities. Doubtless a system of simple geographical representation was suitable enough in the days of the town meeting, when folk, gathered in small communities, knew their neighbors—and the candidate. But as villages became towns, towns cities, when in the flux and flow of a swarming, new population, the town meeting disappeared, no man knew his neighbor any more, nor, often enough, so much as the names of his representatives until he read them on his ballot paper, the system revealed itself as a pathetic anachronism. More and more the business of selecting and seating candidates fell into the hands of small groups of gentlemen anxious to relieve the public of the burden. Adepts these! Rome knew them—in her putrescence. Of all types: the smooth shyster with a social veneer, the raw plug-ugly, the educated schemer, the brawny Irish saloonkeeper, the flash brothelmaster, they had one thing in common: they, as Boss Tweed, with gentle pride, used to say of his associates, "saw their opportunities and took 'em." Largely recruited from the under-world, imbued with its cynical realism, a bit short on grammar but long on human psychology, they operated instinctively on the theory that the average citizen works for nothing but his pocket and his glory all the time. Their technique was to make each supporter, no matter how humble, feel that, in one way or another, he was "in on the game." And theory and technique worked amazingly. Giving three hundred and sixty-five days a year to a matter which occupied the average voter a few hours at most, men such as these found it easy enough to select their own candidates, play boodling benefactor to masses of ignorant immigrants, forge naturalization papers for those that lacked them, vote the same man a dozen times, stuff or steal ballot boxes, organize gangs to terrorize opponents from the polls. And once in control and up to their elbows in the treasury, they found it easy enough to suborn newspapers, bribe off enemies, win the open or tacit support of the various financial groups seeking legislative favors or a blind eye to taxes. . . .

The Founding Fathers could not be expected to foresee that a system based on the odd opposites of economic privilege and town-meeting politics would work out this way. But the logic of events outwits the logic of reason. And the Great Experiment was not fifty years old before its actual result was to crowd municipal councils and legislative halls, not with the intended "chosen best," but, despite splendid exceptions here and there, with the ultimate "unchosen worst," the offal of a social system gone awry. The rise of "machine politics" as the product of geographical representation plus economic privilege and public indifference put legislation on the market, thieves at the public till. It also, even for the honest and aspiring, early and often made itself the sole entrance to political life; and a man had to swim through slime to get to a place where he could bring his own ideas to bear. In New York City the machine—rooted, ironically enough, in America's first organization of defence against aristocratic Federalist tendencies—early had developed into that tenacious political octopus: Tammany Hall—originally a fraternal organization pretending Indian origin, affecting Indian ceremonial dress, and ludicrously organized into "wigwams" superintended by "sachems."

And whatever the Founding Fathers foresaw or did not foresee —and Washington had moments of tragically true prevision—the realistic fact remains that Tammany Hall, born with the Republic, proved to be the archetype and Founding Father of the henceforth actual—as opposed to the intended—administration of American public affairs, municipal, state, national.

And thus in the thirties, amid the drums of hope and hustle, Babel at the Battery, steamboats churning Mississippi mud, settlers and speculators racing to the Rockies, while Tammany Hall set its feet on New York City and with one hand reached for Albany and with the other reached for the Capitol, it happened that the American Dream quietly was folded up and put away in the national garret—to be taken out henceforth, like grandmother's wedding gown, only for Charades. In its place appeared new twin deities in the American Pantheon: the Political Boss, and that "rugged individualist," the Unrepentant Thief.

The American Tragedy—possibly. But it turned out well enough for George Garrett Sickles, sturdy, rigid Knickerbocker, sixth of his American line, proud of his ancestor, Zacharia Van Sicklen, one of the pioneers of New Amsterdam (later New York City) and founder of New Rochelle, proud of deep family roots across the seas, proud also of the fact that he was the first patent attorney in these States. Somewhere in the thirties, growing dissatisfied with much work, modest fees, he plunged into the current gamble in New York real estate. He couldn't miss. Real estate—that marvelous sponge that sops up the community wealth as fast as it is made—was overcharged. He made his bets, took his profits, proved himself an up-and-coming American of his time and place; and, in a few years, amassed such millions as needed a suite of offices at 74 Nassau Street to take care of them. And it was here that his only son, Daniel Edgar —both pride and problem—received his first initiation into law and business.

Little is recorded of Daniel's childhood. It is not until the spring of '36 that he comes fairly to view. Then a few months short of seventeen, he was standing on the stoop of the Glens Falls Academy for Young Gentlemen, viewing the street and the future with a brooding, angry, meditative eye.

A sinewy, good-looking lad, gray-eyed, with a mop of honey-colored hair, dressed substantially in homespun coat, knickerbockers, wool hose and stout brogans, he looked what he was—a sturdy young Dutch American bent on adventure.

Under his ribs pulsed the song of his day: "Believe: take a chance: every man for himself!" He had been marooned in this dull private school upstate because recently typhus had raged in filthy New York; and, also, he had been rather something to handle—even for a Knickerbocker paterfamilias. But the sense of his time stirred in his blood.

Behind the heavy door he had banged on himself, a wizened dominie hugged his haunches, endeavored to resume his dignity and quell the timorous riot of a score of happily scandalized boys. In an unlucky moment the headmaster had undertaken to whip the insubordinate Dan—and had been soundly whipped instead.

On the stoop Dan, still breathing a little hard, looked up and down the empty village street. Suddenly decision snapped. Resolutely he turned north—toward his favorite haunt: the print shop of Stephen Adams, editor of the Glens Falls *Messenger*. Had he not already learned for fun to set type, write up news? Very well, he would get old Adams to take him on as apprentice, give him room and board for a while. Someday he would be the owner, editor, master printer of a great American newspaper. Devil take Glens Falls Academy!

He was not surprised that he felt so calm—or that suddenly everything looked so different! No more than a chick that breaks its shell did he find any need to explain to himself how it happened that in one vicious tussle he had crossed a line, opened a door on himself, passed from schoolboy to man. He only knew that it was so, that school was done, that he was outward bound on his own. Possible objections? In two strides he had forgotten them. Decision —action! Reflection burned to an intuitive flash.

So it was to be with him—in Congress, at Chancellorsville, Gettysburg, in London, Paris, Madrid, and on the bloodstained curb of Washington's Lafayette Square.

CHAPTER III

In Search of an Education

———❦———

IF THE *Messenger* was easily seduced, not so George Garrett Sickles.
He promptly ordered his son to return to school or come home.
Dan did neither, but stuck to his typesetting stick. Finding letters of
no avail, the bearded, strong-jawed father tucked his wife under
his arm and descended on Glens Falls. It was Knickerbocker to
Knickerbocker. Stalemate! In the upshot, Dan's status as an independent wage earner with a lust for printer's ink was recognized
de facto if not *de jure*.

But what gave the meeting a cast of fatality was the presence
of a new friend the parents had contacted en route and brought
along with them—a young professor of New York University. A
fascinating fellow, this Charles Da Ponte—and a member of a fascinating family. His father, the uncannily brilliant Jewish scholar and
poetaster, Emmanuel Conegliano, self-styled Lorenzo Da Ponte—
apparently after the scintillant Venetian Jesuit—was a master of
Hebrew, Latin, Greek, and of most of the languages of Europe.
Formerly Court Poet to the Emperor Joseph of Hapsburg, comrade of Casanova in erotic adventure, librettist to Mozart, and the
intimate of all the great and scandalous in the dying, decadently
iridescent years of Europe's eighteenth-century culture, he had fled
to the New World refuge—for reasons. And, for the past thirty
years, a proud, pathetic sponger, dazzling, insinuating, grandiose,
he had reigned as a kind of seedy social lion over New York's naïve
intellectual circles.

Young Da Ponte, black-eyed, magnetic, speaking with animal ease
the half-dozen languages he had acquired from the cradle, and already, at thirty, America's first professor of the philosophy of history, captured Dan's imagination at a stroke. And with that spon-

taneous outgoing which henceforth was to mark him whenever his eye lit with recognition on man or mistress, Dan grappled him. Da Ponte returned the grip. Raw, rebellious schoolboy and sensitive, sophisticated scholar became classic friends. But it was a year or so before they could get together again. . . .

The Panic of '37—caused by President Jackson's transference of government funds from the privately owned and badly mismanaged Bank of the United States to the regional state banks—brought about a slump in New York real estate; and the elder Sickles was glad, for a while, that his son could prove self-supporting. In fact, during this interlude—when paper fortunes vanished as magically as they had been made—Dan, now a good journeyman printer, came from Glens Falls to New York, and, taking a job with Mr. Turney of Fulton Street, set about contributing to the depleted family exchequer. But in due time the panic passed—as panics will. New York real estate boomed once more—higher than ever. And Sickles, senior, realizing on the market, wisely invested much of his profits in the broad and productive acres of a farming estate at Livingston, New Jersey. To him now—a trifle sobered by his recent experience—the life of a gentleman farmer seemed the better part of valor. He also deemed it a good life for his son; and he set about training him to take over the care of the estate. But Dan had other ideas. Since he first had met young Da Ponte, he had lusted for a college education. Lacking the necessary scholastic equipment, he begged his father to be allowed a spell of precollege preparation in the Da Ponte household. The response was not encouraging; and so, after an honest trial of hogs and apples, Dan, in characteristic fashion, suddenly packed his traps and left home to fend for himself. Then, like a wise man well whipped, George Sickles relented. Once more Dan won his way. A week later he was installed with his dream and his idol in the Da Ponte household.

An island in time, the Da Ponte home was—and for many years, by grace of benignant friends, had been—the center of the last phosphorescence of eighteenth-century culture transplanted to a youthful, blatant New York. The great rambling, half-decrepit house, once the baroque pride of a shipowner, had become both the rookery of the Da Ponte clan and the *Artistenheim* of New York's intelligentsia. And presiding over it, with the aid of seven languages, a gourmet's knowledge of cookery, and a flair for discipline, the signora Da

Ponte, that energetic Italian madonna, managed, on an easily exhausted budget, to prove herself an inexhaustible hostess to her husband's eager and ravenous guests.

The household was large and included, besides the exotic, irresponsible sire and his competent spouse, two unmarried sons, Joseph and Lorenzo, and Charles, the youngest, with his wife, and the clamorous Durant, their two-year-old. Also there was an adopted daughter—now a mother—and her husband. Of course, Lorenzo Da Ponte, barely able to secure his own existence, would adopt a daughter! Not celebrated for conventional rectitude, it is possible that he may have had certain paternal yearnings in the matter. Anyhow, very lovely and seductive, Maria early had attracted the attentions of that constant guest at the Da Ponte table, the maestro of the Montressor Opera Company, Signor Bagioli. The upshot had been a marriage and a new boarder—for opera was no road to wealth—also a baby. And when Dan entered the scene, that baby—a little chuckling imp—already had become the hub of the Da Ponte cosmos.

Her name was Teresa.

Always easily engaged by puppies, kittens, birds, butterflies—anything little, anything lovely—Dan now had his first experience with a human fledgling. And he was her captive on sight. She seemed to know it, always put on an act whenever he came awkwardly diddle-daddling over her crib.

At the same time he found himself in a dumfounding atmosphere where people talked endlessly and volubly in five or six languages—about what, he could only guess; where they greeted each other in French, discussed philosophy in German, criticized the wine in Italian, scolded the servants in English, and quarreled about Mediterranean politics in Spanish. . . .

He felt an outcast, stupidly deficient. But what these people could do he could do. . . . Already he was dreaming of a diplomatic career—as a step to the White House! Someday a command of languages might prove important. He would see what there was to all this!

And the Da Ponte family found him forever eager and questioning. He was young enough, plastic enough, quickly to catch sounds, intonations, phrases. Charles had laid it upon the household that they were to help his student and never give him a word of English. The pupil proved apt. He toiled at his grammars and waded boldly into conversations. A couple of years of this, and he could take tolerable care of himself at table in French, Italian, Spanish—and, at least, swear convincingly in German. At last he felt ready for New York University. And here, under the special tutelage of maestro Charles, he worked well for a few semesters.

Then the elder Da Ponte, well on in his eighties, gathered himself for his last literary effort, wrote an exquisite ode to his own demise, "Parti de la Vita," and within twenty-four hours folded himself to sleep. Three months later Charles, stricken with pneumonia, followed him. And Dan was left to struggle with his first experience of devastating loss. . . . He tried to behave with correct Knicker-bocker phlegm, but once the coffin of his beloved Charles was lowered, he broke down in such grief as scandalized the decent crowd of mourners. . . .

And when he got back to the stricken, shabby old house, there was Teresa—now four years old—puzzled and lonely, wanting to play. He couldn't stand it and fled from her in tears.

Student days were done. Nothing could make him go back to college. But he could not forsake the Da Ponte home. After a while he was in and out again, practicing his languages, romping with Teresa.

For a few months he lent a serious presence to his father's law and real estate practice. Then, sensing his future career, he apprenticed himself to the ranking law firm of B. F. Butler—Attorney General under President Van Buren. He studied hard, passed his examinations with credit, and was called to the bar. He was only twenty-four; and in his first case—involving a question of contested patents—argued before a board of commissioners at Washington, won high praise from Daniel Webster.

Thus ended Dan's youthful educational ambit. On the surface there seems nothing very remarkable about it. Actually it stands unique.

Characteristically, it was self-chosen throughout—and with an uncanny sense of the training his future career would require.

At the age when, as the newest and oldest pedagogies agree, most boys would be benefited by exchanging the schoolroom for the workshop and contact with the world for a while, he forsook desk and bench for the printer's case and a craft that went far to form the orderly prose and trenchant speech of his later life. That step did more for him: it gave him a knowledge of the working world and an understanding of the common man that served him well to the end.

And when he was ready to benefit by it, he chose—what the better type of university regards as its essential value—the informal private tutoring that comes of personal intimacy between student and teacher. And in his case the teacher was brilliant, and the contact a deep mutual attachment that implanted its influence for life. Dan entered the Da Ponte home an awkward, self-assertive lad: he left it with urbane manners, an awakened love of music, painting, literature, and—special gift of a master of the philosophy of history—a dispassionate approach to problems and a sense of historic perspective, that, in later years, distinguished even his minor political speeches.

Thereafter college and law studies were simply means to a clearly grasped end: the White House. When he entered the courtroom for the first time, he brought with him, as aides to his ambition, a trained mind, ease of manner, cultured sense, and a practical knowledge of life. He had given himself precisely the education he needed. It may be doubted if any vocational authority, endeavoring to guide him, could have done better—or as well.

Meanwhile, in New York forty thousand desperate unemployed enviously eyed the pigs fattening in the filthy gutters. The narrow sidewalks compelled them either to walk ankle-deep in mud or humbly to brush against a stream of immaculate tight pants and frock coats escorting velveted crinolines. Arkansas and Michigan were admitted as states. Texas had revolted against Mexico—and the tragedy of the Alamo quivered on the air. Colt invented his handy little tool for clinching arguments. The gentle Audubon issued his classic on American bird life. Longfellow was making neat verses. Congress passed its famous Gag Resolution tabling all further discussion of slavery. A genial Englishman, with half a million dollars to spare, founded the Smithsonian Institution—"for the diffusion of knowledge." And the first three thousand miles of American railroad had been built. French-Canadians revolted against British rule; a group of American enthusiasts tried to join them. The British interposed. And the steamer *Carolina* went over Niagara in flames.

Across the seas Queen Victoria, amid more than the usual palpitations, was perched on a throne long grown sordid, shabby, ridiculous. Promptly demanding a bedroom of her own, she met her ministers with a promise to "be good." Dickens in his Pickwick Papers was splashing the British face with laughter and tears and driving imprisonment for debt into limbo. Thackeray, with suavest irony, was taking the grand bourgeoisie apart. Macaulay was stunning Parliament with his spontaneous perfection of phrase. Wordsworth was in his lovely springtime—never to make summer. Tennyson was tuning up. Browning had taken to visiting the Barretts of Wimpole Street. Wheatstone and Cooke perfected the magnetic-needle telegraph. Ericsson's new screw steamer made ten miles an hour. The English Chartist movement—demanding universal suffrage —bled through riot and massacre. John Talbot first printed photographs on paper.

On the Continent, in these last days of the thirties, a rising ferment of anti-monarchist agitation mingled with a fresh efflorescence of the arts. Louis Philippe again narrowly escaped assassination. And George Sand, Alfred de Musset, Gautier, Heine, and Victor Hugo; Meyerbeer and his jealous rival, Rossini; Berlioz, Bellini, Chopin, and the mighty Liszt were creating a new Maytime in music and letters.

The nineteenth century was well on its way. And so was Dan Sickles. The Tammany Tiger had its eye on him. He had his eye on the Tiger. The question was who would swallow whom.

CHAPTER IV

Tammany Nights

THE FANTASTIC FORTIES! The American populace, groggily recuperating from a couple of panics, decided that it was time for a bold assertion of the rights of man. The presidential election was due. Van Buren proposed to succeed himself. But if we may believe Congressman Ogle, of Pennsylvania, he was not at all the right man to defend the rights of man, but was, in fact, an effete aristocrat spending his days lolling on "arabesqued divans" in the "Blue Elliptical Saloon" of the executive mansion, spraying himself with Parisian perfumes, sipping exotic wines, and gloating over the fabulous furnishings with which he had surrounded himself at the public expense. In a very remarkable speech Mr. Ogle recited the list of these furnishings to a wondering—and occasionally wandering—House. It took him two hours! But his effort keynoted a campaign.

Overnight the "Blue Elliptical Saloon" became metamorphosed into a Red Rag. And rallying all the available political odds and ends —abolitionists, anti-renters, conservatives, Websterites, and so forth— the Whigs prepared for a mighty popular charge upon it. For candidate they selected General William Henry Harrison who—so it was said—had dealt chastisement to the redskins on the field of Tippecanoe. Unwisely the Democratic press, perverting to a sneer what was originally only a pleasant Whig estimate of the candidate, proceeded to damn him as a man who would be content with "a log cabin and a barrel of cider." That was enough! Insurgent America leaped to the challenge.

It mattered not that General Harrison lived handsomely on a two-thousand-acre estate. In the facile fancy of a people bent on a picnic he suddenly became the desire of their hearts—an honest, fighting farmer reeking not of Parisian perfumes but of good, ripe manure; a man who loved his humble log cabin and drowned his sorrows not in exotic French wines but in good, hard American cider. It was a picture of the Plain Man to rouse every red-blooded and cider-loving American to battle.

Soon, in hamlet and city, parades appeared in the streets, shouting the mellifluous war cry, "Tippecanoe and Tyler too!" And the cabins were no hollow subterfuges, but realistically equipped with chimney, coonskin on door, and cider barrel by the steps. And as realistically equipped with gentlemen attending to the cider. Democracy was on the march—and a very delightful march it was! The only platform was the one that bore the barrel. The only issue—"Log Cabin versus Blue Elliptical Saloon!" And this gaily simple method of choosing the Chief Executive amply proved its efficacy. On a sparkling sea of cider Mr. Van Buren was floated out of the White House and General Harrison was floated in.

And when the young democracy finally sobered up (for devotion to hard cider had become a political passion hard to quell), it found itself with hardly time left to get dressed for the millennium. As far back as 1832 a Mr. William Miller, with the aid of the Bible and an astrological chart, had proven conclusively that the world would come to the end it always had richly deserved, precisely on July 23, 1843; and, since that time, he and his preacher cohorts had been admonishing careless Americans to prepare. With the passing years the movement had gained enormous proportions. The great tents of Millerite camp meetings mushroomed wherever city lot or village green offered pegging ground. And, as the time drew near, scores of thousands of crazed folk began casting away their worldly goods, turning their cattle loose, closing their shops, and giving themselves over to "watch-night" services that, often enough, lasted the clock around. "Ascension Robes" were in great demand; and the more wily haberdashers blossomed out with a great variety of cuts and styles. Muslin, however, was the favorite material—since it gave the wearer, according to one advertiser, "a pious and purified appearance," calculated, one may suppose, to deceive even Gabriel. Another advertiser, plastering his window with the sign, "Buy an Ascension Robe *now*—while the stock lasts—and be ready to meet the King of Kings!" did a rushing business up to the last hour. The Hour came—and passed. A hardened old world insisted upon another round or two yet. Mr. Miller, undaunted, announced a new date—but not before some thousands of simple souls who had gone to the hills and the mountains "to watch for the Coming" had suffered severely from exposure, exhaustion, destitution, while no few had slain themselves or gone mad.

And so, in the forties, were educed, in a rather spectacular way, two permanent idiosyncrasies of the national character: a passion for hokum, and a tendency to hysteria. And with them appeared a third: the lusty enjoyment of lofty speech. Sanctimonious grandiloquence, of course, was a characteristic of the age—here and abroad. But here it reached Olympian levels beyond the powers of even a British Chadband. The rising bourgeoisie, schooled but uncultured, got a little tight, in fact, on their first taste of the wine of words, and wishing to impress the world with their new-found superiority, fell,

drunkardwise, upon a virtuous verbosity, amusing and amazing. And
—in an epoch politically sordid, intellectually crass, sexually coarse—
press, platform, pulpit, the courts, Congress, disported themselves
with a tombstone diction suggesting nothing so much as robes and
wings, alabaster fingers pointing to the skies; and upon the slightest
provocation the air pullulated with "domestic altars," "chaste
bosoms," "sainted mothers," "virtuous females," "sublime heroes,"
"deathless deeds," and "elegant repasts."

But out West where sod must be turned—often gun on back—and
babes were thrust into the world with none to aid, there was laconic
stoicism, screaming silence aplenty.

Meanwhile America more than ever was on the move. The Cumberland—longest and most direct highway in the world—was thronged
from dawn to dusk with carts, coaches, cattle beneath a haze of dust.
The seventeen rail and steamboat routes out of Buffalo were blocked
with the migrant mass bound West. Overnight the Indian village of
Chicago had become a braggart, shanty metropolis with nothing to
sell but itself—and selling it big. In Oregon, British and American
settlers squabbled over boundary lines; and the cry "Fifty-four forty
or fight!" made chesty shouting. In California—long since softened
up for conquest by the infiltration of the Yankee mortgage shark—
Frémont, with a merely token display of powder and shot, knocked
the Eagle off his Cactus perch and trussed him up in the Stars and
Stripes. And just in time! Only a few months later a ranch hand,
John Marshall, cleaning the race of Sutter's flour mill, found a hand-
ful of gold in the tailings. After all the cheat and despair—El Dorado
at last!

In schooner keeled or wheeled, by fevered Isthmus, howling Horn,
prairie sprouting feathered death, the last, maddest, and most magnificent of the great migrations set face toward the sinking sun.

At the same time a determined young fellow in the cutaway and
top hat, mustache and goatee fashionable in the period, was getting
his initiation into politics. And Tammany Hall was an exciting school.
Myers gives a picture of one of its energetic discussions: "A row
began in the 'bloody Ould Sixth' by the breaking of some ballot
boxes. Both parties armed themselves with stones and bludgeons, and
the riot became general . . . until the militia hastened upon the scene
and restored order."

Tammany at that time was going through a change in personnel and administration. Hitherto it largely had been governed from above by the sachems of the society; but its dependence upon the under-world coupled with the vast increase of immigrant population rapidly tended to transfer the seat of power to the saloon and the sidewalk—the "ward heeler" and his "gangs."

Against this type of civic administration, the decent citizenry, scattered about in geographical wads, with only sporadic organiza-tion, and unable to give more than odd moments to political affairs, were virtually helpless. But the "heelers" controlling densely popu-lated wards of ignorant immigrant voters were anything but helpless. And for the rest, the bribe or the bludgeon soon persuaded opposition into silence or collusion.

In the forties political morals were, perhaps, no lower than they are today; but political methods were much more frank and crude. A man who proposed office needed a strong stomach. And this young lawyer-dandy and man about town, Dan Sickles, with his air of fashion, honey-colored comb, lean hips and wide shoulders, keen, singularly engaging gray eyes, ready lip and bold port, might be as fastidious as he was assiduous in the matter of wine and women, but when it came to politics his stomach was strong as the best. Tammany he took in stride. It was something you had to go through—if you proposed to be President. And in the decrepitude of the other parties it was obvious to the veriest neophyte that the Tiger guarded the only path to the White House. That was enough for Dan Sickles. That the Tiger had both stripes and claws he knew well enough; but the fact did not deter him.

And at this time the stripes were rather clearly marked. Tammany's complete control of the police department naturally immunized the faithful from arrest—no matter what the crime; and in the event that some policeman proved stupid, Tammany's handmade judiciary provided the necessary acquittal. But nothing is perfect in human affairs. Tammany's control of the state and federal authorities was not always complete; and as a result about half the Board of Alder-men then in session were under indictment for various crimes. What became of the indictments history does not seem to record. If occa-sionally the Tiger lost the first round, he seldom lost the second.

The claws also were becoming full grown. The gangs were loyal, efficacious, immune. Maiming and murder, the bullet and bludgeon were rampant in New York City, although most of the cases of assault never reached the stage of official report. Within or without his belly, the Tiger did not like indigestible persons. Dealing with Tammany required toughness and tact.

And if young Sickles was tactful, he was as tough as the Tiger. He was an American on his way. If this beast of stripes and claws could be used—very well. If not——?

But Tammany received him well. The Tiger was bland. Sickles responded with blandishments. He stroked the striped hide with a first and last issue of his only newspaper: a cleverly worded pamphlet in support of Polk and Dallas, typeset (with boyish satisfaction) by himself. On the platform he won favor instantly, despite a cool and cultured diction that fell strangely upon ears accustomed to coarse harangues. And for one so young he showed himself shrewd in council. The Tiger purred. The Tiger could use him. And he was using the Tiger.

Fundamentally Tammany represented the middle class—the element on the make. Needing the support of the working masses, however, it loudly pretended to be their champion. But it was always secretly subservient to High Finance; and its largest loot came from adroit collusion with railroad and banking interests and the new powerful corporations seeking franchises, charters, legislative favors. Consequently it needed representatives capable of appealing to each of the three classes. Of the mobster and middle-class type it had plenty; but of men qualified to present a convincing front to the wealthy and educated, it never had been able to secure enough. And for years it had been endeavoring to entice into its parlor a few members of the fashionable and literary world. Never did Tammany so proudly boast as when it had succeeded in adding to its roster some naïve scion of an old family, some political innocent among the writers and artists of the day.

And here was a find—a fellow with the dress, manners, speech of a Knickerbocker blueblood. And no fool! The Tiger put him in the New York State Assembly.

For the next few years Dan Sickles levied hard on his Dutch vitality. When he was not debating at Albany, his days were spent in court or at his New York office, 74 Nassau Street, working up one or other of the increasingly important cases that came to his desk. His nights, when he was not attending some turbulent Tammany meeting or convivial powwow, were about equally given to the pursuit of the feminine and to prolonged bouts of private study in his chosen fields of law, history, political theory; and—the uncanny prevision again!—in drilling with the National Guard and conning *Napoleon's Campaigns*.

Often he saw the stars to bed, yet morning found him at work on time—fresh, vigorous, fastidiously groomed. Sleep he did not seem to need.

In law his career was clear sailing. Intellectually he was the athlete. His muscular brains delighted in the tussle of legal exposition and argument, craved the hardy satisfaction that comes of a premise well taken, a definition precisely drawn, a chain of deduction carried to a crushing conclusion. He approached an important case much in the spirit of a general planning a battle—plotting his strategy of position, his tactics of maneuver, arranging his artillery of fact and infantry of argument, and—against crisis—preparing cavalry forays and feints of humor, pathos, irony, the whole co-ordinated to confuse and out-flank the enemy and sweep him from the field. He loved the game for its own sake; and, so long as it did not cut athwart his political ambitions, it mattered little to him what the case might be. As a result newly arising corporations soon began to seek him out. They needed this type of front-line defense.

In politics he was even more successful.

Speeches from the floor in any legislature, of course, are mostly made for home consumption—and the record! Save on critical occasions members—very wisely—seldom even pretend to take each other's wind; and a house in session usually presents the spectacle of some lone individual solemnly addressing rows of empty benches, a crowd of colleagues off in a corner shouting and laughing about something else, a bored Speaker furtively trying to catch up with his correspondence, and a few gentlemen slouched in relaxed attitudes behind newspapers. Nevertheless, now and again, the business of conducting public affairs crops a speaker capable of attracting a corporal's guard to hail or heckle him. Dan Sickles, from the first, was one of these.

When—with *Napoleon's Campaigns*, Montesquieu's *Esprit des Lois*, a battered *History of Greece*, and bound copies of the *Federalist*—Sickles arrived at Albany, the Assembly was struggling with a mass of legislation arising out of the recently revised state constitution. No few of the bills pending closely concerned Tammany interests and were of a nature to require adroit shaping in committee. Also, over and above the routine "fixing" and vote swapping, some of them required unusually skillful defense on the floor. In work of this kind Sickles was in his element. And with one foot on the political ladder, he was not the man to miss a rung. He worked indefatigably, won from his associates a slightly startled respect, and from Governor Marcy the dictum, "As a debater he excels any man of his years in political life." Acute in committee, cogent and crafty on the floor, he soon proved himself, in fact, not only the youngest but the sturdiest "wheel horse" to the dray of dubious Tammany legislation.

Also he was something of a novelty. So suspicious were his opponents of his mystifying allusions that once when, in the course of a speech, he happened to refer to France and her republican institutions, several of them slid from the hall to consult an atlas and assure themselves that such a country really existed and was not just one of his wily fabrications. His pure English—that sounded almost like a foreign language—his scholarship and culture set him apart in an Assembly most of whose members had difficulty with the arts of writing and spelling. In an atmosphere of vociferous rant, his level, polished speech gleamed like a knife. Man of his time though he was, he was curiously free from the customary hokum and grandiloquence. Hokum—as a play upon emotionalized tribal standards and ideas—he understood. But, while he had a sense of theater, he had no taste for the cheap theatrical; and on the rare occasions that he resorted to hokum, it was an intellectualized brand of his own—more a gesture to the mode than anything else. For the most part his speeches were marked by simple statement, clear presentation, persuasive argument. He liked to levy upon history for his illustrations; and from the files of his card-index mind he could draw, at any moment, some apt parallel in the annals of Greece, Great Britain, or early America in support of his view. As for grandiloquence, he was too tough-minded and intent to bother with it. What he had to say he usually put with shrewd choice and economy of words. Not yet had arisen the great moments that would arouse him to classic eloquence.

But as a politician Dan Sickles was completely the realist. He wanted place and power—space for the exercise of the capacities he felt in himself; and he was willing to use his gifts in the service of any man or machine that could help him on his way. For the greed and trickery of little men with little goals he had only contempt; but to get to his own goal he had to deal with them—and did. But

—significantly—he never was charged with complicity in the peculations of his time. Like Lorenzo Shepard, Tammany's most brilliant young orator, he managed to wade the political slime and get ashore with clean hands. As a matter of fact, in these early years he often was hard pressed to pay his way. He had built a fair practice but he was a generous spender. And he could not depend upon his father. The two were not always on the best of terms. And amid the worries of his vast, if fluctuating fortune, George Garrett Sickles had become as careful of cents as his son was careless of dollars. Revealingly, in the fall of his first year of legislative activity, we find Daniel writing his father—a little bleakly—for the loan of fifty dollars, "for a warm overcoat," and not omitting a concrete proposal to repay. A request curtly evaded! A few years later we find the father, embarrassed by a recent slump in the market, humbly writing his son for a quite substantial loan. A request promptly granted!

The tremendous zest he brought to his work, Sickles also gave to his pleasures.

Colonel Henry G. Stebbins, a gentleman full of martial—and sartorial—ardor, had organized the Twelfth Regiment of the New York National Guard as a *corps d'élite* and had designed for its members a uniform copied, with embellishments, from that ultimate of military magnificence—the costume of the Austrian Imperial Guard! If the privates went clad in purple and gold, the officers—plumed, sashed, and sabered—were arrayed in all the splendor of a Chinese cock pheasant. Sickles, a friend of Stebbins, needed no great persuasion to join the corps. He loved soldiering—the whole atmosphere of it: the massed power, blaring brass, throbbing drums, glittering steel, menace of marching feet. And he loved the comradeship of it, the sense of solidarity men don with a uniform, the coarse jollity, all the pride and mischief of the masculine. But if to Sickles this amateur soldiering were a sport, a welcome relief from caucus and court, it was more: an opportunity to learn the rudiments of something that always had fascinated him—the science of war. He studied the military manuals with the industry of a West Pointer and soon was brevetted captain. At the same time he was sufficiently the primordial male to enjoy the sartorial side of the show. He loved to array himself in his plumage, sweat his men through their drill, and then display himself to the girls.

And with the girls—in a parlance vogue then as now—he was the accomplished "wolf." As the son of a sire who in his seventies was to raise a late crop of handsome daughters, he had rather more than his share of the Van Sicklen virility that already had peopled New Rochelle without much other masculine aid! Also he was magnetic, engaging, adroit. Women went to him at a touch. A Knickerbocker of the Knickerbockers, he was much in demand at social affairs uptown. And as irresistible with the matron as with the miss, he soon was trailing clouds of scandal that seemed to make him still more the desire of women and the envy of men. Rumor has it that in the course of these amours he fathered no few offspring—some of them afterwards distinguished in the world of fashion, sport, journalism. Of course there were seasons when the social situation grew somewhat precarious and fathers and husbands uncomfortably alert; but still there were the ladies of the theater, the opera, the cafés, and certain houses—both smart and discreet.

CHAPTER V

Teresa

AND ALL THE WHILE there was Teresa—a little world apart.

Since, as a baby, she first had seduced him, his teasing delight in her, her childish adoration of him, had brightened as she grew. Almost unconsciously she had become to him a pet, private possession, something particularly his own.

He often was at the Bagiolis'. They were his last link with the Da Ponte tradition and the influences that had molded his mind; and their gossip of books and music, their warm, haphazard hospitality were pleasant relief from strenuous bouts of legal battle, political brawl. In the old days Maria—then a child-wife scarcely older than himself—used to help him in his studies. Now she made the house home to him, would coax off his seriousness, whip him up a dish of her famous spaghetti. And the maestro, inclined to peevishness and parsimony, would brace himself to be genial, bring out a bottle of wine; and there would be talk of the opera—a mutual enthusiasm—the brew pot of European politics, racy reminiscences of old Da Ponte.

But even more to him were the moments that he could give to teasing and entrancing Teresa. Always his pockets were full of candy, but she had to plunder him to get it; she was a gamesome sprite, and the ensuing fight would be uproarious. And there would be gifts—gay toys, bits of childish jewelry—mischievously rewrapped a dozen times to drive her frantic with impatience. Sometimes, as she struggled on the floor with knots and seals, she would burst out, black eyes brimming, "Dan, you are the worst friend I have!" Her gaminish spirit released all the nonsense in him. When these two got together the world was fun. It was laughter that did him good.

And through the hoydenish years it was the same—with a difference. Teresa was a natural child, healthy, vital, in love with the open, shinning up trees and tearing her clothes. Ever eager for adventure, she would lure Dan to go berrying or bird-nesting with her, take her to the circus, or the Battery Gardens to see the fireworks. Often enough some client or Tammany colleague would be left to cool his heels while Teresa had her day. At twelve she was demanding a pony of her own. If it cost Sickles valuable time, he presently found her a clever, reliable little mare. It was a gift that marked a change. Completely fearless, she took to the saddle like a gypsy. There came canters together along the woodsy banks of the Hudson. Just to ride was nothing—she wanted to race. Flushed and laughing, while he snatched his breath she would gallop ahead of him to leap a gully or a deadfall. Even while he scolded her he knew well enough that her impetuosity echoed his own.

A creature of moods, she had a language for each one—English for happiness, Italian for excitement, French for banter, Spanish for rage. To him it was an accomplishment that made her a small embodiment of the Da Ponte culture. Drawn into some expedition with her, he would make a stipulation—not without an eye to practice: "Today you must speak only Italian." Teresa on the instant would be one protesting shrug, "*Non, non, monsieur—c'est impossible!*" Sickles would be indulgent. "Very well, then. Let's make it French." But Teresa was not to be caught. "*No, no, señor. Hoy hablo español.*"

Sickles still was amenable to suggestion. "All right, then—it's Spanish." Eyes dancing, she would whirl away. "Why Spanish? I don't feel mad today. Let's speak English." Then, demurely, "I want to improve myself!"

Fourteen—fifteen. And suddenly, with her early Italian maturity, she was a voluptuous little beauty. And Dan Sickles noted, with a flash of fierce male possessiveness, how men, startled, turned to stare at her as she cantered beside him. A natural coquette, she made it apparent to all the world that she had eyes for none but Dan. And he knew that she was completely absorbed in him, never had had a beau—she was still too young for that. But how long would it be before . . . He thrust the thought aside. It still tormented him.

Sixteen—and she was a woman: a sprig of vivacious loveliness, the dark eyes—a bronze glow in happiness, black light in excitement—slightly odalisque, a little too large for the slim, clever face; the trim lips, taut breasts, pouting, expectant.

The two were at crisis. The tiny spark born between a baby and a boy, flickering between them through years of daffing companionship, flashed into flame. Dan, caught in his destiny, suddenly was the mad, romantic lover. Teresa's heart sang.

Assemblyman Sickles, Tammany chieftain with presidential aspirations, was not a man to make a penniless marriage. And by American standards Teresa still was a child. But with him, as ever, it was "Decision—action! Reflection burned to an intuitive flash." He could not wait a day to be wed.

The parents on both sides objected: the old Knickerbocker that she was a "nobody"; Bagioli that she was "much too young." That was enough to make it a runaway match. But within the year the parents had relented; and Teresa had her supreme desire—a church wedding. She had seen herself, veiled and blossomed, walking up the aisle between pews crowded with New York fashion toward a tall, dignified figure at the altar. But when the moment came, she found herself dissolved in music and light, aware of nothing—but her Dan!

At the moment Sickles was at grips with a difficult political situation. For several years past, Tammany had been torn asunder between two bitterly opposed factions: the Outs and the Ins. The first, known as the "Barnburners," supposedly were radical, reformist, and antislavery. The second, known as the "Hunkers," were standpatters, with southern sympathies, and opposed to new policies that might jeopardize the fat offices they now held. But neither had anything in view but control of the municipal treasury. If Sickles served Tammany well, it was with the very clear intention that Tammany should serve him better. Shrewdly judging the situation and its possibilities, he steered a skillful course between the two factions and, backed by his achievements at Albany, secured a place on the General Committee. From that vantage ground he watched for his opportunity.

As usual he proved himself astute in council and at the Baltimore convention played a prominent part in the nomination of his friend, Franklin Pierce, for the presidency. He was gaining power and prestige, but not without cost; for in those days the career of a Tammany committeeman had its inconveniences.

In obeisance to the Democratic tradition, it was the custom of the Executive Committee to hold occasional "open meetings" for the endorsement of their private conclusions in the matter of candidates and policies. And it was in these meetings that the two factions gave to the world some of their most vigorous exhibitions of the Great Experiment in practice. Each side brought its gangs—skilled in every art of thuggery. Preliminary sessions were held in the basement of Tammany Hall—at that time a capacious saloon adorned with mighty mirrors, fat nudes, and the portraits of the great and wise in American history, including Aaron Burr and a line of sachems. Here conviction and courage flowed freely from bottles supplied by both parties. The result always was a series of spirited arguments driven home with fists and bludgeons in which the police—poor devils!—in the pay of Tammany today, but not so certain they would be in the pay of Tammany tomorrow, discreetly took no part.

Once thoroughly loaded with loyalty, the gangs proceeded upstairs to the general meeting and threw themselves enthusiastically into the real business of seating or upsetting speakers, endorsing or downing nominations. In one of these affairs Sickles was tossed bodily into the well of the spiral staircase leading to the upper chamber of council and saved himself only by a wild clutch at the banisters. On another occasion, when, in the midst of a speech, he was stormed by a delegation of the prognathous, only a bold front, a hard eye, and a hand to hip saved him from further adventures. A little later, escorted by a number of the most dignified sachems of Tammany, he was compelled to make a somewhat acrobatic exit from the platform by means of a window and a convenient fire escape.

Sickles took it all like a good campaigner. Nevertheless he was beginning to get a little grim. And when the right moment came—when the "Barnburners" had nominated the popular shyster, Van Schaick, for the mayoralty of New York, and the "Hunkers," hoping to outwit them, had proceeded to nominate him themselves—Sickles gathered about him a small but powerful group of associates, including the redoubtable "Mike" Walsh, and on the very eve of election—when no reply or counterstroke was possible—issued a broadside repudiating both factions and their candidate! In one pounce he had the Tiger down! Tammany's bought-and-paid-for electorate, bewildered, ran amuck. The Whigs rolled over them.

Overnight four thousand key jobholders lacked a meal ticket. The Tiger raged and wept, made public repentance, proposed reform—, and secretly opened negotiations with the rebel "Democratic-Republican General Committee," as the Sickles group styled themselves. After months of cautious poker, Sickles magnanimously consented to reconciliation and a common platform. His reward was the choicest financial and political plum in Tammany's gift—the office of corporation attorney of New York City. The question as to who should swallow whom had been settled!

To Sickles, however, the new office—despite its handsome salary and much more handsome "emoluments"—meant nothing but one more rung on the ladder. And when, a few months later, his friend, James Buchanan, minister to the Court of St. James's, offered him the expensive and ill-paid post of First Secretary of Legation, he accepted on the spot. Within twenty-four hours he was in Washington making the necessary arrangements with President Pierce.

But before relinquishing his office, Sickles was instrumental in fostering a growing demand for an adequate park for New York City and was personally responsible for persuading the Council to take the present seven hundred and fifty acres in preference to a much smaller and less conveniently located area—thus earning for himself the title of "Father of Central Park." To quote from his own report to the Council:

In place of a much smaller and inferior area which within a generation will be utterly inadequate for a rapidly growing city, this park, which we have designated Central Park, will be one unsurpassed in convenience of position; one which our citizens can with honest pride favorably compare with the most celebrated grounds of the chief cities of Europe.

On board, the thresh of the clean harbor breeze seemed good to him . . . Over the prow hovered winged hope . . . And on the dock—eager to join him after the birth of her baby—stood Teresa, all soft excitement, a little close to tears, waving.

PART TWO: A KNICKERBOCKER AT THE COURT OF ST. JAMES'S

CHAPTER VI

Dan Sickles Comes to Town

———◆———

W<small>HEN DAN SICKLES</small> landed in London, what we like to call the Victorian Age was in full bloom.

The well-married Queen and her conscientious Consort were shaming the pertinacity of beavers patching a broken dam in their efforts to strengthen the prestige of the Crown at home and abroad. Spending Spartan hours together daily over piles of state papers and a crushing correspondence, they still found time to supervise the education of a growing crew of not very promising children, open endless bazaars, lay countless cornerstones. Incidentally, they did much more: they provided the British public with the novel and edifying spectacle of marital devotion, royal decorum, industry, dignity, piety, on a throne hitherto occupied chiefly by sots, simpletons, rakes, and rogues. Queen Vic had redeemed her pledge to "be good." Prince Albert had gone her one better.

The spectacle had England enchanted—and a little confused. The Court always had set the social tone—for the most part in some pet key of depravity—frivolous, coarse, or merely dull. Never had it ordained Virtue the fashion! And neither the godless eighteenth century nor the equally bawdy, hard-drinking, gambling first three decades of the nineteenth had prepared the British public for that! But, apart from certain elements of the highest and lowest classes bent on their old unregenerate way, the great mass of the royalty-infatuated bourgeoisie, once it appeared to them that Virtue was the proper thing, hastened to don the robes of righteousness—often enough to quaint result. Lofty sentiments became as much a social necessity as correct attire. Propriety was cultivated as a fine art. Gentlemen were bland; ladies perpetually embarrassed. Trousers could be designated only as "unmentionables." Beneath the bulbous crinoline lurked a discreet vacuum without a name. Moralism chased witticism off the stage and out of the drawing room. Eros, iridescent-winged son of Zeus and Aphrodite, was given a coat of invisible paint, and—

> . . . . *that great force*
> *Which swells and buds and breaks,*
> *And will be life and love and sex and sin,*
> *Adorable, lascivious, sacrosanct,*
> *Forever and forever—*

was politely agreed not to exist. Nude statues were removed from public places or decently swathed to the neck. The legs of the parlor piano were chastely draped. When Lady Beatty, fresh from girlish years abroad with her husband, confided happily to her old friend, Gladstone, that she was expecting a baby, he reddened, turned away, and, in solemn outrage, stalked from the room. Sanctimony reigned supreme.

With the lamplighters' scurrying lope from post to post, London's eighty thousand prostitutes crept forth to peddle used bodies for bread.

Forty years of peace, colonial expansion, the industrial revolution with its new machines and million new machine slaves, had brought England in general, and London in particular, vast new prosperity, vast new misery. If the gentry and upper bourgeoisie enjoyed a mellow life, and the merchant princes and landed aristocracy reveled in new, unguessed riches, down in the gruesome regions of London's East End, in the colliery and manufacturing towns of the Midlands—the smoke-begrimed "Black Country"—the pittance paid miner and mill hand for grueling shifts was not enough to buy meal and potatoes for themselves, much less for a family. And so, in the pits and factories, children of six could be found working ten hours a day for pennies, while, in the piecework sweatshops, wan-faced women treadled their looms from dark dawn to last light for a recompense that seldom equaled the price of six loaves a week. Tom

Hood's cry, "Ah God!—that bread should be so dear, and flesh and blood so cheap!" was no sentimentality.

At the same time, however, the brutishness of the Machine Age had begun to brew its own antidotes. Labor unions were arising. Parliament began timidly to tinker with factory regulation. Thousands of the working classes crowded the new emigrant steamships to the United States. A few years previously some poor weavers of Rochdale had bought a chest of tea at wholesale and divided the contents among themselves at cost—unknowingly founding the greatest co-operative enterprise in history. In a Cheapside lodging-house Karl Marx, driven from Germany for his activities in the Revolution of '48, was toiling—against the drag of disease and destitution—on his *Das Kapital* and organizing the First Socialist International.

And, somehow, amidst all this material expansion and callous exploitation there had come about a new renaissance of British genius. Tennyson, Dickens, Thackeray, the Brownings, Charlotte Brontë, a shy, intense creature who called herself George Eliot, were in full flower. Rossetti, Millais, Holman Hunt, and others just had founded the Pre-Raphaelite Brotherhood, and, ditching formulae and the pernicious imitation of the "masters," had proceeded to work direct from nature and in the open air—with results most refreshing. William Morris—that minor edition of the great Leonardo—driving seven arts abreast, already had linked forces with them in an effort to make the British bourgeois home a little less ornately hideous; and in the Red House, his great studio—with its separate alcoves for painting, printing, weaving, carving, writing, illuminating missals, designing stained glass—began creating furniture, wallpaper, rugs, in terms of a comfort, composure, gay simplicity unknown since the twelfth century.

Meanwhile Charles Kean, at the Princess, was producing Shakespeare in a new mode and engaging his audiences with a natural delivery free from rant. Balfe's pioneer English opera, *The Bohemian Girl*, was charming England and the continent.

Dress and manners reflected the period. . . . It was an interlude of Watteau-like elegance—touched with an affectation of culture and piety, especially piety!—when the writer and artist, even the wretch "without a grandfather," was in demand at the affairs of fashion; and a Disraeli, albeit not without some comment, could appear before Parliament arrayed in slate-colored velvet coat, purple, strapped trousers seamed with gold braid, a scarlet waistcoat grilled with glittering chains, white-gloved, beringed fingers hid by lace ruffles. . . . A time of wasp waists, crinolined flounces, beflowered coal-scuttle bonnets, tiny parasols meant to half-shield nothing more ardent than a coquettish glance.

But across the water there was the European witch's brew! For two thousand years it had seethed without one quiescent decade in its hissing of intrigue, roiling of blood. And it was seething still. The recent anti-monarchist Revolution of '48 had set it boiling from brim to brim. The bubbles—rapid, surface things—quickly burst. But beneath them greater bubbles stirred in France, Italy, Germany. The caldron was getting ready for bigger and better brews: '70–1914–'39! And as though to keep the brew stirring meanwhile, Russia—her decadent aristocracy bored with French novels, Italian opera, idle idiocy, sexual vagaries, and always dreaming of the Black Sea as a Russian lake—suddenly decided that the time had come "to put the Sick Man of Europe to bed." On the pretext that Greek Catholics in Turkish dominions were not treated with due respect, Czar Nicholas, with a truly modern tenderness toward "oppressed minorities," thrust his troops across the Pruth into Moldavia and Walachia. The Lion had no intention of letting the Bear set his paw on the Dardanelles, swallow his Levantine commerce. Louis Napoleon needed prestige, British support. Both promised Turkey their aid. With nothing but an operetta army and a blue Danube to protect her, Austria wisely remained neutral—to the vast disgust of the English masses. But the Sultan, sure of his allies, ordered the Bear back. The Bear was not impressed. The Crimean War—with its official ineptitude, its callous waste of gallant men, its fatuous charge of the Light Brigade, its tart-tongued, magnificent nurse Nightingale —was on.

Soon after he had settled himself in his quarters at the American Legation, the new First Secretary, accompanied by his chief, James Buchanan, repaired to Buckingham Palace to be presented to the Queen. For the occasion he wore—as prescribed by the U. S. State Department—"the dress of a plain American gentleman"; but discovering with disgust that this happened to be also the livery worn by the royal flunkies, he hastened, at the last moment, to buckle on a sword! Despite this unimaginative and rather odd costume he seems to have made a distinct impression at Court. The Queen was more than usually gracious to him. Her ladies, unaccustomed to much personality or style in American officials, apparently were agreeably surprised by his cavalier bearing, bold good looks. Some of them saw further. His air of burnished masculinity struck the Hon. Alice Jenkyns as "both elegant and faintly savage." According to a line or two in one of her gossipy letters, there was quite a ripple of comment around her, most of it in the vein of light mockery with which women usually veil an admiration they would prefer not to show: ". . . Rather high and mighty for an American, I should say! . . . Really, deerskins would be more becoming, don't you think? . . . No, no, my dear—a plumed hat, if you please—seaboots, sash and cutlass!"

Feminine perspicacity, in short, found the First Secretary an unusually vital fellow—born somewhat late. And feminine perspicacity was right!

In truth, the hand Dan Sickles kissed should not have been the soft, fat hand of Queen Victoria. In the right order of things it should have been the sinewy talon of Queen Bess—the dress sword, a battered cutlass!

For centuries before the Van Sicklens took part in the founding of New Amsterdam, their ancestors had played a strong hand in that sea-ravaged, blood-soaked, and erstwhile mythological "kingdom of the many waters," known as Flanders. From generation to generation, with sword and battle-ax, pike and arquebus, musket and cannon, they had been compelled to lead their bearded battalions against the never ceasing attempts at invasion—by the Germanic tribes on the west, the Burgundians and French on the south, and, at last, by the legions of the Spanish Inquisition under the Duke of Alva.

At the same time there was the Sea—and they must leash it with dikes, master it with merchantmen. There were vast fetid marshes—they must reclaim them to flowering fields. Amid the menace of flood and war and want there were cities to be built—and they helped to make them massive, clean, and beautiful. And, as a swift slash at Spain for her cruel arrogance, there were slim privateers to launch and man against the "silver galleons" of the Main. And out of all this struggle with savage seas and savage men, as fighting barons, building burghers, the Van Sicklens had compacted into a family breed fierce and virile as Vikings, stubbornly self-willed, self-assured, indomitably bent upon independence, free scope.

And Dan Sickles was their son. Their vitality was in him; and their stamp was on him—the thrust and thwart of all his character and career. Whether he realized it or not, he was a man fated to pursue his ambitions helped by the power and hindered by the impedimenta—the behavior patterns and impulsions—of a tenacious ancestry who would not let him go.

To him this boundless vitality under his ribs was his daemon. As might some ancient Greek, he trusted it and obeyed it unhesitatingly. Its promptings were all the code he knew or cared to know. Among men it easily gave him the biological leadership of the pack. Among women its magnetic aura as easily played havoc.

His cool, analytical brain, suave demeanor, were simply the instruments and surfaces of this raw force that had its roots in centuries behind him. And just as the pedigreed, gentlemanly Irish wolfhound may revert at a touch to savagery, so Dan Sickles, of the frock coat and immaculate white hands, had it in him to slay with the quick ferocity of his bearded forebears of the Flemish border.

Even his intelligence was the intelligence of vitality.

But beyond this—and entirely crucial—is the fact that this vital overplus dowered him with a sense of inner invincibility, an unquestioning belief in his own rightness, that enabled him to ignore criticism, sweep aside opposition, and, as often as not, impose upon his colleagues and the crowd not only his own views but his own estimate of himself! In an earlier age, as the bantering belles of Victoria's court had divined, he might well have been a buccaneer, another Drake, Frobisher, Hawkins. But Fate had cast him as a Tammany politician, corporation lawyer, diplomat at the most tightlaced court in the world.

He had no realization of his plight, nor that only war itself—war raw, savage, improvisational, such as his forebears knew—could bring the sundered, conflicting halves of his inheritance together in a unity of power: that only in war was he to come to the stature of himself: that only in war was he to know peace.

Such, however, was the man who bowed low before Queen Victoria while her ladies whispered together—in his hip pocket a letter from Teresa babbling of her baby, and, next to it, a crested, scented, clever note from a conquest more recent, less naïve.

For a few weeks there was no great pressure of affairs at the Legation, and Dan Sickles had time to look about him. And first there was the City itself. He knew something of her story. And, as he strolled about her ancient cobbled streets, it stirred him to remember that she had been a busy mart before shepherds heard glad voices from the cirrus wings of the moon; that she had been a citadel of the dark-eyed, skin-clad Brythons, the mailed Romans, the golden-bearded, battle-axed Saxons, the long-limbed, hawk-nosed Normans—the tortured vortex of plague, fire, war, rebellion. And, driving from the Tower on the low east to the Druidic grove of Burnham Beeches and Windsor Castle on the farthest west, he marveled across forty miles of grandeur, grime, and quiet loveliness at this corrupt and unconquerable Londinium, sprawling, relaxed, immense, massively composed, assured, beneath here her innocent skies, there her booming canopy of smoke, here her cloistered peace, there her eternal uproar: home port of the seven imperial seas, hearth of British government, trade, finance, fashion, art and letters —hutch of the foulest slums known to man. He drove and walked and wondered at this that had endured two thousand years and was the county seat for three fourths the world.

But what intrigued him most was the ancient, top-hatted town meeting in its Tudor-Gothic habitation beside the Thames where affairs from Africa to India, Athabaska to Malay, from ducal castle to peasant hut, were settled with the casual dignity, crisp acrimony of well-bred men in a favorite club. Fresh from Tammany brawls, the hoarse harangues of Albany, these clear, cultivated voices, this punctilious politeness, sardonic understatement of bitter issues, tone of hardy good sportsmanship, struck him as nothing had struck him since he had met Da Ponte. His first experience of Parliamentary debate awaked in him dormant feudal overtones, made him believe for a moment that in Europe, at least, monarchy had place and meaning. He did not see that here was only a better-mannered Tammany—a group of expensive gentlemen elected by a limited, bought, or manipulated suffrage, beyond corruption personally, but nevertheless strictly engaged, under one party shibboleth or another, in protecting their own interests—millowner against landowner—at the expense of the great mass of the landless, job-dependent British commonweal. He saw only the manner. The manner was distinguished.

For the moment he was a man struggling with the rather challenging experience of being pitched, without preparation, not simply into the citadel of an alien empire, but into that inmost heart of it where a whisper from the Court shrouds shrewd faces in thought, fashionable dinners decide political destinies, diplomacy weaves her intricate webs, and the late ponderings of elderly gentlemen over their port decide the morrow's spectroscope of Europe. . . . And where women also play their critical, if unscheduled, part. And quickly he became absorbed and alert, aware that he had much to learn in this game where crinkled hands moved peoples as pawns across the chessboard of the world.

Recently there had been political upheaval. Disraeli, Chancellor of the Exchequer, had gone down, fighting with desperate brilliance, before the mordant onslaughts of the apostolic Gladstone—henceforth his gladiatorial enemy. Lord Palmerston, the most dynamic, not to say dangerous, Foreign Minister in a century, had paid the penalty of his final indiscretion—the unofficial recognition of Louis Napoleon's *coup d'état* without consulting Her Majesty—and had been retired to the safe kennel of the Home Office. It was a new era, stolid and respectable, eminently Victorian. To Lord Aberdeen, cautious and commonplace, had fallen the post of Premier; to Lord John Russell, that steady wheel horse of empire, the Foreign Office; and to the disastrously incompetent Lord Newcastle, the critical War Office. The one outstanding political fact was that William Ewart Gladstone, the perfect pillar of propriety, soberly suited, deep-collared, black-cravated, sat himself, not without a grim smile, on the Wool Sack still warm from the poppy-colored breeches of the dazzling, defeated "Dizzy."

And in the sedate West End squares where massive mansions, monotonously alike as barracks, gazed blankly down on tiny, exquisite green parks berailed as for wild beasts, but haunted only by lascivious little nursemaids attending naughty children destined for high places, the hoary British ceremony of Dinner performed its rites.

To be dined officially by an official personage was to be recognized officially; but to be invited to break bread with the same personage privately and cozily was to be accepted socially. Between the two lay the gulf betwixt Lazarus and Dives. With Buchanan,

Dan Sickles made the round of official dinners; and if the British urbane detachment nettled the American in him, he enjoyed the atmosphere of pomp and place, the sense of sitting at the board with men who were shaping the destinies of a vast and ever expanding empire—men with whom, he knew well enough, he soon must match wits, cross swords.

But the other kind of dinners also soon were forthcoming. He had been noticed. The men liked him—especially Palmerston—for his fresh manner of envisaging stale diplomatic problems from a purely American and practical point of view: "The Dardanelles are Russia's front door. No man likes to sneak out of his backyard all the time. The point is: would the concession be worth Russia's gratitude and collaboration? . . . Politically the French are disgruntled Royalists brandishing a broom of Republican feathers—one should take account of that in dealing with them"—things dropped in the casual interchange of men over their wine, but such as frequently made the cautious Buchanan quiver. Without knowing all the intricacies of the trail, Sickles often trod where angels fear, but was not liked the less. The women found his galvanic gray eyes, gallant manner, distinctly disturbing.

Just as it was blossom time in science, literature, technology, painting, so, for some inexplicable reason, it was blossom time for beauty. If the records and the miniatures are to be trusted, it was a decade of English belles. There were the Sheridans—mother and three daughters, each more lovely than the other, and all adored by Disraeli; and vying with them were the exquisite Marchioness of Londonderry, the classic "nymph in crinolines"—as Tom Hood called her—Lady Chesterfield, and those vivacious beauties, Mrs. Anson and Mrs. Austen, and a host of others not so socially prominent as these but any one of them sufficiently the Lorelei to throw susceptible Dan Sickles into a state of romantic furor. Women such as these were a new experience to him. Not simply their delicately bred beauty, musical voices, humorsome manners, had him enchanted, but often enough their contact with political affairs, their knowledge of personalities and the hidden side of events. If he found the Court society rather stiff and uninviting, there was always at hand for relief that other group later delimited as the Smart Set, where, under the very nose of Victorian propriety, a sophisticated obedience to impulse had its day and illicit liaisons flourished in an atmosphere of consummate tact. And in that social penumbra Dan Sickles found himself very much at home. . . . By every packet he wrote to Teresa—brief, gamesome notes. Yet often enough there were moments when, caught in the spell of some new charmer, he found himself wishing that Teresa were more like these women, had something of their intelligent sparkle, sophistication . . . moments when, under the blandishments of this new, exciting world, wife and baby seemed very tiny, very remote indeed. But when after some months Teresa, looking very chic and lovely in her girlish motherhood, arrived with baby Laura, he was once again all ardent devotion, admiration, delight.

It was the magical English May of violets and hawthorn, cowslips and skylarks, and the London season in full swing, when Dan Sickles found himself faced for the second time with sartorial dilemma.

The Crystal Palace—a gigantic cruciform glass edifice originally erected in Hyde Park to house Britain's first Exposition—had been removed to the crest of a noble ridge, Sydenham Hill, on the southern border of London, and there was to be officially reopened by the Queen and Prince Consort. Since the Palace was a pet royal project the ceremony had been planned as a full-dress affair. And that meant one of those rare occasions when the suppressed human male is permitted to emerge for a moment arrayed in all the magnificent plumage stolen from him long ago by his envious mate. It meant smartly uniformed troops lining the streets for miles, the jingle and glitter of beplumed and breast-plated Household Cavalry, the haughty splendor of the Blue Dragoons, the scarlet, jet, and gold of the Honorable Artillery, the vivid tartan of the Black Watch —a processional moving to the skirl of bagpipes, the thunder of drums, the mellow brass of the Guards' Band; and, in the midst of it, the royal coach-and-four with crimson-coated postilions, followed in order of precedence by the carriages of the resplendent royal dukes and the equally resplendent Diplomatic Corps—all the pageantry of a pageantry-loving people, stemming from ages past, Tudor, Elizabethan, Georgian, a belated burst of the ancient British lust for pomp and color and pride, arabesqued by the breedy splendor of the British officer on parade.

To attend a costume carnival of that kind attired in the meek "dress of a plain American gentleman," to present himself a humble crow among stately peacocks, gaudy macaws, dandified flamingos, scarlet cardinals, was more than Dan Sickles could summon himself to endure. And yet, except by feigning illness, he could in no wise escape the gracious royal "command." Dilemma complete! Confronted with it, the unimaginative Buchanan saw no slightest cause for agitation. He argued, a little irritably, that the modest garb he had worn at the Court of the Czar, and for the past year at the Court of St. James's, would serve well enough for the present occasion both for himself and his suite. But Dan Sickles was not so minded. He stormed and fretted, abused the State Department, grew quarrelsome with his patient chief, and had Teresa in tears. Then, at the last moment, a light appeared. Teresa, hushing a squalling Laura in the American rocking chair Dan had imported for her, suddenly looked up with a musical scream, "Dan! Dan! Why couldn't you wear your beautiful State Guard uniform?"

Dan Sickles took one look at his wife and rushed wordless from the room. Half an hour later he was at Buckingham Palace, closeted with the Queen's equerry. Sir William Phipps was all gracious compliance: "Her Majesty prefers that guests holding military rank should appear in dress uniform." The dilemma dissolved in glory!

Out of the moth balls came the gorgeous costume. In the royal procession it blazed like a Crown jewel among ordinary gems, aroused the dazed and whispered comment of the staff officers in charge of proceedings, and the equally dazed—but by no means whispered—comment of the Cockney crowd.

The Crimean War was going badly for the Allies. Consequently Austria—openly suspected of connivance with Russia—was in high disfavor with the British from Queen to coster, and no invitation to attend the Crystal Palace ceremonies had been extended to the members of her embassy. And yet here, in the Queen's immediate entourage, rode an officer of the Austrian Imperial Guard!

There was no mistaking the fact. Londoners, bred on royal pageantry, are experts in the matter of regimental trappings; and at the Coronation, the Wedding, the Opening of Parliament, the inauguration of the Crystal Palace Exposition in Hyde Park, this particular uniform—the most gorgeous in Europe—already had become familiar to the crowd.

Approaching the Palace, the cheers, the trample of hooves and marching feet, drowned out the hostile comments; but within the

gates, as the Queen and Prince Consort, afoot, followed by members
of the Court and the Diplomatic Corps, proceeded upon a formal
inspection of the exhibits and the grounds amid a dense throng held
at bay by ropes and police, the offending costume came in for
painfully apparent attention.

No perter being walks than your true Cockney; and no sooner
had the Queen passed and the Diplomatic Corps come in view than
there broke out a fervid babble and then a barrage of hoarse catcalls—" 'Igh—you wiv all dem fevvahs! Wot yer bloody well doin'
'ere? . . . Ye struttin' Haustrian cock-a-doodle—why ain't yer
fightin' fer yer friend Nick? . . . Gaw blimme, if I 'ad a rotten hegg
I'd give yer a swat on the kisser orl right, orl right!"

Only slowly did Dan Sickles realize that the compliments of the
crowd were meant for him; and only when Buchanan snapped at
him, "It's that ridiculous uniform of yours, Dan—they think you're
an Austrian," did his predicament dawn on him. But he kept a stiff
front, stalked ahead with irritating grandeur. The yelps grew
more menacing. The police were having trouble.

Puzzled, Queen Victoria turned and looked back. Quick as thought
she caught the situation. Not until that moment had she noticed
that for some reason or other the First Secretary of the American
Legation had tricked himself out in the dress uniform of the Austrian Imperial Guard! To her equerry immediately behind her she
whispered a rapid order. At once he dispatched several policemen
to pass the word to their fellows guarding the lines, and through
them to the crowd, that the gentleman in the Austrian uniform was
not an Austrian at all, but a member of the American Embassy, and
wearing the uniform of a crack American regiment.

As the news flashed through the crowd, British good sportsmanship leaped to make amends. Someone shouted "Three cheers for
the Yankees!" And the roar that followed surpassed even the welcome given to the Queen! From that moment the crowd almost
forgot the stumpy little Victoria and her solemn Albert in its sudden
admiration for the handsome, chin-tufted, devilishly resplendent
representative of Uncle Sam!

Buchanan still remained caustic. But on the whole, Dan Sickles
found no cause to be displeased with himself. He had worn the
most gorgeous uniform of the day; he had beaten the British at
their own game; he had focused the entire attention of the crowd

upon himself and had emerged the only member of the royal entourage to receive a personal ovation! So far as he was concerned, the official reopening of the Crystal Palace was a distinct success. One might add: a characteristic success.

A few weeks later the First Secretary again found himself caught in dilemma.

This time the horns were provided by the abounding goodness— and the equally abounding naïveté—of Mr. George Peabody.

Following his long-established custom, that princely philanthropist and merchant genius had invited a hundred and fifty guests to celebrate the Fourth of July with him at the stately Garter Hotel on the wooded heights above Thames-side Richmond. It was to be, of course, the usual stag affair—the honor guests, the members of the American Legation. But for this particular occasion George Peabody proposed an interesting innovation.

As an American of pure English descent, long resident in London, and engaged in vast enterprises and benefactions on both sides of the water, he had come to deplore the rather bellicose tone of previous Fourth of July banquets and had conceived the genial and completely lunatic idea of transforming the forthcoming celebration into an Anglo-American love fest! Accordingly he had invited a number of distinguished Britishers to sit at the board and had been at great pains to provide that the program should contain nothing to offend, and much to flatter, their ancient susceptibilities.

To Dan Sickles, however, love-festing with the British seemed by no means an appropriate way to commemorate the Declaration of Independence; and, the moment that he heard of the project, he sought out George Peabody to protest against it. But the benevolent master of millions was not to be swayed. With gentle calm he assured his visitor that "every honor would be paid to President Pierce." And there the matter had to rest.

Naturally, when Dan Sickles alighted at the door of the Garter that Fourth of July, the Van Sicklen gorge already was disposed to rise. As he entered the lobby the spectacle of a hairy congressman from Arkansas loquaciously croaking his views to a group of ironically amused Britishers started that gorge on its upward course. It rose higher a few minutes later when, entering the banquet hall, he stood staring in dumfounded disgust at two magnificent life-size portraits of the Queen and Prince Consort at the head of the table on either side of a small, inconsequential portrait of George Washington, and noticed that there was not so much as a tintype of President Pierce. It rose still higher when, seated, and wrathfully studying the beautiful hand-painted program at his plate, he observed that it bore the royal, as well as the American, arms: that the toast to the Queen preceded the toast to the President: that to an Englishman, Sir James Emerson Tennent, had been assigned the honor of proposing the toast to George Washington! . . . And it rose to heights apoplectic when he discovered that the lines of "The Star-Spangled Banner" and "Hail Columbia"—printed on the back of the program for the convenience of guests American as well as English—had been revised to eliminate all the good old belligerent allusions to "the haughty host . . . that band who so vauntingly swore . . . their foul footsteps' pollution . . . the hireling and slave . . . the rude foe with impious hands," etc., etc.

But the worst was not yet. In proposing the first toast, "To the Day we Celebrate," George Peabody, not unmindful of Secretary Sickles's recent protests and his present glowering countenance, proceeded to make a few remarks for his benefit: "I am aware that some of my countrymen question the propriety of inviting our brethren on this side of the water to join us in celebrating the birthday of American independence; but these persons are few and know little of the high esteem which, I have reason to believe, English gentlemen have for our country and our countrymen."

Dumb, stiff, red-gorged, Dan Sickles stood staring at the wall before him while the hundred and forty-nine love-festers, greatly helped by the pious printed version, broke into a ragged and raucous effort at "Hail Columbia." Then came the toast to the Queen. This was George Peabody's great moment—and he made the most of it! After a nobly eloquent tribute to Her Majesty, he recited at length how she had generously permitted the Throne Room—yes, the Throne Room!—to be stripped of Winterhalter's famous portraits of herself and the Prince Consort so that the Fourth of July feast of friendship might be graced by the royal presences. According to the newspaper reports, "the speech was received with deafening applause"; and, as the orchestra struck up "God Save the Queen," every man, glass in hand, was on his feet—one foot on the seat of his chair in the traditional fashion; every man, that is, except Dan Sickles. By now rage, too long suppressed, had rendered him red, rigid, mute, motionless. At the moment not the prod of hot irons could have stirred him.

Fortunately—for the love fest, at least—the great length of the table screened by standing guests with outstretched arms, and the fact that, while all eyes were turned toward the royal portrait, the attention of most was also absorbed in trying to remember the words of the ancient doggerel, very few seemed to notice that the First Secretary remained both voiceless and legless. Certainly the Britishers present did not notice it—a way they have! But George Peabody noticed it, was wrung by it, and sat down, at last, so wrought that when, a few minutes later, he rose to propose "The President of the United States," voice and memory faltered. After the recent tribute to the Queen, the little speech sounded strangely flat and inept. It was the last drop in Sickles's cup. And when all arose once more, and the band led off with "The Star-Spangled Banner," he clenched his teeth, gripped his chair, then sprang to his feet and strode from the room. It was supposed that he was ill. He was!

The London press tactfully skirted the incident; and while the New York papers, in various conflicting versions, gave it some attention, only the personally antagonistic *Herald* tried to feature it as a major scandal. No one, however, seemed really to know just what had happened; and Sickles's own lame report made in an anonymous letter to the press did little to clarify the confusion. Some held that he had refused the toast to the Queen, others that he had refused the toast to the President, others again that he had refused to honor either of them. But in the upshot once more an awkward episode redounded to his favor. The great majority of his countrymen concluded that, like a good American, he simply had refused, as the Louisville *Courier* put it, "to play the fawning minion to Royalty"; and they were inclined to give him three cheers and a tiger!

Meanwhile there had been the *Black Warrior* affair, and complications looming—complications highly intriguing to a young diplomat with a name to make.

Cuba, for many years past, had been in a state of insurrection against the complicated deviltries of Spanish rule. Forgetting their own dealings with the red man, Americans, in general, had become duly indignant over this exhibition of barbarism on their own doorstep. Also there were financiers among them who had discovered that Cuba was rich sugar-growing territory and, geographically, within the American sphere. Focused in the sizzling New York headquarters of exiled Cuban revolutionists, a movement for the annexation of the island had been growing steadily throughout the States. In 1848 President Polk, indeed, had offered to purchase it from the Spanish Government for the round sum of one hundred million dollars—to no result. But from that moment filibustering and gun-running expeditions in aid of the insurgents had become an exciting and profitable American sport. The gentlemen engaged in the traffic were not always of the highest respectability, but they usually delivered the goods—and prospered.

Very early in his political career Dan Sickles had realized that decadent Spain's last foothold in American waters must be broken and Cuba annexed. From the day he entered diplomacy he made the project particularly his own, watching developments with jealous care. He had been in London only some six months when, February 28, 1854, the American steamship *Black Warrior* was seized in Havana Harbor by the Spanish authorities and confiscated on charges of filibustering. The news swept the States with the electric crackle of a broken high-tension wire, started editorial fulminations from New York to San Francisco, shocked Congress into crying for immediate suspension of the neutrality laws. In no great while, however, the charge spent itself; and, less hectic counsels prevailing, the clamor for vengeance simmered down to a simple demand for indemnity. But Spain, with her genius for guileful procrastination, delayed the negotiations. Thereupon new filibustering expeditions took on such proportions that President Pierce, in June 1854, had to forbid them by special proclamation. It was a stopgap gesture that loudly touted the necessity for decisive action of some kind. The Cuban question, however, had become international dynamite.

The previous year, alarmed by American sympathy with the insurrectos, the governments of England and France had "invited" the American Government "to decline now and forever hereafter all intention to obtain possession of the island of Cuba and to discontinue all such attempts in that direction on the part of any individual

or power whatever." A piece of tart impertinence that received from
Secretary Everett an equally tart snub:

The question affects American, and not European, policy; and does not
come properly within the scope of the interference of European cabinets.
The United States has no intention of violating existing laws; but the
American Government claims the right to act regarding Cuba independ-
ently of any other power; and it could not view with indifference the
fall of Cuba into hands other than those of Spain.

It was a stout assertion of the Monroe Doctrine that brought an
offended silence from France, a British grunt from Lord John Russell. Stalemate! It was plain enough, however, that unless the United
States Government was prepared to risk hostilities with England
and France as well as with Spain, any move for the acquisition of
Cuba must be made with consummate adroitness and in close consultation with the powers concerned. Once more, therefore, tentative negotiations for the outright purchase of the island—for a vast
sum most useful to the impoverished Spanish Crown—were set afoot.
But the decrepit Spanish monarchy was dependent on the good will
of Louis Napoleon, who in turn found it advantageous to take his
nod from the British Foreign Office—and there sat the imperturbable
Lord John, not anxious to see valuable territory transferred from
a weak and subservient power to one that was neither. Faced with
dilemma, President Pierce suggested to Buchanan that he consult
with Mr. Mason, minister to France, and Mr. Soulé, minister to
Spain, and submit him a report on the whole problem. In the subsequent discussion Sickles took a vigorous part and, to his great delight, was commissioned to present the joint report in person to the
President. Taking fast steamer to New York, he spent a week
domiciled in the White House and attended to his business with
such dispatch that he managed to prepare a lengthy memoir of his
own, "On the State of Europe: Its Bearing on the Policy of the
United States," hold many conferences with President Pierce and
Secretary Marcy, and re-embark on the same boat! He sailed with
special instructions from the State Department for delivery in person to the three ministers. After reporting to Buchanan in London
and Mason in Paris, he entrained for Madrid. There he met General
Espartero—recently premier-dictator by *coup d'état*—and gained from
him the veiled admission that a reasonable settlement of the Cuban

question could be made were it not for opposition elements who would use the occasion to destroy the monarchy and restore a republic. Incidentally, as a matter of routine courtesy, he had a brief audience with Queen Isabella—a fateful moment.

Ten years previously, Isabella and her younger sister had been compelled to wed: the one, her malformed, impotent, feeble-minded cousin, Francisco de Assisi: the other, the Duc de Montpensier, Louis Philippe's son. The scheme had been conceived to outwit Britain. Louis Philippe lusted for a Bourbon heir on the Spanish throne and wished to marry his son to Isabella, the Crown Princess and heiress apparent. Lord Palmerston had objected in his usual hair-trigger fashion. Louis Philippe had bethought himself. The Spanish monarchy—with a republican knife at its throat—was existing precariously from day to day. Under the circumstances he could dictate his own orders to Madrid. He therefore had demanded that Isabella marry her drooling cousin, and that her younger sister marry his own son. The result, he reasoned, would be no heir by the first marriage; several heirs, probably, by the second—a Bourbon on the Spanish throne . . . Britain fooled!

But the young princesses—Isabella was barely sixteen—had shuddered at the proposal. Arguments, inducements, threats proving useless, both had been trapped in a specially arranged Court orgy, taken to the altar inebriated, and married in the same ceremony.

The younger sister had managed to make a forlorn something of her marriage, for the Duc was not quite as much a moral cadaver as his father. But upon Isabella the trick had wrought spiritual disaster. Banishing her pseudo-husband to separate quarters, she had rebelliously turned madcap bawd and had scandalized her conscienceless mother, cynical advisers by openly flaunting her amours not only with one courtier after another but with grooms and guardsmen, any likely lad plucked from the street. In her late twenties she torpedoed Louis Philippe's neat scheme by giving birth to a son begotten of who-knows-whom. And while motherhood brought a new passion into her life, she continued to outrage public opinion at home and abroad by her irresponsible rule, reckless promiscuity, until in 1868 she was banished from the realm.

When Dan Sickles met her she was as yet but twenty-four—a creature of undisciplined impulse, generous and self-willed, full of bright kindness and fierce scorn, buxom, black-eyed, with free, forthright manners well matching her careless costume, picaresque speech. Of what happened in that and several subsequent interviews there remains only a fragmentary and cryptic account to indicate—what later developments amply proved—that here again an unscheduled flash of mutual recognition was to play a critical role in Dan Sickles's career.

In the meantime diplomatic progress in the matter of the Cuban purchase remained nil. Espartero proved noncommittal; Napoleon III gave an imitation of the Sphinx—with an eye cocked across the Channel; Lord John Russell was the Sphinx in person. But the President and Secretary Marcy had requested that the ministers compose and publish a definitive statement of American policy in regard to Cuba—and thus end all futile shadow-boxing. Accordingly Buchanan, Mason, Soulé, and Sickles gathered themselves together at Ostend, where, in season, the bathing, the beauties, and the wines were accounted equally seductive. Diplomatically not one of them had anything to show. They bathed and blathered, dined and discussed, filled one wastepaper basket after another with tortuous solutions. Finally they found themselves, heads together, over Secretary Everett's simple statement: "It is not a matter of European, but of American, policy.". . . It was like a meteoric burst of light in this dark groping to find words ambiguous enough to make it appear that the irreconcilable had been reconciled! Sickles was the first to break the dazed silence. "If this is solely a matter of American policy—then let's state the American policy and be damned!" Four headaches dissolved in what was, probably, one of the most truly American, and at the same time most undiplomatic, documents ever devised: the Ostend Manifesto. It stated that "if Spain, actuated by stubborn pride and a false sense of honor, should refuse to sell Cuba to the United States, then, by every law, human and divine, we should be justified in wresting it from Spain if we possess the power."

The document sent shivers throughout the chancelleries of Europe, provoked hurried consultations between the heads of the French and British admiralties. Secretary Marcy, aware that it stoutly represented the bulk of American street opinion, but that the issue was not worth risking the reception of a *démarche* from London and Versailles, promptly disowned it.

Four gentlemen took their last dip in zebra-striped suits, sipped their last glass of Barsac, shot their last regretful glance at the Ostend demimondaines, and departed wordless and chastened. Dan Sickles, however, soon recovered himself; and, on board the Dover packet, he kept poor Buchanan awake with a masterly dissertation on the pusillanimity of American foreign policy. But Buchanan was sixty-three, a little tired and through with it all. He sank back in his deck chair. "Don't worry, Dan—when Cuba's ripe she'll fall into our lap like a rotten pear." And sound diplomacy went soundly to sleep. Dan Sickles paced the deck.

CHAPTER VII

"The Little Amedican"

MEANWHILE, TERESA, managing her huge, fashionable crinolines rather rompishly, sped about the massive old Legation trilling, and sometimes—to the great scandal of the servants—whistling, with happiness. And there were many things to be happy about. There was the baby; she was glad that it was a girl—found intimate comfort in the cuddle of this small feminine flesh. There was Dan, every day seeming more dashing, popular, important—always terribly occupied, of course, but always exuberant, indulgent. And every morning when she waked there was the perennial surprise of finding herself in the heart of this fabulous Old World of fashion, riches, power, lords and ladies, mighty statesmen, hoary buildings, quaint customs. There was the awesome delight of her presentation at Court, and all the exciting business of preparing her costume: hours of driving hither and thither in her smart brougham, diving into ancient, exclusive little shops with diamond-paned windows sporting the royal arms, where one was treated as a queen amongst courtiers, escorted to a high-backed tapestried chair, and—while Dan, with the decisive air of a man of taste, hovered over every detail of the purchases—the host-proprietor, himself, wheeled up a wine-table set with cakes and fine old sherry. But, perhaps, what she most enjoyed was the fashionable early morning ride in Rotten Row between her two cavaliers—Dan curbing a breedy mount and his own high spirits with assumed nonchalance, Buchanan stately as a statue—exchanging greetings with bewhiskered gentlemen in box hats, deep-skirted riding coats, gay plaid waistcoats; relishing the appraising, and sometimes envious, glances of ladies arrayed like herself in tightly buttoned black habit; now and again catching a reflection of herself in the young girls—their faces, beneath their beplumed tricorns, dewy pink as the heart of a dog rose with the thresh of damp air, the pulse of the canter. . . . And always on her escritoire a stack of invitation cards—teas, dinners, theaters, balls, receptions.

A gay life! Separately or together, both spun on a social whirligig pleasurably confusing—numbing reflection. A busy life, too. Dan, of course, always had seemed to have engagements the clock around. And soon Teresa also found herself well occupied.

Buchanan, a bachelor, had come to be pathetically dependent for feminine social aid on his niece—Miss Harriet Lane. But that mistress of the punctilios—chill and firm, despite violet eyes, auburn hair—had returned to New York to adjust some important property matters. Diplomatic custom decreed that the wife of the First Secretary should assume her place as the official Legation hostess. But here Buchanan needed no support from precedent. To him Teresa, with her buoyant *esprit*, her easy command of half the languages of Europe to aid his own weak smatter of French, seemed less decreed by custom than by Heaven! And he insisted that she help him out. To her alarmed protests that she lacked the necessary social experience he argued that all she needed was her own natural good sense and tact plus a little schooling in the curiosities of British etiquette—something he could give her as occasion required.

And so it came about that this oddly assorted pair—a tall, gray-pated Pennsylvania-Scotch politician, timorous of soul but handsome despite a squint eye, a head forever held askew above choker collar, enormous white cravat; and an iridescent little Italian-Viennese beauty not long out of school—stood side by side at receptions, presided together at Embassy dinners, attended functions, made calls, and—unconsciously if inevitably—aroused a certain speculation. Teresa met the challenge of it all with youthful verve; and if her Latin blood sometimes prevented her from quite catching the casual yet circumspect British tone, she nevertheless made an instantly happy impression. In an age which confined women strictly to the home she found in her position all the exciting novelty of a "job"—a rather royal one as to its trappings, but exacting enough as to its duties. She enjoyed both the trappings and the duties, and was wildly elated when her efforts brought some word of praise from Dan or Buchanan. To her it was praise earned.

Fashionable London—impervious to the native parvenue—watched the new Legation hostess cautiously, then—as it has a way of doing—suddenly smiled. This "little Amedican," apparently so unsophisticated yet able to converse freely in French, Spanish, Italian with the foreign diplomats at her table, and who, without experience of the beau monde, behaved as though she were born to it, had everyone charmed. If her candor and freshness had a tang of the New World, her great dark eyes, quick eloquent gestures, a touch of the exotic in her jewelry, a trick of slipping, in excitement, from one language to another, had all the flavor of the Continent. Not without some kindly amusement, she was accepted as a law unto herself: in the British sense—an aristocrat. And when those social arbiters, Lady Clarendon and Lady Palmerston, took her under their capacious wings, it was conquest complete. The society columns greeted her lyrically, created her third person of a new trinity; and, thereafter, the auburn and alabaster Miss Lane, the gorgeous Mrs. Lawrence, and "the new American beauty, Mrs. Sickles," were stylized in the press as "The Three American Graces."

Curiously, however, praise of her beauty left Teresa cool. She accepted her odalisque eyes, cleverly carven face, figurine physique as something with which she had nothing to do. She was too much a Latin not to be a coquette, with a dainty flair for dress and flirtation, but, at heart, she had little personal vanity. There was, in fact, something boyish and forthright in her nature, a certain unguessed realism and firmness of mind, that shielded her against playing admiring audience to herself. Beneath her deceptive air of slim fragility lurked a lithe body and healthy spirit then called "hoydenish." There was that in her that craved the outdoors, the wind across the heath, the long ramble, the cross-country canter; that hated crinolines, corsets. Curiously, just as there was much of the sixteenth century in Dan, so there was much of the twentieth century in Teresa—a spirit that would have found itself much at home among our modern free-mannered young Amazons of saddle and surf and golf course. But Fate had doomed her to Victorian hoops, mincing modes . . . devout conventions discreetly ignored!

At The Hague and Paris—accompanying Dan and Buchanan on brief diplomatic visits—Teresa's popularity was even more marked. Here, as she had not in London, she felt herself instantly *chez elle*. The fact that her father had conducted the opera in both cities, and that she often had heard him describe those events in nostalgic detail, may have had something to do with it; or it may have been because her blood was purely Continental. In any case, these cultivated Hollanders and Frenchmen seemed to her, in a sense, her own people. They fascinated her, and she them. That Buchanan gallantly gave her the spotlight particularly pleased the Parisians. The boulevardiers drew their own conclusions.

But beneath all the pleasurable excitement of her new position, social success, Teresa secretly was troubled, a little bewildered. The trouble was Dan; the bewilderment, that she could not find herself with him, that while everyone else treated her as a woman, he still seemed to see in her only the child of other days. He was, she realized, more indulgent, more lavish than ever—when she saw him. But then she hardly ever saw him save for a few minutes at breakfast, and then he would be so gay, gossipy, full of solicitous questionings, paternal advice—so generally endearing—that there was nothing she could do but respond.

But always it was the same—a kiss and a pat on the shoulder, and he would be off again! And if she protested against seeing so little of him, there would be some smiling evasion, "Diplomacy, Terry, has no hours. Conference work has to be done late. You never can see the important people during the day. Buchanan is not the man he was, and I have to shoulder most of the load." And if she begged, he would come striding over to her, toss her up in his arms. "All right, then—I'll risk an hour or two off duty. How about getting that new bonnet for the garden party, eh?" And he would whisk her away on a whirlwind shopping spree. And then, once again, with that affectionate pat, he would be off about his affairs—or an affair!

An affair! There was the rub. That side of his life she instinctively shut from her mind.

Who was she to judge Dan—the good genius of her days, Dan—

the future President of the United States? Rather she blamed herself, her own inadequacy beside these brilliant London women, for the fact that he so often sought his pleasures elsewhere. It was a situation that she could only quietly ignore. Nevertheless she had enough feminine spirit to make a play for her own. She held but one card: Buchanan.

For a variety of very human reasons, the infatuations of elderly bachelors seldom are conducted discreetly. And Buchanan was both elderly and infatuated. For him it was "last call" to romance in a rather pallid and barren life; and like all lovers who have failed to equilibrate their passion in private, he tended unconsciously to make undue display of it in public. And Teresa, in pique, boldly played to his lead.

Naturally their occasionally unguarded behavior aroused comment —comment that the sharp difference between the British and American psychologies made rather tart. Nothing horrifies the Englishman so much as even a slight display of the more intimate emotions in public; nothing bothers an American less! A British ambassador, enraptured with a pretty hostess, would have trod the social rounds with no more manifestation of regard for the lady on his arm than he would show for his umbrella. His studied indifference would be a tacit "Damn your eyes and hold your tongue!" to all beholders— a signal that, in his own circles at least, would be accepted in the spirit of *noblesse oblige*. But Buchanan, thoroughly the American, behaved more naturally and, by his obvious attentions, innocently invited his audience into a secret that they would rather not be burdened with. The consequence was that while the ladies pounced upon the supposed "affair," the men were irritated by what seemed to them its needless exposure. The more sensible, of course, smiled at the idea that a slightly shaky gentleman of sixty-four could be a rival to the masterful, magnetic Dan Sickles. But Teresa's youth, beauty, popularity with the men, had not failed to arouse the usual meed of envy. And there were plenty of agitated ladies to make the most of the gossip, and even to conjure up other lovers for good measure. Teresa was a quite simple person. Only slowly did she come to realize what a teapot typhoon she had stirred up. And the storm was just beginning.

It happened that unpleasant rumors seeped back to Miss Harriet Lane in Washington just as she was giving a little farewell tea for her friend, Mrs. Thomas, wife of General John A. Thomas, Assistant Secretary of State—recently appointed solicitor to the American Claims Commission then sitting in London. Miss Lane was outraged; Mrs. Thomas, loyally furious. Both proposed righteous retribution.

Upon reaching London, Mrs. Thomas immediately went to see Buchanan. Her mission was twofold: to ask him to arrange for her presentation at Court—and to get in a smashing slap at Teresa. The affable Buchanan agreed to make the required arrangements and added that, as was the custom, she would be sponsored by the Legation hostess, Mrs. Sickles. Mrs. Thomas was waiting for that! In a passion of propriety she demanded to be provided with a more suitable introduction. Buchanan, for once, was neither timid nor irresolute. He smartly refused. The lady was not presented! But her social entrée was wide; and in the drawing rooms of her friends she took luxuriant revenge.

Strangely late Dan waked to the growing gale of gossip. Then, suddenly, he was jealous, alert. Bounding up the Legation steps, he burst in on Teresa, dressing for dinner. For a moment she was terrified. Often she had seen his gray eyes glint white flame—but not when he was looking at her! Then, as she caught the gist of his fury, her heart sang again. So, after all, he did care! She could afford to play with the moment, equivocate, taunt. "I don't know what you mean, Dan. I have to take care of everything for Jim. And if he seems to appreciate it, what can I do?" It was a feeble attempt, but the tone was stab enough. The retort came like a bullet, "You don't have to be with him day and night—behave like a hussy in public—make a fool of me!" Teresa was demure. "But I hardly ever see you, Dan—and you can't expect me to live like a nun." Dan stopped dead. "What —was that?" On the instant Teresa knew that she had overplayed her hand. The man who stood over her was a stranger. She cowered. "But Dan, Dan, what have I done? What do they say I've done?" The ingenuous cry quivering to tears, the crumpled, crinolined figure, were answer enough. They choked the words in his throat—made him feel ridiculous. In a breath he found himself patting a sleek, jet head. "It's all right, Terry—it's all right. I know you didn't mean any harm. But you're too impulsive, my dear. In a position like yours, you can't be too careful. And you really must be more circumspect, Terry. This isn't New York, you know. It doesn't take much to set all London talking." Wet, obsidian eyes were half smiling up at him.

"I see it now, Dan. I just didn't understand. After all, they talk about you, too, don't they?" Dan, startled, turned away with a forced chuckle. "I suppose they do—the damned cats!"

CHAPTER VIII

Iceberg in the Sun

———◆———

DAN AND TERESA—what of them really? One can only say that at this moment they were like twin peaks of a glittering emerald and turquoise iceberg drifting southward in the sun, unmindful of the hidden, already creviced mass beneath—lord of their ways, threatening to break them asunder.

Beneath the scintillant surface these two presented to the social sun lay something very different—something fateful, dark, unheeding: the hidden reality of a marriage that never was a mating; and, that, because it was seemingly predestined, was only the more poignantly mistaken.

In the subtle realm of the erotic emotions, it is very easy to mistake the true nature of a relationship: very easy to mistake a gay child, a charming schoolgirl, for something entirely different—a wife; very easy to mistake the generous, playful benefactor of one's rompish days for something equally different—a husband. Very easy, in short, to mistake a marriage for a mating! For the one is a matter of the romantic emotions; the other, a matter of dictatorial molecules.

Precise as the laws of the test tube are the laws that govern the coalescence of man and woman. Far below a surface attraction, "compatibility," lies that master and mystery of human life—biologic rapport. Where that spontaneous, molecular recognition, with its rhythmic mutuality of need and response, exists between lovers, peace descends, quest is transformed into fusion and new growth. Where it does not exist there is no peace and—whether one will or no—the quest goes on; it goes on even when it appears to die in mutual flaccid friendliness or mutual dull endurance. In the unconscious it never dies but persists as long as life itself.

Had there been this real rapport between Dan and Teresa, then nothing else would have mattered.

It would not have mattered that the one was nearly twice as old as the other; that the one was sophisticated, the other naïve; the one complex, the other simple; the one mature, the other undeveloped; the one keenly aware of his own demands upon life, the other barely awake to her own womanhood. It would not have mattered that Dan was decisive, resistant, resilient, while Teresa was pliable, impressionable, easily crushed. But as it was, these contrasts of temperament, that otherwise might have proven happily complementary, merely set these two at poles apart.

Swept by Teresa's virginal loveliness, Dan genuinely had thought, for the moment, that here at last was the end of his search, the end of an overprolonged youth filled with fleeting affairs. Naturally enough, under the circumstances, Teresa was equally swept. And what was—and should have remained—virtually a charming godfather-child relationship suddenly ignited in a brief, fallacious lover relationship; and then inevitably began to revert to its original pattern.

Dan was too instinctive not to realize almost at once the true nature of his marriage. He knew that no one else ever could take Teresa's place in his heart, that she always would be his cherished charge, an esthetic delight; but he also knew that she never could be to him the wife he craved, that he never really could be to her—a husband. And from that moment, regretfully, he lavished upon her everything in his power—everything but himself.

Over and above all this, it would seem that Dan Sickles was a man constitutionally unfitted for marriage. Like many men of unusual caliber—a Goethe, a Liszt, a Guy de Maupassant, an Aaron Burr, a Pancho Villa, to cite wildly contrasting examples—his restless vitality and tremendous erotic energy apparently made it impossible for him to confine himself within the bounds of a relationship with one woman. To him marriage was simply a fetter.

For Teresa—given her simple, natural, ardent temper—it was, of course, a marriage situation more intricately tragic, delicately damning than fiction has yet dared to propose. A child had become a child-wife—the "child" still pampered, petted, adored by all the ardor of a dominating nature; the "wife"—ignored!

But Teresa, in the midst of her new distractions, was only vaguely aware of a haunt in her heart, a lack in her life; for Dan, with his prodigal kindness, simply muffled her mind. Immature, plastic, accustomed from childhood to take her cue from him, she now, in her dawning womanhood, responded to his masterful lead as does a rhythmic but unschooled dancer to her partner on the floor . . . a Dance of Death!

Under the circumstances hers was inevitably a precarious predicament. Unconsciously she was savoring the girlhood she had never known—with the disadvantage that she was a married woman—spiritually unprotected. And she would not have been a warm-blooded daughter of the South if she had not enjoyed a sense of her own allure, the admiration of the men about her, her obvious conquest of "Minister Jim." Yet, at the same time, she was mystified by the response she provoked in men. They not only gathered about her wherever she went, but seemed to regard her most innocent sallies as deliberate enticement. Often she was afraid to play too much, more often was glad that she had the superficial refuge of a social position, a husband. She did not know, could not know, that a woman whose marriage is incomplete consciously or unconsciously carries about her an atmosphere of quest; and that there is nothing so patent to the masculine instinct as a woman erotically aroused but emotionally unappeased. And thus there were moments when, guiltily, she wondered how it could be that the touch of a stranger's hand could arouse in her a response that Dan, with all his ardor and *adresse*, never had aroused.

Suddenly, with the air of a man trying to think of a dozen things at once, Dan was bursting into Teresa's dressing room. "Jim wants me to go back at once and start the campaign for his nomination. With Jim in the White House—I'm next! . . . Hurry up, Terry!"

PART THREE: MASQUE OF DEATH

CHAPTER IX

Fighting Escalade

———◆———

THE PERFERVID FIFTIES!—born with the Gold Rush, dying amid the bruit of Civil Havoc. . . . Years of social fever, political ferment, sizzling crusades, rant and riot. . . . Mad years!

Slavocracy and Plutocracy; the agrarian South and the industrial North; chattel slavery and the wage system, were about to fight it out—with the States for prize. No one wanted to believe it. The gold of the Incas was pouring into New York! And a people torn between a crackling get-rich-quick excitement and a stifled foreboding of Things-to-Come gave itself over, on the least excuse, to such outbursts of mass emotionalism as could not be matched even in its own phrenetic history.

At the dawn of the decade New York City was rent by so simple a thing as jealousy between the English actor, Macready, and the American actor, Edwin Forrest. Argument concerning the respective merits of the two grew to bloody, feuding proportions. On the night that Macready attempted to play *Macbeth*, the opposing faction stormed the Opera House and then turned on the militia summoned to restore order. The ensuing battle strewed Astor Place with a score dead, filled the hospitals with the wounded.

Healthier vent for the popular need to emote was "the furor." It was the age of Barnum in mind and scene, and of clever "managers" quick to cash in on the American attitude of doting adoration toward any foreigner of note—duly advertised. As in the preceding decade,

Dickens, Ole Bull, Fanny Elssler, Jenny Lind, Kossuth, each in turn were met and feted by enormous outpourings of howling humanity such as no victorious warrior king ever encountered. Thackeray, appealing only to the intellectual class, escaped being mobbed—but did extremely well!

At the same time there was the drama of the Atlantic telegraphic cable. Its completion—marked by the exchange of Morse-code compliments between Queen Victoria and President Pierce—sent the nation wild. Promptly the tortured cable broke—to lie silent while a palpitant public waited.

Politically it was a decade of perpetual crisis. Abolitionism, at first the field of a few fanatics, rapidly had become the major escape valve for the repressed passions of a people still largely cowed by the crude moralism, morbid theology of Puritanism. No piston-and-cylinder for a steaming unconscious like a good excuse for righteous indignation! And the same force that could blast a Cellini from a fevered bed to the casting floor, a Schicklgruber from a Vienna slum to the throne of World Dementia, was driving the whole North blindly on the road to war. All Boston turned out to liberate a single bewildered Negro escaped from the South, imprisoned—and reclaimed. "A lot of folks to see a colored man off!" he muttered, as, escorted by a powerful detachment of over a thousand cavalry and infantry—at a cost of $40,000—he gloomily headed back to Dixie. Hordes of Boston's jobless mill hands—hunger-gnawed men and women, work-weazened children—watched and wondered; wondered, perhaps, that black flesh and blood could be so dear, white flesh and blood so cheap.

From day to day the headlines crackled the news of a rending social structure. In "bleeding Kansas" the struggle between Free Soiler and Slavocrat reeled from riot to raid, from mobbing to massacre. Both Congress and Senate witnessed bitter brawling, fisticuffs. Senator Butler, of South Carolina, was ill and absent from the House when Senator Sumner, of Massachusetts, singled him out for an unusually vituperative attack. Whereupon young Congressman Preston Brooks, Butler's nephew, sought out the acrid old abolitionist and, catching him bowed at his desk, beat him into insensibility and years of invalidism with the butt of his heavy, gold-headed cane. In the ensuing months, Brooks's stately plantation became cluttered with heavy gold-headed canes sent him by his Southern admirers.

There was the fateful Dred Scott decision—"The black man has no rights which the white man is bound to respect"—striking the States asunder with apocalyptic sword. . . . And, presently, there was John Brown's mad, moronic raid on Harpers Ferry.

In literature, likewise, it was crisis. With the appearance of Walt Whitman's *Leaves of Grass*, Thoreau's *Walden*, Melville's *Moby Dick*, Hawthorne's *House of the Seven Gables*, Emerson's *Representative Men*, the early fifties witnessed the last sundown flair of America's "Golden Day." At the same time, headstones carven with names destined to become familiar to every schoolboy began to dot American graveyards. James Fenimore Cooper, John James Audubon, William H. Prescott, Washington Irving went their way . . . and among them others—Clay, Calhoun, Webster—the oratorical "elder statesmen" of an age born to the beat of the British drum and about to die to the skirl of the Rebel yell.

A decade of death—and birth: death of the sober years of New England strength, intellectual passion: birth of the hectic years of Blather and Best Seller. Like fireweed amid a burnt-out forest there sprang up a lush crop of propagandists—abolitionist, temperance, feminist—cracker-barrel humorists, lachrymose female fictionists, petty versifiers. And the crop throve mightily. While *Leaves of Grass* sold not one copy, and Thoreau had to take back and store in his garret the unsold first edition of his immortal pond-side report (with the dry remark: "I now have a library of four hundred and fifty volumes each one written by myself!"), the new effusions ran into printings of hundreds of thousands, and in half a dozen instances into the millions.

Fanny Fern's *Fern Leaves*—a delicious decoction of tear-bedewed fronds from Fanny's mental fernery—sold seventy thousand copies off the press and held a place among best sellers throughout the decade. *The Lamplighter*, by Maria S. Cummings ("There was a sweet soft moan of tender unrest, and she flung herself on his heaving bosom") sold, naturally enough, over a hundred thousand copies the first few months and continued to do land-office business down the years. Susan Warner's *The Wide, Wide World* and *Queechy*—with a freshet of tears to the page—deservedly did better. Timothy Shay Arthur's soul-saddening *Ten Nights in a Bar Room* surpassed both. All four made the million mark.

And then, of course and at last, there was *Uncle Tom's Cabin* and

Hiawatha—the Plantation as imagined by a lady who never had set foot on one: the Red Man as observed from a Harvard window! Longfellow, in fact, knew no more about the Indian and the West than Mrs. Stowe knew about the Negro and the South. But the sobbing saga of slavery and the tepid, epicurean epic of the tepee outbested all the best sellers of the day.

Despite their reformist tendencies—not forgetting a bravura attempt at bloomers, and Elizabeth Cady Stanton's bold foray for Woman's Rights—the fifties wanted to feel, not think. They were uncritical years!

And Sickles felt and shared the tumult of the time. Returning to New York clad in the éclat of his recent diplomatic jousts, he plunged at once into a campaign for the state senate. The odds were all against him. Tammany at this time was rent into viciously feuding factions. The "Soft-Shells," comprising the cream of the criminal element, were preparing to strong-arm their leader, the lean, lecher-faced Machiavellian, Fernando Wood—first of the tough dynasty of Tammany "bosses"—into the mayoralty. The "Hard-Shells," avid for office, sported fake reformist policies under a less accomplished corruptionist, Wilson G. Hunt. At the same time the Native American Party or "Know-Nothings," springing to life again, put forward another candidate, James W. Barker; while the Whigs supported John J. Herrick. "The ensuing contest," remarked the polite *Harper's Magazine*, "was the most bitter and relentless ever waged in New York." Gustavus Myers was more detailed:

The competition for the millions of city plunder was so terrific that the Wood and anti-Wood men fought savagely. In the Sixth Ward the Wood partisans, upon being attacked, retreated for a while, and coming back, armed with brickbats, clubs, axes, and pistols, set upon and routed their foes. The police, meanwhile, calmly looked on.

It would not have been the fifties, of course, if the brawling had not been a little more fervent than usual! And Sickles, once more, had to bear the full brunt of it. With the Whigs, the Know-Nothings, and half Tammany against him, he waded into the melee; and, with no organized backing worth mentioning, made his campaign a test of the endorsement of Buchanan's nomination by the New York electorate. It was a critical moment in his climb. If he failed to gain a seat in the state senate now, it would dim his prestige at the forth-coming Democratic convention, detract from his influence in aid of Buchanan's nomination, vastly diminish his chances of election to the next Congress. And to enter Washington an "Honorable" aboard the presidential train of his own victorious nominee was for him a maneuver essential to his ultimate march on the White House. It was a moment not to be missed. It needed all his wiliness, energy, eloquence, personal popularity, all the support a few stanch friends could give him. The combination served him well. He emerged from a chaotic, unpredictable campaign an elate, if rather breathless, state senator—the vital rung secured.

But there was no time to lose. In the view of his friends, the color-less Buchanan's chances of receiving the presidential nomination were decidedly slim. Arrayed against him were: the popular President Pierce, the volcanic, rhetorical Stephen A. Douglas, the cautious and astute Secretary William L. Marcy—candidates long in the public eye, wielding powerful political influence, and each boasting a large per-sonal following. But in the preconvention caucuses Sickles cleverly used Buchanan's very defects as convincing persuasions in his favor. He argued that Pierce, Douglas, Marcy were strong personalities, jealous of each other and easily able to split the party ranks if brought into opposition; and that all three were much too involved in the fierce factional disputes created by the disastrous Kansas-Nebraska bill to be trusted with the task of consolidating the Democratic vote: that Buchanan, on the other hand, was a quiet, sensible man, with no pronounced views on anything; that his prolonged absence at the Court of St. James's had removed him from all contact with the caldron of domestic politics; that, in short, there was nothing to be said against him—a supremely important qualification for a successful presidential nominee. Secretly and persistently, in season and out, Sickles pressed his friend's claims. His efforts proved effective. When the Democratic convention opened in Cincinnati in June 1856, the result already was foreknown. Quickly the delegates by-passed all rival candidates and chose the inoffensive and highly esteemed "Old Buck" to lead them to victory at the polls. Five months later the country endorsed their decision. It was a narrow squeak, however. The newly arisen Republican party, skippered by the opéra-bouffe "conqueror of California," John C. Frémont, polled only half a mil-lion less votes.

Meanwhile, at Albany, Dan Sickles found himself condemned to opposition—the leader of a small minority. But, with his aptitude for guerrilla tactics, it was not long before he had harassed the Senate into the conviction that it could get little business done without him. And, as usual, there was nothing of bravura in his manner. In opposing a measure not to his liking, his attitude was, in fact, rather amusingly akin to that of a skilled surgeon excising a tumor for the instruction of a group of raw medical students. The dissection finished—always to the last fine filament—there remained, as a rule, small room for further discussion.

A typical instance of this was his treatment of the Registry bill. There had been much outcry against the abuse of the polls—particularly against the wholesale frauds practiced by Fernando Wood and his acolytes. To still the clamor, the astute mayor of New York, certain Tammany chiefs, and a few purchasable Whigs themselves had engineered the introduction of a bill drawn ostensibly to prevent illegal voting. The measure actually was a most ingeniously camouflaged device for delivering the power to qualify voters entirely into the hands of the Wood machine. Forced through the Assembly, the bill was well on its way to endorsement in the Senate when Dan Sickles rose to speak. He was in his most polite and surgical mood. Before the eyes of a silent, uneasy audience he proceeded, with quiet, exasperating thoroughness, to dissect the measure and expose it fragment by fragment for exactly what it was—a cleverly conceived fake. When at last he sat down no one seemed anxious to rise; and the bill was shuffled off into committee for "reconsideration," surreptitious burial.

But it was the Trinity Church bill that gave Sickles his first outstanding parliamentary victory.

Under a grant by Queen Anne, Trinity Church had been chartered in colonial days as a parish of the English Episcopal Church—with, as was the custom, a substantial "glebe" for its support. In the course of New York's Jack-o'-the-Beanstalk growth, the "glebe"—once innocent pasture and tilth—had become metamorphosed into blocks of enormously valuable real estate in the city's heart. At the same time a thrifty board of directors—nominally elective but virtually self-perpetuating—had steadily improved the property with buildings commercial and residential, and now was drawing princely income from its leaseholds and rentals, while expending only very modest sums for charitable and religious purposes. Naturally the newer, smaller, less fortunate Episcopal churches of the diocese began to feel themselves entitled to representation on the Trinity Church vestry—with a corresponding share in its swollen emoluments. In 1847, in fact, they had submitted their claim to the state legislature in a measure known as the Trinity Church bill. Eventually it had been killed in committee; but Sickles, then an Assembly neophyte, had attended the discussion with alert interest. Now, once more, with powerful support, the measure was re-introduced. And, as the senator for the district served by Trinity Church, Sickles was importuned by the vestry, and even by his own devout mother, to secure its defeat. It was an opportunity not to be missed—and Trinity a political power not to be despised. Technically the case was clear; and, in the course of a brilliant ten-hour speech, Sickles not only defeated it, but in so doing established an "opinion" as to its illegality that, a hundred years later, still remains, for good or ill, unquestioned.

Trinity Church, of course, was, and is, an anachronism—a fragment of the English state church left thriving on American soil, drawing its income from British grants, re-established by Congress in 1784 and 1814. And whatever may have been its Christian duty toward the smaller churches, its status as a business corporation, subject only to the electors of its own parish, was legally unassailable. And Sickles wisely centered his attack on the purely legal aspects of the bill. But, understandably enough, there was a vast amount of sentiment in its favor. Cleverly, therefore, he begged the whole case, treating his auditors not as a legislative body with power to enact, but simply as a court with power to try—a procedure that inevitably threw into the sharpest relief the legal decrepitudes of the measure. At the same time, with consummate wile, he masked his tactics with a display of sentiment, sarcasm, ridicule such as seldom crept into his speeches. Did the proponents of the measure weep for the plight of the small churches?—Sickles, too, could draw tears:

I was born and reared within the bosom of this church, and in this parish. The graves of my humble ancestors lie within its sacred enclosures. The marriage vow, the baptismal blessing, were pronounced upon those from whom I sprang, by the side of its altars. It is the only church that now remains within my district to take care of its poor; to relieve their wants, to visit them when sick, to clothe them when naked, and to guide them to a happy immortality hereafter.

Was the behavior of Trinity Church unethical, non-Christian? Very well! Not content with the clear, legalistic proof that the parishioners of the complaining churches had no electoral rights in the Trinity vestry, he mischievously embellished his argument with an amusing word picture of the disastrous results likely to befall their own Christian behavior were they given the vote.

You array churches that should be the sisters of Trinity, against her. The friends of Trinity in the other churches will be eager that Trinity shall be sustained in the elections. A majority of some congregations will be for Trinity, and a majority of others will be hostile to her. Thus you will array church against church, congregation against congregation. St. George will be against the Holy Innocents; St. Matthew's will be against St. John's; Grace against St. Paul's; St. Luke's against All Saints'; St. Mary's against the Annunciation; and the Holy Evangelists, perhaps, against them all!

Well, sir, here we have fifty-four angry ecclesiastical elections going on in one day in New York—an exciting issue, a heated controversy, a bitter conflict! It is not too much to fancy that we see the omnibuses rattling through the streets, crowded with eager voters, and vocal with strange election cries: "Three cheers for Grace Church! . . . Hurry up more votes to Ascension! . . . Trinity is ahead! . . . Ho! for the Evangelists!" See the inflammatory handbills, "Up with Trinity! . . . Down with St. George!" Ah, it will be no longer the St. George we have been accustomed to regard, but St. George and the Dragon—eager to enter the field of strife, burning for the foray! But let us hasten to the churches, hear the crowd around the doors—the police vainly endeavoring to preserve order—give three cheers for the Low Church, three groans for the High Church, and a tiger for the Bishop! Now approach the door and see the eager ticket peddlers pay their respects to each newcomer: "Are you against Trinity? . . . Can't you give us a vote for Grace Church?" Mark how they follow that opposition voter along the aisle; how closely they watch him to see that he is a duly qualified voter; how spitefully they challenge and wrangle with him about his vote! . . .

Followed a note of solemn mock reproach:

And what a time have you chosen for these extraordinary proceedings in the Church? The season of Lent!

Then, suddenly, he is majestic:

Sir, I would maintain always and everywhere, by my voice, my vote, and my best labors, *vested constitutional rights;* and if there be any nation on earth—if there be any form of government devised—if there be any people under the sun that more than any other must be dependent on the scrupulous preservation of private rights and constitutional guarantees, it is this government of ours. It is a people who believe in the democratic faith, in the capacity of man for self-government.

We have a government which has surmounted all other dangers. We have a constitution under which we can hold elections, choose legislatures, elect and install presidents, and in one brief hour transfer the power of a mighty empire from one hand to another without tumult, without resistance, without the presence of a single bayonet. We have educated a people to a point where they can intelligently exercise the exalted function of electors. But, sir, we have yet to undergo a higher test—whether or no we can respect, preserve, and maintain inviolate the vested rights of citizens and communities. If we can do this, then, indeed, shall we have triumphed. Then our august experiment stands out to mankind a victory— an example to be followed by all other nations and by all other races throughout time. But if we fail here, we send an arrow through the very heart of free government, and the whole magnificent fabric falls.

The defense rested its case. It is still resting!

1856. The presidential election. Buchanan swept into power— largely by Sickles's efforts. And, after a brief and brilliant campaign against the forces of Whigs and Wood-ites, Sickles himself emerging congressman from the Third District of New York City. Feeling himself well on his way, he purchases a beautiful estate at Bloomingdale, New Jersey.

A few more rungs well won. Washington at last! And a fashionable residence—within pistol shot of the White House!

CHAPTER X

Swampoodle Palmyra

——————◆◆◆——————

STRANGE THAT A PEOPLE sporting the eagle for oriflamme, and long nurtured in a log-cabin tradition, should have chosen a malodorous mud flat as the site of its capital and a pseudo-Greek type of architecture for its national edifices! The resulting mélange bewildered the visitor, touched off many a quip. Henry Adams, revisiting it after twenty years, found it, ". . . the same rude colony set in the same rude forest, with Greek temples for workrooms, and sloughs for roads!" Dickens, with genial sarcasm, hailed it "the city of magnificent intentions." To Thackeray it suggested "the ruins of Carthage." And Anthony Trollope, complaining that, to explore it, one must have "breeches tucked well above knees," dubbed it "the new Palmyra." . . . Swampoodle was its aboriginal name.

In the fifties, in fact, Washington, already fifty years a-building, still was a forlorn embryo. Most of the streets marked on its pretentious map remained rabbit runs and cowpaths; and such as actually existed on earth were deep in muck when not deep in dust. Pigs wallowed and goats browsed on Capitol Hill. The disused Canal, riving the city's heart, and now a popular dumping ground, was foul with offal, excrement, dead dogs and cats; and the southern half of President's Park was rendered unusable by the stench from the neighboring swamp—formerly the sewage outfall. Pennsylvania Avenue, the one important thoroughfare—much affected by flocks of peripatetic geese—frequently was impassable afoot. Nevertheless its broad-brick northern sidewalk—peopled promiscuously by politicians in Yankee stovepipes, southern broad-brimmed Barcelonas, western sombreros, by behooped ladies and colored maids, liveried Negroes lounging around hotel doors, red-shirted river toughs, dandified gamblers, government clerks and fancy-girls—formed the only fashionable promenade. Even the lonely, incongruous, unfinished temples, spotted haphazardly about, stood knee deep in their own debris; and, with all the embarrassment of maimed and naked Greek statues exposed to public view in some dejected shanty town of the lower Mississippi, gazed upon each other across blowsy vacant lots, patches of pristine brush, rubbish heaps, open sewers, dingy boardinghouses, saloons, and brothels.

For all its malaria-stricken, mosquito-infested dreariness, however, Washington could boast, at least, one ultrafashionable district—and that, at the moment, quite the most important, not to say explosive, spot in the highly disunited States. North of Pennsylvania Avenue, and the littered lawns of the unfinished White House, stood blocks of solid, handsome residences. A sprinkling of these belonged to northerners—among them Stephen A. Douglas, Charles Sumner, Charles Francis Adams, William H. Seward. But the great majority of them were owned by planter-politicians—men such as William M. Gwin, the proslavery senator from California; Jacob Thompson, of Mississippi; Aaron Brown, of Tennessee; Justice Campbell, of the Supreme Court; Senator Toombs, of Georgia; Senator Slidell, of Louisiana; those social arbiters, the Riggses, Clays, Parkers, Tayloes; the Washington Croesus and art collector, W. W. Corcoran; Vice-President John C. Breckinridge, of Kentucky; and Jefferson Davis, of Mississippi—Southrons (their pet self-styling) knit in a tight phalange. And it was here, in these ponderous homes, amid an atmosphere of prodigal hospitality, revel and vaunt and intrigue, that the whole social and political power of the South clotted in ceaseless watch over its own.

Chattel slavery, of course, long had ceased to pay. Cotton sold at a profitless six cents a pound. But a prime slave might cost as much as two thousand dollars. The average plantation failed to net one per centum on its investment. And southern adoption of the northern wage system plainly would have proven much more efficient and profitable—if less merciful—than the patriarchal exploitation and support of the unwaged black man. But the South was besotted of its own institutions and stood ready to rend the Union to preserve them —and establish the right to expand them upon the western territories.

Significantly, as the rumblings grew louder and the earth began to crack between states and parties, between friend and friend, father and son, brother and brother, the Washington whirl of balls and banquets quickened with the gathering pace of a tarantella. And if the pace was set by the southerners, the northerners were not slow to follow. The Blairs kept open house for the young Republican party; Stephen A. Douglas and his bride—the famous Washington beauty, Adele Cutts—entertained the Free Soil Democrats. And the dinners given by Adams and Seward and Sumner were second to none. In these homes, too, often were held certain "secret suppers" where anxious discussion—aided by cold duck and Rhenish—brooded deep into the night. In the teeth of the abolitionist threat from the North, the secessionist threat from the South, the opening years of Buchanan's administration were by far the gayest the capital ever had known.

Political hospitality, indeed, had become so lavish that the President, to maintain his own standing, had to draw largely upon his private account to supplement his meager salary of $25,000 a year. And so the Executive Mansion, too, blazed with light—even if the light were a little austere, Miss Lane's ideas of etiquette a trifle stiff for Washington taste.

Much of the social life centered about the three fashionable hotels —Brown's, intimate, southern, exclusive; the National, favorite spot for political conferences; and Willard's, large, noisy, always overflowing, famous for its cuisine and ballroom, every night the scene of informal hops. And since not everyone wished to be bothered with the upkeep of an establishment, many politicians preferred to live at one or other of the hotels; and their wives and families often formed congenial groups—"messes" in the local idiom.

Desolate and deserted throughout the long, unhealthy summer, with the autumn reopening of Congress, Washington leaped to life. The grimy little station thrummed with the incoming crowds of northern and western congressmen and senators with their families, political hangers-on, office seekers, lobbyists, salesmen, gamblers, government clerks, and a due proportion of befeathered girls and enterprising thieves. The wharves were crowded with southerners arriving by every steamer from Aquia Creek, surrounded by darky retainers and piles of baggage. Pennsylvania Avenue swarmed with hacks, smart broughams, lumbering wagons loaded with produce for the markets; and its flyblown shop windows newly polished off made bold display of the latest wares from New York, London, Paris; while the sidewalks, cluttered with the influx of boxes, barrels, crates, were rendered almost impassable to the hurrying throng. In a day or two the lone Washington theater would open; perhaps with a minstrel show, possibly a dubious opera company; or, with luck, there might be Joe Jefferson or Charlotte Cushman, Edwin Forrest or Edwin Booth to lend a New York touch to the still rustic capital. And, at night, mansions that had stood silent and dark for months would become battlements of glowing windows; the sedate avenues would echo the trample of blooded horses, the growl of carriage wheels; massive doors, long locked, would swing ceaselessly in the hands of liveried darkies grinning welcome to streams of guests—ladies with the silhouettes of hand bells, gentlemen still arrayed much in the fashion of "Uncle Sam."

And what if the Treasury lacked steps; the White House, pillars; the Capitol, a dome—it was of no consequence. For the actual government long had been handsomely housed elsewhere—in a score or two of Washington's bemirrored and chandeliered drawing rooms. Let Congress puff and palaver as it might, Washington society remained the government. And Washington society was the southern hostess.

Seldom, indeed, have feminine hands daintily wielded more dangerous power—or afforded a more cogent anti-feminist argument for woman suffrage! For if it remained for the twentieth century to discover that a woman in Congress is just another politician, prewar Washington amply proved that a diplomatic fragility in the drawing room was more than a match for a dozen politicians!

Amidst rancorous debate in the House and Senate, laughter and wine, dining and dancing in the great homes, the North and the South were preparing for the death grapple in a struggle old as burgher and baron. Brewing for five hundred years, blazing out in the prophetic British civil war between Cromwellian Roundhead and Stuart Cavalier, transplanted to the New World in the guise of Yankee against southerner, it was essentially a struggle for political supremacy between the rising industrial bourgeoisie and the old feudal aristocracy—between the masters of steam and the lords of the manor. And what lent shrewd edge to the feud was the human fact that just as the curled and cultured Cavalier had been the hated darling of the shaven, uncouth Roundhead battling for place in British life, so now the leisured, romantic South was no whit less the hated darling of the hustling, money-mad North—while, most curiously, soil and climate had served sharply to accentuate their divergencies of temper. Settling on the bleak shores of New England, the hard-fisted, psalm-singing Puritans had grown still more acrid and parsimonious in their wrestlings with the red man, with rain and snow and frozen ground; and their tone pervaded the whole North. On the other hand, the indolent, roistering, hard-riding British thoroughbreds pledged to Prince Charlie, establishing their plantations in the sunny, fertile South, had simply re-created the old feudal regime and, taking the Negro for serf in place of the rebellious English yokel, had continued to develop a luxurious and prideful way of life.

Side by side, Cavalier and Roundhead had ventured the Great Experiment together—the ancient issue between them still unsettled. But now the hour of final accounting had come. And in the paneled library of many a Washington mansion men—such as the defiant Georgians, Toombs and Iverson and Clay; Louisiana's haughty Slidell; Wigfall, the bleak-faced Texan; the cool, scheming Jefferson Davis—gathered to plot secession, pore over maps, prepare for war. And—what was equally important—in the adjacent parlors their wives and daughters artlessly wove a seductive web for the unwary opponent, the possible influential friend.

Even more fiercely than their men, southern matron, southern belle reacted to the North's impending threat to their seignorial traditions, cherished culture, political power. For them it was a blood issue. And their beguiling ways hid many a subtle deception practiced in loyalty to their own. National coquettes, they understood their lure, deftly exploited their prestige in northern eyes. Experts in the masculine, they knew how to touch the keys of ambition, inferiority, vanity, greed in veteran and neophyte alike and set them to harmonizing on a Dixie theme. And to them, in larger measure than history accords, was due the fact that even now, as the Union approached its zero hour, the Administration continued to be—what it always had been since Independence—virtually a southern preserve. The amiable Buchanan's southern predilections were obvious. Vice-President Breckinridge was a proslavery son of Kentucky. Minister of War Jefferson Davis, an avowed secessionist, was already dreaming upon a conquest of Mexico and Cuba that should make the Gulf the "*mare nostrum*" of a new slavocratic empire. And while proslavery Democrats had a clear majority in the House, practically all the important army posts had been assigned by the deliquescent old General Winfield Scott to what he admiringly called "southern rascals"—among them a certain Robert E. Lee.

And Dan Sickles, entering Washington—as he had proposed—on the train of his own presidential nominee, was quick to sense the new milieu. If, in New York, political advancement depended upon strong-arm mobs, mayhem, and ballot snatching, here—he saw clearly—it would depend largely upon social prestige, and that from the conquest of Ward and Wigwam he must now proceed to the conquest of the Drawing Room.

Politically, of course, as a Democrat, a protagonist of states' rights, Sickles already was *persona grata* to the southern representatives. But socially—well, in their eyes that was another matter. He was a "northerner." It was a situation that he did not grasp at first. He never had met—and, Knickerbocker that he was, he never expected to meet—such a thing as a social barrier. He could not know that while the planter-politician noblesse might exchange routine courtesies with northern Democrats sympathetic to their cause, they rarely welcomed them into their own inner circles; that, clannish by tradition and snobbish by temper, their attitude toward anyone so unfortunate as not to have acquired a grandfather among one or other of their reigning families was simply: "Paul I know, and Peter I know—but who are ye?" All that Sickles saw was the prospect of a political game tinged by the glamour of a social tourney—something very agreeable to his taste and talent. And he entered upon it with more than his usual zest and assurance.

His first need was an impressive address. Luckily, while staying as a guest with his old friend Jonah D. Hoover, ex-United States marshal, he managed to secure the fine old "Stockton Mansion" on Lafayette Square—practically a part of the White House grounds. Here, around a tiny green park adorned with a grotesque equestrian statue of Old Hickory, stood some of the most fashionable and historic homes in Washington—including the dignified pile where Commodore Decatur had lived and died, now the British Legation; the Dolly Madison house; the home of Thomas Swann, wealthy Baltimorean, now the Russian Legation; Corcoran's imposing mansion; and the handsome residences of the Tayloes, the Blairs, the Slidells, and the Adams family—not to omit the Cosmos Club, rendezvous of masculine fashion, and St. John's Church, punctiliously attended Sunday mornings by the President and the Washington elite. For Sickles, the aristocratic locale and substantial old house were ideal. And purchasing for Teresa a handsome brougham and pair, he prepared to match hospitality with the best.

CHAPTER XI

Dragon Couchant Gripping a Key

PHILIP BARTON KEY stood at crisis. Six foot of fastidious nonchalance, his clear, well-bred features, large blue eyes, luxuriant sandy hair and mustache, rather Byronic speech and manner, contrived an effect highly disturbing to the feminine. Washington knew him as United States attorney, dilettante politician, modish captain of the crack green-and-gold Montgomery Guards, but better as eligible widower, dean and darling of the drawing rooms. Keener eyes, however, might have divined, beneath the pallid skin, the drooped lids of disillusion, sad disdain, the gifted drifter and philanderer, confronting invalidism and the "dangerous forties" with nothing but an emotional fatalism to aid.

Of distinguished pedigree, his family relationships ramified throughout Washington society. His father, Francis Scott Key, also United States attorney, leader of the Maryland bar—and something of a hymnist and minor poet—had become identified with the national spirit as the author of "The Star-Spangled Banner." John Ross Key, his grandfather, descendant of a fine old Highland-Stuart family, had distinguished himself in the Revolutionary War and subsequently had married the daughter of the governor of Virginia. Congressman Phil Barton Key, his granduncle, was still remembered for his eloquence and parliamentary ability. One of his father's sisters had achieved some fame as a poet before her marriage to Senator Blount. And another, in marrying Chief Justice Taney of the Supreme Court, had become a Washington institution as the leading hostess of the Judiciary set. His sister, a woman of notable charm and intelligence, had married the genial "Gentleman George" Pendleton, congressman from Ohio, and now reigned over a coterie of her own. Fourteen years before, he himself had married Sophie Swann, daughter of a wealthy Baltimorean whose capacious mansion on Lafayette Square subsequently housed the Russian Legation.

Eight years of a love-match marriage—and Barton Key had stood distraught over the body of his dead wife, while in the next room four small children played. It was a loss that had left him too nerveless and disordered for family cares; and leaving his young son and three little daughters in charge of a competent housekeeper at his home on C Street, he had taken up quarters with his sister and her husband. The Pendletons were a charming, congenial pair. He was devoted to them both, and they to him; but even their companionship, warm and cheery as it was, had not been able to prevent him from falling into prolonged spells of depression. Presently heart trouble had intervened. Too weak to make his grief a way of growth, he had sought to evade it with social distractions. But, at last, his one real solace was his horse Lucifer—a nobly bred, dapple-gray hunter.

Those were days when Washington's winter mud made riding or driving a necessity for those who objected to being mired to the knees. But to Barton Key, riding was not simply a matter of transportation. With a true horseman's instinct, he sought in the saddle a peace and sense of health that he could find nowhere else. And for riding, his location gave him plenty of opportunity and excuse. The Pendletons' big rambling house stood far out on the city's outskirts. Thence customarily he rode to his engagements—unless they were such as made the use of his carriage imperative. And thence, when his hours were free, he could canter north along the virgin trails of the beautiful Rock Creek country. In horsemanship, as in everything else, he displayed his characteristic flair for style, grace, distinction. Astride Lucifer, arrayed in the ultimate of equestrian fashion, in white whipcord breeches and top boots, plum-colored hunting coat and flat-topped white cap, his was one of the most familiar and picturesque figures on Pennsylvania Avenue. Riding kit became him well—and he knew it. In daylight hours he rarely appeared in anything else. And Washingtonians long had agreed to be only pleasantly shocked at meeting him at court or at afternoon teas and at-homes, looking much like an English huntsman—crop still tucked under arm. On the other hand when he appeared afoot he was always impeccable in frock coat, silk hat. No one could swing a gold-headed cane with more grace. And at a time when, in even the most correct Washington circles, men made little distinction between their day and evening attire, he invariably changed for dinner—British fashion—into black broadcloth, ruffled white shirt, and white cravat.

And so Barton Key had lived, horseman and man of fashion, dividing his time with increasing ennui between his slender official duties and the onerous social round, playing up to a role he had come to despise but had no energy to change. Not a matron with a marriageable daughter but had her net spread for him. Well aware of it, he walked warily, amused himself with a flirtation here and there, and passed on, evading capture. None of these buxom Washington belles seemed able to touch the springs of his nature. Perhaps his recurrent ill-health gave him pause. He was like a man waiting for some new tide, some renewal of life, some passionate adventure—or death. Too intelligent for his trite round, lacking heart to seek anything more meaningful, he had exhausted the present—without hope of the future. With the indecision of the frustrate, he even had begun to dally with the dream of joining the westward pioneer stream—to hunt buffalo, face life afresh in the raw.

Actually he merely pursued his usual role as—in Mrs. Clement Clay's enthusiastic dictum—"the handsomest man in all Washington society," a romantic figure with his sad eyes, languid charm, deft touch upon the feminine, and, by way of salty contrast, his huntsman's garb, his often ironic brusqueness of address. His mysterious malady—which a modern diagnostician might have found to be mainly psychologic—haunted him with the shadow of death. He could not forget his dead wife or his two dead brothers—one killed on the frontier, the other shot in a duel over a woman. And often when he sat down to write in his small scratchy hand on his elegant buff stationery, he found himself brooding over the embossed family crest—a Dragon Couchant Gripping a Key.

In the fall of '56, as the result of an unusually bad spell, Barton Key decided to take sick leave and try what a few months in Cuba might do for him, but first—since he was a Pierce appointee—he must make sure that Buchanan would maintain him in office. Just then his old friend and confidant, Jonah D. Hoover, formerly United States marshal, invited him to attend a stag whist party. Among the players was a dynamic, stylish fellow, one of Hoover's Tammany cronies, recently elected to Congress and now in Washington, alone, seeking a house for the forthcoming term. Barton Key and Dan Sickles already knew each other by repute. Now on sight they took to each other and before the evening was over had arranged to meet again. Shortly, thereafter, Sickles, who was having some legal difficulties in the matter of the Stockton Mansion lease, engaged his new friend as counsel. In the ensuing weeks, at Willard's or Brown's, at Attorney General Black's, or at the home of the ever hospitable Hoover, the two men saw a good deal of each other. Politician and social arbiter had valuable hints to exchange. Liking grew to warm comradeship. And when, presently, Sickles gathered that Key was concerned over his reappointment to office, he promptly undertook to intercede for him with Buchanan; and a few days later brought him the signed confirmation in person.

Anxious now to be gone, out of this cold slush and sleet, Barton Key made his preparations for departure. Racked by a cough, dogged by fatigue, his heart playing tricks, he longed for lazy days by palmetto-fringed beaches under the healing warmth of soft Cuban skies. But at the last moment he hesitated. He had been too ill to attend the Presidential Reception. And to absent himself from the Inaugural Ball as well might be interpreted as a discourtesy to Buchanan. And then, he had not missed an Inaugural Ball in twenty years; and who could tell if he would live to see another? The change in plan would detain him only a few days—and by the next boat he would be off.

Barton Key left the Inaugural Ball profoundly perturbed. He could not believe that in one glance—as might some callow lad—he had lost his wits over a woman. Back at his quarters, far too excited for sleep, he paced the floor, restlessly poked the fire, poured himself one whisky peg after another, conning again every moment of the evening. It was not just that she was petite and dark, incomparably lovely; it was the extraordinary sense of rapport that had fused them the instant their arms had encircled for the waltz. Suddenly he was standing very still. "Dan's wife, by God!" Slowly, absent-mindedly, he began packing his traveling bag.

The dawn was up. He had bid good-by to the Pendletons the night before so as not to disturb them so early. His carriage, piled high with trunks, was at the door. It was a haggard Barton Key who stepped in. He had been looking forward to this holiday for months. Now he felt like a man going into exile.

CHAPTER XII

Washington Hostess

THE NEW HOME, standing a little aloof from its neighbors on the west side of the pretty, tree-shrouded park, had been built by Commodore Stockton during the administration of John Quincy Adams. And everything about it—the primly symmetrical architecture, severe chimney stacks, fashionable whitewashed brick, the paneled library, carved staircase, heavy, bronze chandeliers—bore the stamp of the old sailor's taste for shipshape, solid distinction. Secretary of the Navy Woodbury and, quite recently, Speaker of the House James L. Orr, of South Carolina, had occupied it—entertaining in the grand manner. And a few years earlier the wife of a certain scholarly statesman, adorning it extravagantly with imported paintings and tapestries, had made it the pet resort for the members of the various foreign embassies—before flitting away, with mysterious suddenness, to her former gay life in Paris and Vienna. In one way or another, the Stockton Mansion, as it invariably was called, had become something of a legend. And Washingtonians, impressed by the hospitalities of its line of hostesses, its antique span of two generations, always referred to it politely as both "famous" and "historic."

But to Teresa, the morning after the Inaugural Ball, as she stood amid half-opened crates of new costly furnishings—still quivering from the touch of a hand, the pulse of the dance—the old place seemed chill and menacing, a little like the unlit stage of a dress rehearsal to a leading lady absorbed in something else, and, even so, by no means sure of her part. For the moment she could think of nothing clearly. But at best she felt no confidence in her ability to play the role of Washington hostess—particularly here, where so many accomplished women had presided before her. It was a role more critical than she knew.

In Washington of the time, the wife's social enterprise was a vital factor in her husband's political success. Particularly was this true in southern circles. Reared in a matrix of chivalrous masculine adulation, trained from infancy to be homemaker and hostess, the southern woman usually brought to marriage not merely the sparkle of well-nourished femininity and a keen social sense, but an alert interest in her husband's affairs. Transplanted to Washington, she naturally re-created for him her own atmosphere of warm and winsome hospitality—and as naturally made it a means of furthering his ambitions. Who can say how much Senator Clement Clay of Alabama owed to his lovely Jinny—"the belle of the fifties"—with her bountiful kindness, quick intelligence; the harsh, unscrupulous Slidell to the graceful, tireless efficiency of his French Creole bride, Mlle. de Londes, formerly the toast of New Orleans fashion; the sturdily unsocial Senator Fitzpatrick to the energy and popularity of his youthful Clara; the jolly epicurean, Secretary Cobb, to the intellectual little beauty, née Clara Lamar; or Senator George E. Pugh to the grave and gracious Thérèse Chalfant, "the most beautiful woman in Washington"? We know only that wives such as these created and maintained a golden social background for their men, and that whether they confessed it or not, the gay southern quip, "Friendship is the better part of politics," was writ on their rings.

But of marriage of this kind, marriage as a working copartnership, Teresa had no conception. Her experience in London—on the arm of a popular diplomat, bemothered by great British ladies—was small preparation for a Washington, where the social life so largely was concerned with the enmeshment of political support. Furthermore she never even had been called upon to play a part in Dan's public life. Nor, as a matter of fact, had she shared more than a small, if de luxe, compartment in his private life. Thus inevitably her marriage relationship lacked the needful experience of teamwork, the still more needful spark of spontaneous co-operation—so manifest in many of the rich unions around her. It was a spiritual lack that could not be hid, and that neither skill nor unusual effort on both sides could overcome.

But this was only one of the handicaps. Washington was a honeycomb of cliques. There were, of course, the usual highly exclusive circles of the Cabinet and the Supreme Court. But, apart from these, House and Senate were viciously divided on the overarching issue of states' rights and the extension of slavery, and splintered again into warring factions, centered about certain dominant personalities, a Douglas, a Sumner, a Breckinridge, a Davis, representing every shade of the controversy. Under such circumstances even the experienced hostess often found herself in a quandary over her guest list—where a single *faux pas* might bring embarrassing consequences. To Teresa, with her bohemian background, it was a situation utterly confusing. To her, people were simply people, to be honestly liked or disliked for themselves, and quite apart from their views. And when Dan tried to sketch for her Washington's social-political topography, she found it terribly complicated and a little boring. Willing as she was to try to do what was required, she felt helplessly dependent upon him for guidance. But when it came to the feminine sphere of social strategy, Dan himself—for all his personal polish—was more or less the average helpless male. Two babes in the Washington wood!

Also there was the matter of family. Dan, at least, was a Knickerbocker—and, at a pinch, the Southrons might condone that. But Teresa, despite the fact that she was the daughter of a notable maestro of grand opera, was to them a "nobody."

And, at last, there was Miss Lane. Buchanan never had forgiven Mrs. Thomas for her London scandalmongering. And, despite her friendship with his niece, one of his first acts in power was to dismiss General Thomas from his position as Assistant Secretary of State. It was a gesture that gave Dan the keenest satisfaction. But Teresa received his report of it with pure dismay. "Don't tell me that! I shall be blamed for it all—and they'll be spreading their poison about me again!" Not till then had Dan realized how much the London affair had unnerved her. For an eloquent hour he tried to reason her out of her fears: Buchanan's action only showed what a loyal friend he was; Miss Lane would have to take her cue from him; Mrs. Thomas was a gossipy nobody—and out of the picture. As for friends, they had a host of them. They had a home distinguished as any, perfect appointments, a smart turn-out. She was far more lovely than any of these plump Washington belles, her gowns and jewels not to be matched in Paris. All she had to do was to pluck up heart, let Gautier do the catering, dress her charming best —and she would be the most popular little hostess in town. It was as if Dan were trying to reassure a child—a child he himself had kept from growing up.

But Teresa knew the intensity of Dan's ambition, knew that behind his efforts to encourage her lay his own urgent need of her cooperation; and she was woman enough to respond. She bit her lip; and with Dan's supervision, Buchanan's discreet support, Gautier's superb catering, and a staff of efficient servants to aid, gamely essayed her role of political hostess.

And so, every afternoon, the modishly dressed Mrs. Dan Sickles daintly maneuvered her crinoline into the crimson-leathered brougham and set forth upon her round of calls—a dutiful gesture, even if, for the most part, she merely left her card. Her small dinners, wisely grouped, at first, around intimate friends among the northern Democrats—such as the Hoovers, Haskins, Secretary Lewis Cass and his wife, the massively bearded and bespectacled Edwin Stanton—were in the best Stockton Mansion tradition; and, as hostess, her girlish warmth and naturalness won even the captious inclined to deplore her lack of discrimination in showing as much attention to a raw western congressman as to a cabinet minister. But her at-homes—the real social barometer—met with only a faint response from the notables. True, Mrs. Slidell might graciously descend now and again for a few moments—possibly with Mrs. Clay and some of her friends of the Brown's Hotel "mess." But this was a feather not to be flaunted too much. Dan recently had been giving Senator Slidell expert counsel in the framing of a measure for the purchase of Cuba, and etiquette prescribed a wifely courtesy of the kind. Also, despite Buchanan's unfailing friendliness, his offer to stand godfather for Laura, there was no escaping the fact that an invitation to a formal Executive Mansion dinner—that final social accolade customarily delivered in Miss Lane's precise calligraphy—was *not* forthcoming.

That first season Teresa's social success could not be called more than modest. Dan likewise had failed as yet to set the Potomac afire. The political tension created by the ever impending crisis between North and South threw all lesser questions into the discard. Burning to make a record for himself, he could find no dramatic measure to his hand. And to take open sides in the main issue was still premature. His sole contribution to the record was to secure the passage of a bill providing for the observance of Washington's birthday as a national holiday.

For both Dan and Teresa, recess—and a long vacation at quiet Bloomingdale—came with a sense of relief. For Dan it was an opportunity to catch up with much overdue legal work. For Teresa it meant leisure at last to play with Laura to her heart's content, enjoy an occasional canter over the hills—and dream disturbing dreams of a tall, pallid figure. From time to time she entertained a few of Dan's friends, played hostess to her gentle, emotional mother, the crotchety maestro, burly, dogmatic Sickles Sr.—the simple kind of thing that delighted her. For the most part she felt like a girl out of school, Washington and its problems forgotten.

CHAPTER XIII

Tarantella

———◆◆———

During the season of '57–'58, Washington's pulse quickened giddily. Never had the capital witnessed, never would it witness again, such a vivid and feverish social display. Southerner and northerner vied in a carnival of balls and banquets. If Postmaster General Aaron V. Brown's extravagant wife led the dance, surpassing all others in prodigal entertainment, she was closely followed by the cabinet hostesses—Mrs. Lewis Cass, Mrs. Howell Cobb, Mrs. James Thompson, by the great southern families—the Slidells, Tayloes,

Toombses, Parkers, Clays—pivoted about Jefferson Davis; and by the northern and western cliques attached to Seward, Stanton, Adams, Sumner, Douglas. The usually rather staid legations also flared with the general spirit of revelry. The at-homes of the gifted writer, Mme. Calderon de la Barca, wife of the Brazilian minister, and of the Comtesse de Sartiges—formerly Miss Thorndike—wife of the French minister, were not unworthy of the First Empire; and their dinners and dances among the gayest. The Baroness Stoeckl, wife of the Russian minister, played hostess with Slavic opulence at the old Swann house. And even the unworldly Lady Napier, presiding shyly over the British Legation, found herself swept into the glittering swirl.

The fall session of '57 scarcely had opened—with a virile exhibition of nose punching, hair pulling, spittoon hurling on the floor of the House—than Mrs. Gwin, wife of the millionaire senator from California, decided to inaugurate the season with a fancy-dress ball. It was the first event of this kind in Washington annals, and the announcement caused a great scurrying to dressmakers and tailors, much anxious searching of the Congressional Library for authentic pictures of classic and medieval costumes.

Unprofited in health, Barton Key just had returned from Cuba. Scarcely had he reached his quarters and changed to correct attire when he was driving nervously to Lafayette Square. Dan Sickles gave him a royal welcome, insisted that he was looking splendid, made him promise to stay to dinner. Teresa's hand in his trembled a little. The three talked late into the evening: Dan of the dangerous Kansas-Nebraska situation, the increasing political bitterness, the gathering strength of the Republicans; Key a little of his experiences in Cuba, but more of the forthcoming season. With tactful suggestions here and there he made it clear that he wished to be useful. Dan, realizing what his sponsorship would mean, was frankly appreciative. Teresa glowed with delight. The talk turned on the Gwin ball. Dan chuckled that he would go as a pirate if he could get the costume in time. Key, with a mock serious bow, suggested that Teresa would make a matchless Titania. She caught at the idea, but when he added that he thought he would adopt a fancy version of his usual English fox-hunting kit, she seemed to lose interest in it.

The night of the ball found Dan Sickles in bed with lumbago, but propped up with pillows and still struggling—his law books about him—to make notes for a forthcoming speech in the House. Key arriving—for the three had agreed to go together—promptly went upstairs to see him, full of sympathy. But Dan was quite cheery and matter-of-fact: "Barton, my boy, you'll have to do the honors for me tonight." Then—critically conning the cherry velvet coat, white satin breeches, lemon-colored riding boots: "You damn Britisher! A smart outfit if ever I saw one. But I'd have knocked you sidewise with that Laffite costume of mine." At that moment, a chic Louis Quatorze duchesse, equipped for the deer hunt in green velveteen habit and white-plumed tricorn, appeared smiling mischievously at the door. Key gave a light unconscious gasp. Dan, with a chuckle, eased himself up in bed: *"Mon Dieu—voilà Madame la Duchesse!"* He watched her quizzically as she went to shake hands with Key. "You certainly will be the belle of the ball, Terry. Damn this lumbago. You two—what a pair!"

Washington, since it rose out of the swamp fifty years before, had not witnessed such a throng as filled the ballroom of the Gwin Mansion—knights and troubadours, sultans and savages, crusaders and clowns, nymphs, houris, harlequins, gypsies, fairies, priests and pierrots waltzing, quadrilling, galloping in a motley, iridescent maze. And none seemed to enjoy the nonsense more than Teresa and Barton. If La Duchesse was all vivid delight, her huntsman escort seemed entirely to have forgotten his semi-invalidism, and every now and again would raise his silver bugle to his lips and blow a blast that echoed around the room most jollily. And often, as the two passed in the dance, other couples would pause a moment to watch them.

"Barton," said Mrs. Slidell, "you are surpassing yourself tonight—evidently Cuba was good for you."

He turned mockingly. "I find Washington much better, thank you."

It was after two in the morning when Barton and Teresa took carriage home. Reluctant to part, they directed a rather scandalized coachman to drive them by side streets about the city for an hour or more. When at last they alighted at the Stockton Mansion steps, they separated quickly without a word.

Thereafter, on one pretext or another, or with none at all, Barton Key was a constant visitor at the Sickles home. With his passion for the saddle, his need to spend the early hours in the open, he tried to lure Dan and Teresa into joining him on riding jaunts. But Dan professed himself much too busy. Unwilling, however, to deny Teresa the pleasure of an occasional canter, and knowing that she could not well do without an escort, he suggested that now and again, when circumstances permitted, she invite Barton to ride with her. There was nothing unusual in such an arrangement. Not a senator or congressman but was bedeviled with the constant conflict between masculine political duties and feminine social engagements. When debate was hot in the House, or important measures pended, the Washington wife—a dance or dinner invitation in hand—often enough found herself a "Washington widow," without escort unless some friend of her husband's would obligingly come to her aid. And, as a matter of simple necessity, emergency courtesies of this kind had become quite customary and *en règle*. As a consequence the society matrons of the capital enjoyed a freedom quite unknown elsewhere in the States at that time. So long as they preserved the amenities of the situation, they might appear shopping, riding, at hops, teas, and at-homes with any of their husbands' acknowledged friends without exciting remark. Barton understood this even better than Dan; and at every opportunity he calmly constituted himself Teresa's cavalier.

Before the last days of Indian summer died in sleet and slush, farmers on the city outskirts sometimes stopped to stare at a striking couple cantering by—the one in plum-colored riding coat and white breeches, the other in severe black riding habit—and wondered that folk could so laugh and talk and seem to enjoy being splashed to the eyes with mud. At the same time Washington drawing rooms also noted, with no more than an appraising smile, how sedulously the uncapturable Barton Key danced attendance upon the charming Mrs. Dan Sickles. And soon the southern elite, playing follow-the-leader, began appearing frequently at Teresa's Tuesday at-homes. Barton likewise saw to it that her Thursday dinners, smartly catered as any, now should include more of his own set—the Pendletons, the Slidells, Chief Justice Taney and his wife, the Comte and Comtesse de Sartiges, the Breckinridges, Tayloes, Parkers. And Dan, gratified with the changing social complexion, Teresa's poised, blithe manner, gave credit where credit was due. Barton appeared to think nothing of it.

After the Christmas holidays and the President's New Year's Day Reception, the season started off again fortissimo with the long-remembered Napier Ball. The popular British minister had been re-called by his government, and Senator William H. Seward promptly had organized a subscription farewell ball in his honor. It proved to be the most prodigious affair of its kind in Washington history. On the great dance floor of Willard's Hotel, over a thousand celebrants jostled one another in relays of several hundred at a time. The corridors, parlors, bars were jammed with a crush highly promiscuous —for while Napier's personal friends were all on hand, anyone who had the price of a ticket could attend.

Among the guests was George B. Wooldridge, one of the assistant clerks of the House. And with him had come two young friends, Marshall Bacon and S. K. Beekman, junior clerks in the Interior Department. All three, as Tammany henchmen indebted to Sickles for their present jobs, had been visitors at Stockton Mansion. And Beekman, a callow product of Albany, with a little New York pavement polish, had fallen into a mooncalf infatuation for Teresa. In the course of the evening he made several attempts to claim her for a dance—only to find each time that a supercilious Barton Key had forestalled him. Gloomily, at last, he retired to the bar to souse what he deemed to be a most magnificent jealousy. A trifling episode—with consequences!

Came February with clearing skies. Dan, summoned to New York on an important trial case, left hurriedly. And the next morning Barton Key on his dapple-gray was at Stockton Mansion. Teresa, expecting him, already was in her riding habit. Not until late afternoon did they return—to take a snack in the little study. The next day, and the next, it was the same. But before the week was over, clouds began to gather. Determined, however, to snatch one more ride ere the March rains should bog the trails, they set out on a jaunt to Bladensburg, intending to lunch there before returning. But well on their way, the already threatening skies clotted in a black, driving downpour. Disgustedly they wheeled and started homeward at a gallop. A few miles of this and they were wretchedly sogged in their saddles, scarcely able to catch their breath against the threshing sleet. The Greystone Tavern, looming up ahead, was a welcome sight. With a burst of speed they reached its shelter, turned their horses over to the groom. Amid the stares of the loungers at the bar, Barton engaged a room for Teresa and bade her tuck herself into bed while her habit was dried. At the same time he asked that he might be allowed to warm himself in the kitchen. The landlady ushered them both through a door at the end of the bar. And while Teresa trailed her wet garments upstairs, Barton sought the kitchen range and draped his coat over a chair before it. Then he ordered tea and toast sent up to Teresa and settled himself by the stove with a hot whisky punch. An hour and a half later, the storm lifting, he called for their horses. It was not until then, when they were passing through the bar together, that he caught the snickering glance of a slight, dapper fellow drinking with a group at a corner table. Faintly he remembered him as the aggressive young man at the Napier Ball. He knew then that there would be malice afoot; but he shrugged it aside. Nevertheless, on the canter home he broke a long silence to remark casually, "I think you should tell Dan about this." Teresa's tone was limpid: "Why of course, Barton—I expected to."

When Dan returned, Teresa, in the course of breakfast chatter, casually mentioned the episode of the storm and the tavern. But Dan, deep in the *Globe*, listened more politely than attentively. "Too bad. Lucky you found shelter. Might have caught a beastly cold."

Beekman, however, could not wait to pour his version of the affair into Marshall Bacon's ear. With vengeful chuckles he recounted how he had seen the high and mighty Barton Key and Mrs. Dan Sickles come dripping into the Greystone bar, engage a bedroom, and disappear for over an hour and a half together, and how, when the kitchen door had swung open, he had caught sight of their clothes drying before the stove. And as Beekman knew very well he would, Bacon, garnishing the story with his own relish, promptly passed it on to Wooldridge.

Meanwhile Sickles had gone to Baltimore for a week. Upon his return Wooldridge sought him out and, speaking as a matter of duty, hesitantly confided to him Beekman's gossip. To his astonishment, Sickles waved it aside. "Oh—that? Teresa told me all about it long ago." Wooldridge, suddenly wishing that he had kept out of the affair, urged Dan to examine Beekman himself and get the facts. "I don't believe it myself, Dan, any more than you do. But the point is that Teresa is being slandered. And if this story gets around, it won't do you any good either. It has to be scotched right now."

Summoned to Stockton Mansion, Beekman, first confronted by the irate Mrs. Bagioli, crawfished, evaded, denied that he had done more

than make a few joking remarks on "the feminine sex in general."
Scared by the mounting menace in Sickles's manner, he threw the
entire blame on Wooldridge and Bacon, accused them of distorting
and falsifying his statements; and, finally, throwing out a panicky
screen of righteous indignation, fled the room. Feeling that the whole
thing was a miserable canard, Sickles called in Key and frankly placed
the facts before him. Key was icily furious, retorted that anyone
who made such an assertion would have to meet him at the point of
a pistol. His decisive "Let *me* handle this" sounded completely convincing.

Commissioning Hoover to act as his personal messenger and secure
replies, Key dispatched formal notes to Wooldridge, Bacon, and
Beekman in turn, demanding in each case an immediate explanation
in writing. Wooldridge, of course, merely cited Bacon as his in-
formant. Bacon, in an insolent note, cited Beekman. Terrified, Beekman once more flatly denied having made any of the accusations
attributed to him, pretended to challenge Bacon to a duel, and wrote
an elaborate apology to Sickles. Key pinned the correspondence together and turned it over to Hoover for delivery at Stockton Mansion. Then, to clinch the matter, he sent a verbal message to Dan
through their mutual friend, John B. Haskin. In it he was at pains to
explain very precisely that he regarded Teresa simply as a child, felt
for her only paternal affection, considered himself as standing toward
her—to use his own legal phrase—*in loco parentis*. It was an attitude
cleverly calculated to win Dan's sympathetic comprehension. Then,
returning wearily to the Pendleton home, Barton changed into riding kit and rode off along the Rock Creek trail.

The crisis had unnerved him. He needed space and peace to settle
his course. So far he had managed to preserve the technical proprie-
ties—by the skin of his teeth. But he knew that he could not preserve
them much longer; and that if he could, Teresa would not. Their
bodily need of each other had become such as to reduce all other
considerations to dust. They had been wrongfully accused once.
They probably would be accused again. But the next time—would
he have the boldness of, at least, his own conventional rectitude? He
doubted it.

The next day Dan, after a talk with Haskin, and feeling that he
had been made the fool of busybodies, sought Key out in his office.
His tone was ingenuous and disarming. "Barton, my boy, don't let

this thing make any difference between us—or between you and
Teresa. I want everything to be just as it was. I know you're a man
of honor. I've never thought of you as anything else. But for Teresa's
sake, and for yours and mine, I simply had to run this damned gossip
to earth. I know you understand." A strong, vital hand crunched a
hand moist with cold sweat. Key was gracious but very pale. To hide
his inner wretchedness he complained of his heart, suggested they go
over to Brown's together and get a julep. The drinks served, Dan
insisted they cross glasses through linked arms—pledge *Brüderschaft*,
German fashion. Then, as though nothing had happened, both fell to
talking politics. The two men parted, apparently, with more warmth
than usual. But never again, they knew, would it be with them as
once it had been.

CHAPTER XIV

Mad Honeymoon

———————◆●———————

So FAR AS THE feminine portion of Washington society was concerned, Teresa, with her dark Latin beauty, fluency in foreign
tongues, aura of scandal, remained something of a curiosity—not to
be cultivated too closely. And Teresa herself was aware of it. After
a year of conventional social acceptance she still could not name a
woman in Washington whom she truly could regard as friend, and
had come rather wistfully to prize her gentlehearted mother's occasional visits. Then, at a tea, soon after the Napier Ball, she had met
Octavia Ridgeley, a sensible, liberal-minded New York girl, now
living with her parents quite close to Lafayette Square. The attraction between the two had been instant; and, from that moment,
Octavia had become almost an inmate of Stockton Mansion, often
calling in the morning, running over for dinner two or three times a
week, and sometimes staying all night. The sudden friendship gave

Dan a distinct sense of relief. He had been bothered by the fact that Teresa seemed to make little contact with her own sex and that when business took him away he must leave her without feminine companionship. Now that problem was solved. Nevertheless, when, just after the Beekman episode, his practice called him back to New York for several weeks, he asked Haskin—faithful henchman that he was—in a casual but guarded way to drop in on Teresa now and again and see if she needed any help. On the surface it was a natural enough request, for Teresa was not too expert a manager; and Haskin, a constant visitor at Stockton Mansion, was always craftily alert to put himself at the service of the man he expected to see President. But there was more to it than that. Dan trusted Teresa's good faith— but he did not trust her judgment. He knew that just as her youthful naïveté and impulsiveness had gotten her into several predicaments provocative of scandal, so they might again. And scandal was the one thing he could not afford. There must be no more of that! And without stressing the point, he was plainly asking Haskin to keep a friendly watch over her.

The situation for Barton and Teresa now had become dangerously tense. Suspected, made the target of malicious attack, surrounded, wherever they went, with whisperings, they still had refrained from the final step. Now suddenly, by ironic decree, while all eyes seemed centered upon them, and tantalization had keyed their passion to torture, they found themselves alone—in the stolid privacy of Stockton Mansion. With Dan gone, Octavia absenting herself soon after dinner, the servants assumed to be safely asleep, the little library with its deep divan, cozy fire, and double-locked doors offered treacherous security. Restraint fled down wind—and, down wind, the simplest sense, the plainest caution.

Haskin was a diligent fellow, but a coarse and crafty son of the Wigwam—hardly the man to be entrusted with a mission of tactful surveillance. The day after Dan's departure, returning from a shopping trip with his wife to Georgetown, he espied a dapple-gray horse hitched outside Stockton Mansion and suddenly decided that this would be an excellent time to pay a call. Driving up to the stoop, he hurriedly assisted his wife to the pavement, ran with her up the steps, quietly opened the unlocked door, crossed the empty parlor, and burst without knocking into the little library beyond. The door flung wide on Teresa and Barton just come in from a canter and still in their riding clothes, standing at a little table discussing light lunch and champagne. Teresa, in the midst of tossing the salad, looked up with a startled gasp, flushed with confusion. "Why, Mr. Haskin! Has anything happened?" Haskin was all facile apology: Dan had asked him to drop in. . . . He just happened to be passing by—was in quite a hurry—couldn't find anyone about and so . . . His voice trailed off a trifle sheepishly. Barton, refilling the glasses, had quietly put down the bottle and now was standing very still, subjecting Haskin to a relentless blue stare. Teresa, recovering herself, was greeting Mrs. Haskin, endeavoring to smile into a fat face just now twisted to a nervous smirk. Hastily she introduced Barton to her, then was offering both visitors wine. Conversation distinctly lagged; and so, with more shambling apologies, the pair backed out. Champagne and salad *à deux*, at four in the afternoon, seemed evidence of deviltry enough. But Haskin, cowed by the cold challenge in Barton's eyes, thought better of reporting the matter to Dan. Mrs. Haskin, scrambling into the carriage, snapped open a tight jaw. "She's a bad woman, John—a bad woman!"

Now it was mad, stolen honeymoon. For the next two or three weeks the lovers were inseparable. There were long rides in the forenoon, cozy teas together as the day drew down, sometimes the theater at night—and then the library until dawn. And perhaps with a sense of the close kinship between love and death, often they trysted at the still half-wild cemetery and wandered together among its trees and tombs—while Teresa's coachman snoozed on his seat or, waking, grumbled his disgust to the pricked ears of the two blooded bays. For the nonce two tragic beings moved in a happy delirium, rapt beyond fear, and by that very fact stilling all titterings to an expectant silence.

When Dan at last returned, Washington was already emptying; and Teresa's hours were prosaically crowded with supervising the rolling up of carpets, the covering of furniture, mirrors, and the packing of multitudinous trunks. It was time for Bloomingdale again —and the long vacation.

As for Barton, his world on the instant had become a complete blank, with but one living image—Teresa. Dan he had not seen and hardly dared face. But on the morning of their departure, in his role of friend of the family, he rode over to the shabby little station to bid them good-by. One last glimpse of Teresa he must have. And then there was the aching, shamefaced hope that possibly Dan might invite him to Bloomingdale. When he arrived he found Dan in the midst of a back-slapping group of politicians who had come to see him off. A hurried farewell to Teresa, and there came the cry "All aboard!" Dan, breaking away from the group, for the first time spied Barton and came forward with outstretched hands. "Barton! I was hoping you'd show up. We want you to come and see us this summer. I'd like you to see my place." The engine was tooting loudly. As he dashed toward the already moving train, he shouted over his shoulder, "And bring your boots—it's fine riding country!"

Pale and shaken, his ears still ringing with Dan's warm voice, Barton stood motionless, oblivious of the greetings of friends, watching the train vanish down the tracks.

CHAPTER XV

"Whom the Gods Would Destroy——"

IN NOVEMBER, Dan Sickles would have to stand for re-election; and in face of the rapidly growing power of the Republican party, the vicious Tammany feuding between Wood-ite Soft-Shells and Tiemann Hard-Shells, and the ever-widening split in the Democratic ranks over the extension of slavery, his political chances seemed completely unpredictable. Under the circumstances he decided to organize his own support and conduct a virtually independent campaign.

Soon Bloomingdale began to take on the air of a busy country resort. From early morning to late evening, groups of Sickles's many friends—Tammany chieftains, Democrats of every shade, ranking members of the New York bar such as James T. Brady and Thomas Francis Meagher, and, significantly, even a sprinkling of Republicans, including the pontifical Edwin McMasters Stanton—crowded his library or roamed with him over the lawns in close discussion. All day long, Mose, the colored boots, ran hither and thither with trays of cooling drinks. Lunch, often served in relays for late-comers, loafed along into midafternoon. And usually a knot of guests stayed to dinner.

Dan Sickles was a thoroughly social being. He enjoyed people, liked to be the hub of a crowd, loved to play host, was indefatigable in doing favors for his friends. If he had the trick of popularity, he also had its substance—and, with it, a magnetism that knit men to him with a curiously strong devotion. Throughout his public life he had spent himself freely in friendship. Now that friendship was flowing back to him. The tide of response surprised and touched him, stimulated all his energies. Never was he more heartsome, more impressively keen, assured. And few of those who visited Bloomingdale that summer failed to arrive at the conviction that Dan Sickles was the coming man.

For Teresa the long vacation was a period of respite—respite from the exacting duties of Washington hostess and, what was far more imperative, respite from her own inner tumult. At last she had a chance to rest and collect herself. And, relaxed in the knowledge that Dan was happy and unsuspecting, she let herself drift through the long lazy days, fending off, with a kind of animal instinct, the shock of realizing that Barton had taken possession of her entire being. To her the interlude of half-somnolent peace seemed a gift from the skies. And she was Italian enough, youthful and sensuous enough, to abandon herself to it: to enjoy while she might her hours with Laura, her morning canters along the woodsy Jersey paths, the quiet evenings *en famille*. The household management gave her little concern, for the servants, under Mrs. Bagioli's watchful eye, took care of that. But she was always on hand to play her part in greeting newcomers— often, with as much pride as Dan himself, would show them about the rose gardens and orchards, the greenhouses and well-kept stables. Outwardly her life seemed placid as the ornamental lake beyond the lawns. . . . Then one morning a tall, fastidious figure came slowly up the steps, followed by a coachman laden with bags. Peace fled with her smothered cry!

There were few formalities at Bloomingdale. Dan greeted Barton heartily, saw to it that he was comfortably quartered, then, with the injunction to make himself free of the place and pick his own mount, amicably left him to his own devices.

However, amid a house full of guests, including the Bagiolis and

Grandfather Sickles, the situation for Barton and Teresa was full of constraint. Their only opportunity to be alone together was in the saddle; and, even so, after the first few rides, they often found themselves jogging along together in silence, oppressed by a sense of foreboding they could neither admit nor shake off. And so, after a few days, Barton, not wishing to overstay his visit, took moody departure. And, with the exception of a brief meeting at the Atlantic Cable celebration in New York some weeks later, they saw no more of each other until the reopening of Congress early in October.

In a final burst of campaigning, "as brief as it was brilliant"—to cite a contemporary issue of *Harper's Weekly*—Dan Sickles piled up a decisive majority at the polls. The victory—won amid the wild enthusiasm of his supporters and against all the predictions of the wiseacres—now definitely established him in national politics. And upon his return to the House, the fact was signalized by his appointment to the Committee of Foreign Affairs. It was an assignment peculiarly advantageous for him at that moment. It not only enabled him to exploit his diplomatic experience abroad, but—what was far more important to a man with his eye on the presidency—it saved him from embroilment in the bitter feuding at home. Also it put him in a strategic position to promote his pet project—the acquisition of Cuba. And, for a while, completely absorbed in his new duties, he had eyes and ears for little else.

Made more reckless than ever by their recent separation, Barton and Teresa now again were seen everywhere together. As soon as Dan left home—usually about noon—to attend the House, Teresa would run upstairs to make a hasty afternoon toilette and then would order her brougham. By one o'clock she would be on her way; and almost always, within the first few blocks, would be met by Barton, ostentatiously ceremonious with his "Good morning, madame!" Thence the two would drive off together, sometimes on a shopping expedition, sometimes on a round of calls among their more intimate friends, the Slidells, Claytons, Browns, Thompsons, and the intriguing Mrs. Greenhow, occasionally even dropping in for a chat with Old Buck himself, as he sat erect and immaculate at his desk, still patiently endeavoring to portray a gentlemanly President beset by political ruffians. Or sometimes they would direct the coachman to take them to their old rendezvous, the Congressional Cemetery, or the burying ground at Georgetown, where among the tombs and trees they could enjoy a secluded hour. Scarcely a day passed that they did not meet—to spend most of the afternoon in each other's company, and, when Dan was away, most of the evening also.

They could not escape noticing, of course, that they were stirring up a fresh outburst of gossip, and that even the Stockton Mansion servants—particularly Bridget Duffy, the Irish chambermaid, and John Thompson, the Scotch coachman—had begun to assume an impudently knowing attitude toward them. But they paid no heed. Nothing mattered to them but to be together—and for that no risk seemed too great.

Their friends began to become worried about them. Presently Hoover took it upon himself to drop Barton a kindly warning. But, although it startled him into recognizing his own inner tension, Barton shrugged it aside. No longer was he the philandering poseur who once, at the Cosmos Club, had boasted of his taste for "French intrigue—with a spice of danger." For the past two years his passion for Teresa had led him to play dice with his office, his social position, even his life. And now, with the bravado of a proud weakling, he still held on his course. And Teresa, ductile, enamored, blindly followed his lead.

But a little later came a warning that could not be shrugged aside. Casually but decisively, Dan made it plain to Teresa that he wished her to refrain from inviting Barton to the house except when he himself could be present. He offered no explanation, and in her panic she dared not question him. And, what sharpened the significance of his request, he now made a point of accompanying her to market himself—ostensibly to select the Madeira and Rhenish from Gautier's or consult with butcher Emerson on the choice cuts and game for the increasingly distinguished Stockton Mansion dinners.

Now, at last, and too late, Barton and Teresa began to make a feeble effort at circumspection. To everyone's amusement, when paying calls or attending teas they would arrive and leave separately; and, when returning from a drive with Teresa, Barton would be careful to alight before entering Lafayette Square—naïve measures that deceived none, and only added to their own dejection as they watched their former means of privacy vanish one by one. Stockton Mansion was barred. The rains forbade riding. The coachman's suspicious surliness ruled out their long drives into the country. Only in the gossipy drawing rooms of their friends could they meet. And

VIEW OF THE HOUSE, 383 WEST FIFTEENTH ST. (WASHINGTON), HIRED BY KEY, FOR HIS MEETINGS WITH MRS. SICKLES

From *Harper's Weekly*.

PHILIP BARTON KEY

there, they soon realized, their sheer frustration trapped them into betraying themselves in every glance and gesture. They had arrived at impasse complete. And with that, they began to lose their wits.

So far as its residential districts were concerned, Washington of the fifties was a quilt of satin rags and sackcloth patches. Here an ultrafashionable section ended abruptly in a foul slum; there, a solid, middle-class locality changed, in the width of a street, to a colored shanty town.

And within three minutes' walk from Lafayette Square, going north on Fifteenth Street, suddenly one came upon a quarter once decent enough but now badly run down and taken over by Negroes.

Two blocks up the street—where it makes a slight jog between K and L streets—stood a narrow, two-story house flanked by vacant lots, and with a large rear yard—stoutly fenced to the height of a tall man—opening on a filthy alley. The flyblown, warped "To let" sign in a lower window suggested that it had been untenanted for some time.

Barton, roving the neighborhood meditating a mad plan, espied it; and, apparently unmindful of the fact that he was one of the best-known figures in the city, alighted, tied his horse to a tree, and proceeded to make inquiries about it from a Negro woman next door. Nancy Brown scanned his stylish riding clothes with suspicious appraisal, tartly reminded him that it was against the law to use her tree for a hitching post, and somewhat grudgingly told him that the owner of the house, a colored man named Jonathan Gray, lived on Capitol Hill. Barton, apologizing for using her tree, thanked her and rode off. To the puzzled owner he naïvely explained that he thought of taking the house for "a friend—a congressman." After examining it and assuring himself that it was usably, if scantily, furnished, he paid down one hundred dollars for the first two months' rent, requesting that it be thoroughly cleaned for occupancy by the first of December.

If the appearance of a dandified horseman seeking a house in the colored quarter had aroused the curiosity of the block, his reappearance three weeks later in overcoat and silk hat, entering by the front door, did nothing to lessen it. And when, on his subsequent visits, a puff of smoke soon was seen to belch from the chimney, and hands from behind the drawn blind of an upper window tied a piece of white string to the shutters as though to make a signal, and a slight figure in plaid dress, black cloak and bonnet, a black velvet shawl half shrouding her face, presently hurried in after him, the neighborhood was all agog. But when, after a while, the lady came no more to the front door, but was seen furtively picking her way through the muck of the alley, creeping into the house by the back door, the whole street became electrically watchful, convinced that "dem white folks was up to no good."

A curious place for the amour of two fastidious beings!—a shabby old house, a drab bedroom with mildewed paper, ancient iron bedstead, dubious mattress, and only a wood fire in the grate to give it some cheer—while outside, on the pavement, at every door and window down the street, great blackberry eyes rolled on each other knowingly, and Mrs. Nancy Brown cursed the blinds that were always drawn.

But to the lovers this was the way it had to be. They never had contemplated a future together, for they knew there was none, that for them was only the hour they could snatch. To Teresa divorce—on the only admissible grounds: adultery—obviously was out of the question. Elopement was equally so. She was as incapable of leaving little Laura as she was of taking her—and so depriving Dan in one stroke of wife and idolized child. And Barton, with his pampered soul, sick body, was hardly the man to play Lochinvar and boldly take his woman West—child or no. They dared not think beyond the fact that, at last, they had a hideout where they could be alone together. That it was in a quarter where they ran small risk of meeting anyone they knew, and that it yet was near enough to Stockton Mansion for Teresa to reach it alone afoot—without need of summoning her coachman—seemed boon enough for the moment. And the very complications they faced in arranging their meetings, their naïve set of signals—the string at the window to say, "At home"; Barton's flourished handkerchief, as he passed Stockton Mansion, to telegraph to Teresa behind her blinds, "All's well, will be there as agreed"—the very excitement of watching, dodging loungers, scheming to arrive unseen, gave to each tryst a thrill of surreptitious, tragic adventure that, despite the bleared wall paper, musty odor, creaky bed, had its own fatalistic fascination.

And Dark Town watched . . . and Dark Town talked.

CHAPTER XVI

"*I Have Killed Him!*"

———◆———

THE CHRISTMAS HOLIDAYS came and passed. And again a gray wisp of wood smoke hung above the chimney of No. 383 Fifteenth Street; and again a piece of white string dangled from an upper shutter; and again a veiled figure picked her way through the muddy alley and darted in at the rear gate—while pickaninnies peeked around the corner behind her, and Mr. and Mrs. Seeley, churchgoing colored folk, whose house commanded a view of the yard, took scandalized note of the visitor's dress—even to the bugles on her velvet shawl.

But now the wisp of smoke was seen more often. And Barton and Teresa, emboldened by their apparent immunity from detection, sometimes would arrive hurriedly together. The last time that they dared this piece of indiscretion, however, the interested scrutiny of two policemen on the corner caused them at the last moment to stroll on past the house without a glance at it. And the mammies gossiping on their stoops, peering knowingly from the policemen to the elaborately unconcerned couple sauntering down the street, smothered chuckles behind their aprons. And Mrs. Baylis who ran a rooming-house across the way, watching the ruse with a mingling of caustic comment and Scriptural quotation, called upon her shambling son Crittenden to witness that "dem white folks sho' act mighty guilty."

That night Teresa sat down to struggle with her weekly problem, the guest list for the Thursday dinner. When at last she had finished, she handed it to Dan for his approval. Running his eye rapidly over the names, "Slidells, Claytons, Parkers, Pendletons," he paused at the initials P. B. K. "Don't you think we are rather overdoing Barton, Terry?" Teresa was flustered. "But Dan, you said that you wanted to invite those who had entertained you, and Barton has had you to lunch at the club several times. Besides, he lives with the Pendletons." There was no mistaking Dan's indifferent, "Do as you choose," as he tossed the list back to her. But the hand that began scratching out monogrammed notes still trembled a little.

The following Sunday, Laura was to have been christened—with Mrs. Slidell as godmother and none other than Old Buck himself as godfather. But in the meantime she had developed a temperature, and the ceremony had to be postponed. From day to day her condition worsened. The doctor was noncommittal. Dan and Teresa, taking turns in watching by her bedside, remained tense with anxiety until—on the morning of the dinner party—the case was diagnosed as nothing more than an attack of measles. That night, host and hostess were all relief and laughter. The guests quickly caught their tone. The dinner was long remembered. It was the gayest Stockton Mansion was to know.

Four or five times, during these last days of February, Barton and Teresa foregathered at their shabby rendezvous—but each time with mounting trepidation. No longer could they hide from themselves that their comings and goings were closely watched. On Wednesday, February 23, quite early in the morning, they met at Maury and Taylor's bookstore, on "the Avenue." Teresa—little Laura, now fully recovered, trotting beside her—was finishing her day's marketing. Barton accompanied her to the butcher's to help her select a joint, and thence to the dairy. But, taut as they were with the sense of impending crisis, they found it impossible to talk to any purpose in public; and, presently, Barton took Laura over to the nearby home of the Hoovers to play there awhile, arranging to meet Teresa at No. 383 as soon as she finished her shopping. Twenty minutes later he was letting himself into the house—aware, more than ever, of heads slewed to watch, faces peering from windows, dusky figures appearing at doors. And when, shortly, Teresa arrived by the rear entrance, she was breathlessly agitated. On the way she had run into several people she knew; a group of darkies at the corner had burst into insolent chuckles as she passed; pickaninnies, whispering and pointing, had followed her right to the yard gate. Barton cursed his own nerves as he tried to soothe her. But it was plain to them both now that these walls, that once had seemed so shelteringly opaque, had turned to glass. Feebly Barton declared that he would set about finding a safer place. It was an empty gesture. Both knew it. Fatalistically they soon ceased to talk. . . . An hour later they parted with the premonition that they would never meet there again.

The next day Teresa, accompanied by Octavia, set out to pay some overdue calls. On their way to Mrs. Greenhow's they encountered Barton on horseback. After chatting for a moment he dismounted, tied his horse to a hitching post, and joined them. It was late afternoon when the brougham drew up beside an impatiently pawing Lucifer. Barton seemed loath to leave, and with foot on step, elbow on knee, remained, stooping forward into the carriage, earnestly scanning Teresa's face. Her distraught appearance had been troubling him all the afternoon. His solicitous, "Your eyes look badly, my dear," carried more than the words implied. Shakily, Teresa admitted that she was not feeling very well. Since it was Thursday, and he knew that after the usual Stockton Mansion dinner, it had been agreed that the whole party would attend the hop at Willard's, he asked if he would see her there. She drew a deep breath. "If Dan will let me go." Octavia, a self-effacing shadow in the background, pretended neither to see nor hear. But John Cooney, the new coachman, already put on the alert by belowstairs talk, listened with cocked ears.

After dinner that night, as the whole party was preparing to leave for Willard's, the butler brought Dan a letter. The cheap, yellow envelope suggested nothing of any importance, and he stuffed it into his pocket unopened. When most of the guests had driven off, he found that a couple of out-of-town friends who had come in hacks had no conveyance. Promptly he seated them with Teresa in the brougham, cheerily declaring that he would follow on foot, since it was a matter of only a few blocks.

When, a little later, he entered the ballroom, he noticed Barton and Teresa sitting on a sofa in close conversation. The curious seriousness of their manner was something that he remembered only later. As he came toward them Barton jumped up as if he had forgotten something and, with a bow, hurried away. Just then Dan was intercepted by Wooldridge; and when he saw Teresa again, she was dancing with Senator Slidell. Barton had disappeared.

Returning from the dance well after midnight, Teresa, exhausted, went off to bed. Dan, however, still had work to do; and poking up the fire in his own combination of study and bedroom, he sat down to con over the speech he was to deliver the next day on the Navy Yard appropriation bill. It was not until the task was finished and he was emptying his pockets to undress that he came upon the forgotten yellow envelope. Opening it carelessly, he suddenly went still, staring blankly at a few precise, incredible lines, written rather illiterately in a distinctly literate hand:

FACSIMILE OF THE ANONYMOUS LETTER INFORMING HON. DANIEL E. SICKLES OF THE INFIDELITY OF HIS WIFE

Washington February 24th 1859

HON. DANIEL SICKLES

Dear Sir with deep regret I enclose to your address these few lines but an indispensable duty compels me so to do seeing that you are greatly imposed upon.

There is a fellow I may say for he is not a gentleman by any means by the name of Phillip Barton Key & I believe the district attorney who rents the house of a negro man by the name of Jno. A Gray situated on 15th street btw'n K and L streets for no other purpose than to meet your wife Mrs. Sickles. he hangs a string out of the window as a signal to her that he is in and leaves the door unfastened and she walks in and sir I do assure you

with these few hints I leave the rest for you to imagine

Most Respfly
Your friend R.P.G.

Dan crunched the note to a wad, tossed it on the desk. "Damnation! What do they take me for?" His mind flashed back over the Thomas affair, the Beekman affair . . . He had risen to the bait twice; they wouldn't hook him again. Anonymous—of course! He reached for a cigar and, chewing on it, strode about the room irritably. Then involuntarily he was straightening out the wadded paper, scanning it again—"a negro man by the name of Jno. A Gray . . . 15th street btw'n K and L . . . hangs a string out of the window . . ."

Like most public men he had received the usual meed of anonymous notes—abusive, insinuating, driveling—and always had destroyed them without a thought. But he could not blink the fact that this one was different. Here was no threat, no innuendo—only a factual statement that could be checked in an hour. Again he was pacing the room, chewing savagely on his cigar. Very well, he would say nothing about it. First thing in the morning he would check the trash—and be done with it!

But even as he started again to undress, the detailed circumstantiality of the note began to claw at him. Who would invent such a thing? Was some political enemy trying to trick him into making a public ass of himself? Possibly. He must be on his guard about that! Of course, he could take the note straight to Teresa and clear up the matter at once. But the Thomas episode had come close to shattering her social confidence for life, Beekman's scurrilous talk had caused her days of wretched humiliation. He was not going to expose her again to anything of that sort. Then suddenly, with a queer mixture of relief and grim amusement, he was reflecting that, in all likelihood, Barton was meeting one of the fancy-girls about town at that address, and some snooping idiot had mistaken her for Teresa! It was a mistake easy enough to make, too, for of course Barton and Teresa had been seen together often enough. The more he thought of it, the more he felt that this was the real explanation. And with that he went to bed—to lie wide-eyed while, despite all he could do, a hundred hitherto unremarked incidents in Teresa's association with Barton paraded before him—a dance of devils clad in new, and torturing, significance.

In the morning, without waiting for breakfast, while Teresa slept late, he went on foot to the address given in the note. A few seemingly casual inquiries among the Negroes of the neighborhood assured him that it was none other than "Phillip Barton Key" who had rented the house, also that the owner indubitably was "a negro man by the name of Jonathan Gray." Shaken with misgiving, he rushed to the telegraph office. Well he remembered how once, in stress of violent grief, he had gone completely out of hand; and now, like a man facing an emergency operation yet still collected enough to send for the right surgeon, he wired his old friend, Collector Hart of the Port of New York. His message was brief, "Please come at once. I need you."

It was already eleven o'clock; and snatching breakfast at Willard's, he walked to the Capitol. The House was just about to go into session, but he knew that it would be an hour or so before he would have to speak. To avoid conversation he went to his chair and pretended to be absorbed in making notes. Presently a page brought him a telegram from Hart, regretting that he could not get away for a few days. Able to stand the suspense no longer, Dan sent for George B. Wooldridge. For the past year that good friend and efficient congressional clerk had been intimate in all his affairs—even to the point of taking over much of his correspondence. Now at the summons he promptly appeared, leaning on his crutches, at the door. Dan led him into a foyer behind the Speaker's chair and, struggling to keep a calm front, drew the note from his pocket. "George, I want to speak to you on a very painful matter. Late last night I received this letter." Steadily he forced himself to read aloud. But at the words, "and sir I do assure you," he choked. Handing the note to Wooldridge, he turned away. And it was a minute or two before he could control his voice enough to explain that he had just come from Fifteenth Street and had established all the facts but one—the woman's identity. His tone turned firm. "My hope is that it is not my wife but some other woman. As my friend you will go there and see whether . . . it is or not. Get a carriage—I'll show you the house." During the drive, Wooldridge, his arm about Dan's shoulder, declared that he would rent a room opposite the house and remain on watch until he could ascertain definitely, as he hoped and believed, that the woman was not Mrs. Sickles. After pointing out the house to Wooldridge, Dan, a little comforted, returned to the Capitol, to labor, like a man in a dream, through a long and tedious analysis of the Navy Yard bill.

That same afternoon Barton met Teresa—again accompanied by her little chaperon, Laura—at Green's, the cabinetmaker's. A moment before, a colored messenger had thrust a cheap yellow envelope into his hand. He had only just opened it, and while Teresa and Laura went on into the shop, he lingered outside to read it. . . . Across the street two curious loafers, a William Ratley and a Frederick Wilson, watched him. Presently, when Teresa reappeared, and he strolled on down the Avenue with her, still frowning over the folded sheet, Wilson, with a remark that set Ratley chuckling, crossed over and nonchalantly planted himself against a lamppost where the two must pass. Just then Barton, without a word, handed the note to Teresa. She read it swiftly, gave a quick gasp, and turned it back to him. And with Laura holding a hand of each, they walked on past the loiterer by the lamppost, unseeing, blanched, speechless.

Upon reaching the house, Teresa, pleading indisposition, immediately went to her room. Dan Sickles dined alone. And Barton Key, feeling himself a man foredoomed, went to his house on C Street and spent an hour with his children.

The next day, haggard and hollow-eyed, he haunted Pennsylvania Avenue for hours, mechanically returning greetings, pretending haste when anyone tried to detain him. But no Teresa appeared. He could not know that she lay abed, stunned and still, awaiting the stroke. Finally, in desperation, he went to the Cosmos Club, and taking an upper room facing Stockton Mansion across the square, he remained frozen to the window, watching through his little French opera glasses for some glimpse of her.

Meanwhile Wooldridge, returning to the room he had rented from Mrs. Baylis, had been prosecuting his inquiries. From Crittenden he gleaned—among a lot of inconclusive details—one fact that seemed important: it was on the previous Thursday afternoon that the lady last had been seen entering No. 383. With this he went at once to Stockton Mansion, taking the young Negro with him for further questioning. Dan, at the mention of the word Thursday, stopped pacing the floor and sank into a chair. "Thank God, George, it wasn't Mrs. Sickles! Thursday afternoon she was paying calls with Miss Ridgeley—I know that. And now I must ask you to be very careful in your inquiries not to mention her name—the mere suspicion could be as bad as the terrible reality."

The next day, Saturday, Wooldridge again went back to talk to Mrs. Baylis. But now he had no need to ask questions. Word had spread around the block that the white folk at No. 383 were being investigated; and the Negroes, eager to tell all they knew, crowded around him, talking each other down. Most of what they told him he already knew, but from Mrs. Baylis and Mrs. Seeley he obtained, for the first time, a minute account of the lady's dress. Darkly he realized that the description tallied all too closely with some of Teresa's elegant costumes. Then suddenly both women were correcting Crittenden, affirming that the lady's last visit was not on Thursday—but on Wednesday! Insistently Wooldridge questioned them on the point. But they could not be shaken. All the colored folk around agreed with them that it was Wednesday; and at last Crittenden himself admitted that he had made a mistake.

Wooldridge knew then what he had to do. Returning home to an early dinner, he found a note from Dan, stressing his previous request: "Please be very tender in your inquiries; for I am satisfied now that Mrs. Sickles is not involved." Sick at heart, Wooldridge forthwith took a hack to the Capitol and sent in for Dan. Silently the two walked down the corridor, away from the congressmen clotting the lobby. Then Wooldridge rested on his crutches. "Dan, I am afraid I have bad news for you. Crittenden was wrong about the day. It was on Wednesday, not on Thursday, that the lady was last seen at Gray's house. All the colored folk of the block say the same thing." Doggedly he sketched the costume, reading from his notes, "plaid dress, handsome black velvet shawl with bugles, beaver hat." Before he had finished, Dan with a hoarse cry flung himself against the wall, bursting into such a convulsion of sobbing that Wooldridge hastily drew him into an anteroom.

It was half an hour before the tempest died down. Then a spent Dan Sickles was quietly asking Wooldridge to bring his hat. A few minutes later, striding down the Avenue, looking neither right nor left, he failed to notice the greeting of the Reverend Smith Pyne, who was to have officiated at Laura's christening. Puzzled, the clergyman remarked to his son, "Mr. Sickles certainly has a peculiar appearance." Looking back, he added thoughtfully, "I never saw such an air of desolation . . . defiance."

At Stockton Mansion dinner already was laid. But Teresa did not come down; instead she sent word by Bridget that a headache kept her abed. Mechanically Dan took his place at the table, then, with a groan, jumped up and ordered the dinner sent upstairs. The bedroom was empty. When Bridget had set down the tray and closed the door behind her, Dan called sharply, "Terry." Wan and disheveled, she came from the dressing room. One glance and she knew! Despite his effort at control, his voice blasted from him like a pistol shot, "Where were you Wednesday afternoon?" Teresa blenched, swayed, sank down on the little slipper chair at her side. "Why . . . I—I think I was shopping, Dan." In two strides he was standing over her, his fists knotting and unknotting spasmodically. "Weren't you at a house on Fifteenth Street with Barton Key?" Teresa drooped her head. Stooping, he shouted, "Tell me!" He shook her violently. "Were you?" Her nod was almost imperceptible. A hand seized her left wrist. A wrench—and her ring was gone. She slid to the floor, fainting.

A little later the servants heard loud voices in the room—tones of fierce rage, wild protestation, broken pleading, shrill weeping, guttural sobbing.

Presently all was quiet. Teresa, a lifeless image, sat at her escritoire preparing to write, lip and pen aquiver. Dan deliberately opened the door wide, then came and stood beside her. Hair shagged, face streaked, vest torn open, he looked like a maniac, but his manner was tensely alert, collected. "Now write—write down in your own words what you have just told me." The pen dropped on the desk. "Dan . . . I can't." He picked up the pen, put it in her hand, and as though she were a child, closed her fingers over it. His voice was terrifyingly quiet, emphatic. "You must. You owe it to me. It is all you can do for me now. God knows what may come of this!"

Slowly, laboriously, hypnotically, in a quaking, almost indecipherable hand, Teresa began to write—halting, disjointed dabs of words. But Dan, now seemingly galvanized by his agony, remained clear-minded, focused on what must be done. Two lines, and Teresa's mind refused to work further. And again, as though she were a child at her lessons, he prompted her, by question, suggestion, correction, to set down just those precise details that he knew would be required in any legal statement of the facts. But he wished that statement to be her own; and only when her crawling pen came to a dead halt did he offer her a word, a phrase. It was a slow, crucifying process. But at last the blotched scrawl lay between them:

I have been in a house in Fifteenth street, with Mr. Key. How many times I don't know. I believe the house belongs to a colored man. The house is unoccupied. Commenced going there the latter part of January. Have been in alone and with Mr. Key. Usually stayed an hour or more.

There was a bed in the second story. I did what is usual for a wicked woman to do. The intimacy commenced this winter, when I came from New York, in that house—an intimacy of an improper kind. Have met half a dozen times or more, at different hours of the day. On Monday of this week, and Wednesday also. Would arrange meetings when we met in the street and at parties. Never would speak to him when Mr. Sickles was at home, because I knew he did not like me to speak to him; did not see Mr. Key for some days after I got here. He then told me he had hired the house as a place where he and I could meet. I agreed to it. Had nothing to eat or drink there. The room is warmed by a wood fire. Mr. Key generally goes first. Have walked there together say four times— I do not think more; was there on Wednesday last, between two and three. I went there alone. Laura was at Mrs. Hoover's. Mr. Key took and left her there at my request. From there I went to Fifteenth street to meet Mr. Key; from there to the milk woman's. Immediately after Mr. Key left Laura at Mrs. Hoover's, I met him in Fifteenth street. Went in by the back gate. Went in the same bedroom, and there an improper interview was had. I undressed myself. Mr. Key undressed also. This occurred on Wednesday, 23rd of February, 1859. Mr. Key has kissed me in this house a number of times. I do not deny that we have had connection in this house, last spring, a year ago, in the parlor, on the sofa. Mr. Sickles was sometimes out of town, and sometimes in the Capitol. I think the intimacy commenced in April or May, 1858. I did not think it safe to meet him in this house, because there are servants who might suspect something. As a general thing, have worn a black and white woollen plaid dress, and beaver hat trimmed with black velvet. Have worn a black silk dress there also, also a plaid silk dress, black velvet cloak trimmed with lace, and a black velvet shawl trimmed with fringe. On Wednesday I either had on my brown dress or black and white woollen dress, beaver hat and velvet shawl. I arranged with Mr. Key to go in the back way, after leaving Laura at Mrs. Hoover's. He met me at Mr. Douglas', as we would be less likely to be seen. The house is in Fifteenth street between K and L streets, on the left hand side of the way; arranged the interview of Wednesday in the street, I think, on Monday. I went in the front door, it was open, occupied the same room, undressed myself, and he also; went to bed together. Mr. Key has ridden in Mr. Sickles' carriage, and has called at this house without Mr. Sickles's knowledge, and after my being told not to invite him to do so, and against Mr. Sickles' repeated request.

TERESA BAGIOLI

This is a true statement, written by myself, without any inducement held out by Mr. Sickles of forgiveness or reward, and without any menace from him. This I have written with my bedroom door open, and my maid and child in the adjoining room, at half past eight o'clock in the evening. Miss Ridgeley is in the house, within call.

Teresa Bagioli

Lafayette Square, Washington, D.C., Feb. 26, 1859.

Mr. and Mrs. Pendleton dined here two weeks ago last Thursday with a large party. Mr. Key was also here, her brother, and at my sugges-

FACSIMILE OF PART OF TERESA SICKLES' CONFESSION

tion he was invited because he lived in the same house, and also because he had invited Mr. Sickles to dine with him, and Mr. Sickles wished to invite all those from whom he had received invitations; and Mr. Sickles said "do as you choose."

TERESA BAGIOLI

Written and signed in presence of O. M. Ridgeley and Bridget Duffy. Feb. 26, 1859.

Octavia, aware of grave trouble impending, had kept close to Teresa all day, and still lingered downstairs in the library, pretending to read, but actually listening dry-mouthed to the ebb and flow of the storm overhead. It was eight o'clock when Dan appeared and in a strange voice asked her to come upstairs for a moment. Tremulously she followed him. At the top of the stairs he looked into the nursery and beckoned Bridget Duffy—just then putting Laura to bed. Carefully covering the main part of the confession with a blotter, he asked both girls to witness Teresa's signature. Now at last his forced composure gave way. And as Octavia, and then Bridget, in embarrassed silence put their names to the strange document, he began pacing the floor, fingers pressed to his temples, moaning, in a brutal, husky staccato, "Laura! My little Laura! My little Laura!"

When the girls had gone, Teresa, dazed, feeling her way as though she were blind, staggered across the hall to Octavia's room and, closing the door, stumbled to the floor, her head on a little Victoria chair by the bed. Unable to obtain any word or sign from her, Octavia tried to lift her. But it was as though she struggled with a creature turned to lead. Far into the night she crouched by Teresa's side, patting her, talking to her—without sign. At last, utterly wearied, she undressed and lay down—still, between broken patches of sleep, maintaining her vigil. In the morning Teresa still lay where she had fallen. And Octavia, thinking now that, perhaps, in God's mercy, it were better so, left her. And Bridget, coming to make up the room, took one glance at her mistress and tiptoed out.

Dan, meanwhile, had gone to his room. All through the night, from time to time his bursts of grief shook the house. Presently Laura began whimpering. And Dan, suddenly shamed, stilled, crept to her room, took her up and carried her to his own bed. And as he held the tiny replica of Teresa against him, he began to realize in more dread clarity that what had come upon him was more than loss—a rending mutilation. He knew now that Teresa was not to him what she might have been had he met her a woman, but that from infancy through childhood, girlhood, wifehood she had become meshed in his fiber, a private delight, a pet possession, secure in a special place in his heart—a place so secluded from all his passing affairs with other women that he never even had thought of them as touching her skirt. Bitterly he realized that sometimes he had neglected her, been impatient with her immaturity. But no more than he had ever dreamed that another man could supersede him had he dreamed that another woman could take her place as his wife—and he knew now, too late, that no woman ever could. And it was as though he saw a Great Hand reach out and take her—and with her, child, home, honor, place, leaving him in howling darkness, all ambition turned to dust.

Yet he knew there was something to be done.

Sunday morning, while Octavia breakfasted with Laura, Dan mournfully roamed the house, upstairs and down, rambling aimlessly from one room to another, every now and again breaking out into wild weeping, and Bridget, meeting him on the stairs wringing his hands, fled tearfully to the kitchen. Presently, realizing that he must have some human help or go mad, he sent for Wooldridge and that much-trusted Tammany friend of his, Samuel F. Butterworth, just then visiting Senator Slidell. When Wooldridge arrived, Dan thrust the confession into his hands and rushed upstairs to his room. There, a few minutes later, Butterworth found him prone on the bed in a state of incoherent grief, able only to wail, again and again, "I am a dishonored and ruined man, I cannot look you in the face." Finally dragging himself to his feet, apologizing for his behavior, Dan wearily recited the story, ending despairingly, "What shall I do—what shall I do?"

In contrast to the silently sympathetic Wooldridge, Butterworth, a hardheaded practical politician, was quick with his advice. "If I were you, Dan, I would send Mrs. Sickles immediately to her mother in New York. It's near the end of the session, and her going would excite no remark. It will be half a year before the House meets again. What you should do is take a trip to Europe—meanwhile arrange a separation. I don't suppose the affair is known to more than two or three persons—although doubtless a good many may have their suspicions. Think of your own future, man."

Dan listened to the cold, matter-of-fact tones with bitter disbelief.

"It's no use, Sam. They were too utterly reckless. All the Negroes in the neighborhood know about it—and God knows how many others."

Butterworth seemed to hesitate, then rose. "I'd like to talk to Wooldridge about this." In the library, Wooldridge handed him the confession. After prolonged scrutiny, he put it down. "I don't know what to say. Think I'll go over to the clubhouse—tell Dan I'll be back soon."

Across the square Barton, fruitlessly watching Stockton Mansion through his binoculars, could stand the suspense no longer. For two nights he had not slept, scarcely had eaten, sustaining himself with whisky that affected him no more than water. Now he plunged outside, flourished his handkerchief three times, peering through the screen of budding trees at Teresa's window. There was no answering signal. What had happened? Had Dan——? Trying to think what to do, he jerkily walked a few blocks, turned back. Passing along the south side of the park, he waved thrice again. Still no sign. Hopelessly he entered the clubhouse and went to his room, snatched up his binoculars and watched and watched. Several times he was on the point of going boldly over and meeting whatever was to be met. At least he would know . . .

When Butterworth entered the library again, Wooldridge hastened to tell him that he had just seen Key pass and repass the house on the opposite side of the square, waving his handkerchief. And Bridget, in the kitchen basement in the front of the house, witnessing the waving, had called the cook, crying, "There's Disgust signaling his Disgrace again."

In the meantime Barton, with a last desperate ruse in mind, had left the club and, circling the eastern end of the park, had mingled with the stream of worshipers coming from St. John's Church, hoping to use some of them for cover. Singling out a young couple, slight acquaintances, sauntering in the direction of Stockton Mansion, he linked stride with them. Despite his affected casualness, his pallor and his bloodshot eyes startled them. Solicitously they asked if he had been ill. Barton clutched at the passing sympathy. "Yes, and I am not feeling very well." Then, with a last gesture of bravado, "In fact, I have a mind to go West and hunt buffalo. It would either cure me or kill me—and I don't care much which."

Abreast now of Stockton Mansion, Barton, with a wide flourish,

From *Frank Leslie's Illustrated Newspaper.*

HON. DANIEL E. SICKLES SHOOTING PHILIP BARTON KEY,
IN PRESIDENT'S SQUARE, WASHINGTON

TERESA SICKLES

whipped out his handkerchief. At that moment Dan's little Italian greyhound, Dandy, ran across the street and began to frolic about him in greeting. Cleverly pretending to play with the dog, he flicked his handkerchief at him three times—while keenly watching Teresa's window. Still there came no sign. . . . At the corner, half a block away, he bade good-by to his friends and continued around the park to the club.

At the same moment Dan was stumbling downstairs, bursting in upon Wooldridge and Butterworth in the library, shouting wildly, "I just have seen the scoundrel making signals. My God, this is horrible!"

In a curiously unconvincing tone, Butterworth urged him to sane consideration of the matter. "Calm down, my friend, and look this thing squarely in the face. So long as there's a possibility of keeping it quiet, you must do nothing to destroy that possibility." Then very deliberately, "You *might*, you know, be quite mistaken in your belief that the whole town knows about it."

Dan, goaded, cut him short with a grim gesture toward the window. "After that? All Washington is talking about it."

Butterworth's shrug was spark to the tinder. "If that be so, then there is but one course left to you. As a man of honor, you need no advice."

It was sentence of death. Suddenly Dan knew it—knew now that nothing but blood could wash this smirch from his life. With no more ado he made for the door, beckoning, "Come on. I am going to the clubhouse."* In the hall, however, motioning Butterworth to go ahead, he ran downstairs to the room in the basement where he stored his saddles, guns, and heavy New York winter wear. There he hastily charged a large-bore, single-shot Derringer—deadliest of short-range weapons; and a clumsy, muzzle-loading Colt revolver discharged by means of separate caps affixed to the butt of each chamber.

Slowly making the necessary half-circuit around the sleepy, deserted, little park, Butterworth, at the southwest corner—as by some fateful decree—met Barton just coming from the clubhouse not forty yards away. Courteously Barton greeted him. "Good morning, Mr. Butterworth—what a fine day we have," and was passing on, but a

---

*In his own report of the matter, Butterworth pretended not to know Dan's intentions—obviously to clear his own skirts. It was not credited.

hand detained him. "Have you come from the club?" The reply was curt. "I have." Butterworth drew out his words. "Do you know . . . if Mr. Stewart . . . is in his room?" and moved on a pace, forcing Barton to turn around as he answered, "Yes, Mr. Stewart is in his room, and he is quite unwell." Looking past him, Butterworth saw Dan rapidly approaching, and noticed that, although it was a warm day, he had donned a heavy ulster. He bowed pleasantly. "I am going up to see him. Good morning." Turning, he walked deliberately, ears alert, toward the club, then suddenly wheeled, backing against the park rails. A tenor scream split the silence: "Key, you scoundrel! You have disgraced my house—you must die!" There came the crash of a revolver shot. Barton, staggering, instinctively reached in his inner breast pocket. But he had changed his coat a few minutes before. His hand closed on—a little pair of French opera glasses! Dan placed a fresh cap in his Colt, aimed. But the trigger clicked harmlessly on a dud. In a wild effort to forestall a third shot, Barton lunged at him, grappled him, weakly endeavoring to batter his face with the binoculars. But Dan flung him off, thrust the revolver in his pocket, backed away into the middle of the street, and whipped out the Derringer. Reeling, Barton retreated backward toward the club and desperately hurled his binoculars at the approaching muzzle. But blasting, "You villain! You have dishonored my house! You must die—die—die!" Dan came on, and within ten feet, fired. Mortally wounded, Barton doubled up, lurched toward a tree, clutched it, crying, "Don't shoot—don't shoot!" Remorseless as fate, Dan tossed the Derringer aside, drew his Colt again, set a cap, and still blasting "You must die—you must die!" fired once more. Crouching, gripping his guts, Barton slumped to the ground. Grimly as an executioner Dan, setting a fresh cap, strode down on him and put the barrel right to his head. But a member of the club, running up, stopped him. "Mr. Sickles—for God's sake!" And Butterworth, coming forward, took Dan by the arm. Without a word, they walked away together.

It was done! Suddenly as calm as he had just been frenzied, Dan, thrusting Butterworth quietly aside, announced that he was going over to the home of Attorney General Black to give himself up. At this, Butterworth turned back and followed amid the rapidly gathering, excited crowd as Barton was carried to the clubhouse and laid on the parlor floor—his head propped on the rung of a tilted chair.

There Butterworth waited until the dying man's last faint gasps had ceased and the doctor had pronounced life extinct. Then he walked over to Judge Black's with the news.

Meanwhile a hastily organized coroner's jury prepared to hold inquest over the blood-dappled but still dignified figure on the floor— the face strangely composed as though the reft spirit were already aware of atonement, release. It was hours before the troubled jurors could agree on a statement. Guardedly they concluded that "the deceased met death from the effect of pistol shots fired by the Hon. Daniel E. Sickles."

After a prolonged and painful interview with Judge Black, Dan and Butterworth took carriage to Stockton Mansion—to find an excited crowd about the steps and a group of friends and newspapermen in the hall. Dan, a tousled demoniac, pushed through the crowd and went immediately upstairs. Alarmed at his murderous appearance, a young Tammanyite, McCluskey, followed him halfway up, then hesitated, listening. At that moment Mayor Berritt and Chief of Police Goddard, with several officers, arrived from the clubhouse. Upstairs Dan went straight to the front bedroom, closed the door. Teresa, still in her dressing gown, her black hair wild about her, turned from the window, her great dark eyes one crazed question. His stare was as crazed. "Yes, I've killed him!" The door slammed on a scream.

Heavily he went downstairs. There he briefly greeted some of his acquaintances—Senator Slidell, J. H. McBlair, and several others—but at sight of his beloved friend, Congressman Robert J. Walker, his voice broke. "A thousand thanks for coming to see me at a time like this." Unable to say another word, he gripped Walker's sleeve, pulling him into the back parlor. Butterworth followed, closing the door behind him. Ensued a terrifying scene. With the howl of a wounded wild beast, Dan flung himself upon the sofa. For some minutes his hoarse cries, unearthly sobbing, screaming protestations to God, rang through the house—while, in the hall and parlor, talk died down and men looked uneasily into one another's eyes. Before such paroxysms of despair, Walker and Butterworth stood helpless, aghast. At last Mayor Berritt strode into the room and, taking Dan by the shoulders, sternly bade him compose himself and get ready to go to jail. With a tremendous effort at self-control Dan rose and, accompanied by Walker, Butterworth, and the mayor, re-entered the parlor, where Chief of Police Goddard awaited him. As he appeared at the street door the crowd outside burst into hoots, jeers, catcalls. Seeming not to know what he was doing, he vaguely waved to them; but Mayor Berritt at his side sharply warned him not to attract attention and hustled him into Senator Gwin's proffered carriage.

At the jail, after a cursory examination, he was committed on a charge of homicide, and, refusing bail—despite many urgent offers— he walked resolutely to his cell with Walker and Butterworth. Once more he broke down—but now quietly, in utter emotional exhaustion. And saying little, his friends stayed with him until, just before dusk, he became more tranquil.

CHAPTER XVII

Tragic Interlude

———◆◆———

THE DISTRICT JAIL was a foul hole, swarming with vermin, destitute of sewage, bath, water, ventilation, and so inadequate to its purpose that often a dozen or more prisoners were herded into a single narrow cell. That in refusing bail he was consigning himself to intolerable filth and stench was something that had not occurred to Dan Sickles; but, confronted with the fact, he was steadfast in his decision. It was, and was meant to be, a challenging gesture to his fellow citizens: "In doing what I had to do I have broken the law. Therefore I have placed myself behind bars. It is for you to set me free!" And to deliver that challenge he was willing to face reek and wretchedness, to say nothing of the severe disadvantage of presenting himself in court not a free man under bond but a jailbird between guards.

Unable to change Dan's determination, Walker insisted that at least he must be given a clean cell; and volunteered to see Warden King about the matter in the morning. Wooldridge, equally concerned, crutched it over to his friend, the Reverend Haley—a man full of good will, and a constant visitor at the jail—and asked him to call at once upon the prisoner, do what he could to comfort him, and use his influence to see that he had fresh blankets and, perhaps, a decent meal sent in from one of the neighboring chop houses. Haley, eager to be of service, promptly complied. Dan received him with appreciative courtesy, but set aside all talk about his own needs. His only concern was for Teresa. "I should be grateful if you would go to see her, and tell me how she is."

And so it came about that the good minister, besieged by the curious mob hanging about the jail and about Stockton Mansion, plied back and forth between stricken husband, frantic wife.

In utter contrition, agonized atonement, Teresa had sealed her mind, if not her heart, against sorrow for the dead; all her suffering now was for the living—for the irreparable disaster she had brought upon husband and child. And Haley, alarmed at her frenzy of remorse, reported back to Dan that he feared for her reason, even her life, unless she were given some help, some hope. He brought from her a heartbroken note pleading for forgiveness, pleading especially for the return of her ring. Dan was wrung but adamant. Having no other paper, he wrote in pencil on the back of the note: "Do not accuse yourself any more. It is useless. I have no reproach for you, only pity; but I cannot return the ring." Sadly Haley left him. In an hour he was back, deeply troubled. He brought news that Teresa, discovering that he had come empty-handed, had collapsed in a heart attack. The benevolent old face grew stern. "My friend, consider what you do." Slowly Dan drew out the ring, placed it in Haley's palm. "Tell her I send it for what comfort it may give her; but the bond between us never can be restored." Day was already breaking when Haley returned bearing a fervent scrawl of thanks and blessing.

In the morning the warden, blandly surprised to learn that his distinguished prisoner had suffered much from the bedbugs and fetid air of the jail, promptly gave up his own room to him. To Dan, sleepless through four days and nights of emotional storm, the change of quarters came as a vivid relief. He now had a decent room on the second floor, equipped with a clean bed, table, several chairs, and lighted by a large—if well-barred—window. Presently

Octavia, acting for the still prostrate Teresa, sent him a trunk packed with wearing apparel, cigars, books, and writing materials. And when lavish boxes of flowers began to arrive, and Dandy—that most fanatical of his devotees—leaped at him from Walker's arms, suddenly the bare boards and whitewashed walls seemed to lose some of their dreariness.

Tuesday afternoon, James T. Brady arrived from New York to take charge of his friend's defense. He had not waited for the wire that he knew would come, but had already packed his bags before it was delivered. To him, as the ablest criminal lawyer of the day, Dan gratefully assigned full charge of his case. Followed a long and harrowing consultation. And at its close it was agreed between them that Edwin McM. Stanton and John Graham, outstanding members of the Washington bar, should be called in to assist.

That night George Garrett Sickles burst in upon his already exhausted son. The stout old Knickerbocker was stormful: "You hotheaded fool! That's no way to settle things! No woman's worth it! No matter how you come out of this, you've killed your career—White House and everything else." Dan's tone had the firmness of a man surmounting his own weariness. "Don't you think I know that? And if I had to, I would do it again!" Sickles Sr. gave up. One sharp look at his son's fagged face and he mellowed down, began to growl encouragement. Energetically, for a while, he discussed the organization for the defense, ended by drawing out his checkbook.

The next night Mr. and Mrs. Bagioli appeared with Collector Hart. They just had come from a hysterical scene with Teresa. The Maestro seemed to have lost his voice. But Mrs. Bagioli burst immediately into a torrent of lamentations, accusations, wild supplications for *"mia carissima bambina,"* imploring Dan not to cast her off, to remember how he had played with her as a tiny baby. In the midst of a sentence she collapsed in a faint. When she revived, the Maestro led her weeping from the room. In momentary bitterness Dan turned to Hart—standing sympathetically silent. "I might have been spared this, at least!" Then, with a swift glow of warmth, "It's good to see you, Manny! God knows how I've wanted you." Far into the night the two friends talked, fell amicably silent, talked again.

In the course of a week, while Teresa lay in a state of dangerous collapse, Dan, regaining something of his old poise, set himself with military self-discipline to cope with the crowding demands of his situation. He rose early, took a sponge bath, made his toilet with scrupulous exactness, then, after breakfast, sat down to read the pile of letters received the previous night. One of the first of these was a kindly note from the President. Practically all of them were expressions of sympathy. To the many proffers of aid—no few of them, significantly, from bitter political enemies—he had but one answer, "I leave everything to my counsel and the law." As a man of many friends, popular with the crowd, and, beyond that, a national figure on trial for his life, his mail, naturally, was burdensomely heavy; and scarcely did he have time to deal sketchily with it before visitors began to arrive. Early in the afternoon came counsel—Brady, Stanton, Graham, and soon with them four lesser assistants, Magruder, Chilton, Ratcliffe, and Phillips. There would be hours of close conference. Then, toward dusk, came more friends —and sometimes they would bring small hampers of food and wine and share the evening meal with him. Every evening the Reverend Haley visited him. And one friend, usually Walker or Hart, always stayed with him until he was ready for bed.

Meanwhile the body of Barton Key, followed by a few friends, was borne to the Georgetown Cemetery—scene of so many stolen hours. Shortly thereafter his effects, even to his old horse pistols and gay Montgomery Guard uniform, were sold off to a morbid, bargain-hunting, souvenir-hounding crowd. The ladies, however, were puzzled and disappointed by the plain, substantial character of his furnishings.

Dan's first act in confinement had been to arrange that Teresa, taking Laura with her, should go at once to New York and remain there in the care of her parents. But it was March 10 before her condition permitted travel. Before going she begged Dan for a parting interview. The request, however, met with a gently worded refusal: "A meeting at this time only could inflict torture on us both." Nevertheless he asked to see Laura. The child had been told that her father was in New York, and he did not like to think of her bitter disappointment when she failed to find him there. There was the risk, of course, that she would be shocked by his surroundings; but even so he thought it better for her to be brought to him. When, presently, she appeared with Mrs. Bagioli, she ran into his arms, all joy, full of questions. But as she began to look about this strange bare room, examine the cheap cot, the rack of old muskets on the wall, and peer out of the barred window, her face puckered in bewilderment. One troubled question followed another. Dan's answers were deft and quick. But she only shook her head. Suddenly she began to cry bitterly. Nor could she be diverted or coaxed into telling the reason for her tears. Dan could stand no more. Hastily composing a little bouquet from the flowers on his table and putting it in her hands, he motioned the signora to take her away.

The next morning Teresa, heavily veiled, half carried by her father to the carriage, left Washington forever.

"The Washington Tragedy"—as it quickly came to be known—created an extraordinary reverberation throughout the country. Even while crowds of the morbidly curious were clotting about the jail, Stockton Mansion and No. 383, the newspapers, North and South, East and West, wherever wires ran, were front-paging the story under screaming headlines and, in the larger cities, rushing out extras every hour or two, as fresh details came to hand. At the same time a corps of correspondents and pencil-sketch artists arrived in Washington to supply the popular demand for full-length, illustrated accounts of characters and scene. It was in New York, however, where for years Dan Sickles had been a prominent and popular figure, that the excitement flared to its highest. There, for days and all day long, the papers refurbished and blazoned the story from every angle, while hordes of newsies ran through the streets howling, "Pi-per! All about the moi-i-i-der!" Everywhere, in the home and on the street, in hotel lobbies, clubs and cafés, offices and workshops, Dan Sickles was on every lip. And what was true in New York was in lesser measure true of the country at large. Even in the western wilds where the story only could be carried by diligence, steamboat, pony express, it became as much the absorbing topic in cabins and camps as on the streets of the cities. And, what was more important, wherever it was discussed it aroused the most energetic debate. For here was dramatic news that also was a challenge to the judgment of everyone who heard it. From Maine to Alabama, from the eastern seaboard to the Golden Gate, folk fought over the question: was Dan Sickles justified in slaying the man who had betrayed his confidence and seduced his wife? And if down on the Tammany East Side the raucous caucus of saloon and sidewalk voted him right, and the metropolitan dailies—including even his enemies, the *Herald* and the Wood-ite *News*—were scarcely less emphatic in his favor, elsewhere a deeply troubled public opinion stood divided. As a consequence the whole country turned jury. And it was this that served to sustain a nationwide interest in the case far more intense than its merely sensational features warranted.

Of course the fact that the victim was United States attorney, son of the revered Francis Scott Key; the aggressor a member of the Foreign Affairs Committee, intimate friend of the President; *la femme fatale* a youthful, engagingly lovely Italian—added rich color to the picture. But what gave "The Washington Tragedy" its unique importance was the fact that on the national stage had been enacted a "morality play" of helpless passion, drifting treachery, heartbroken vengeance, old as human history, universal as human wrong, appealing and violent as any theme transmuted to literature by an Aeschylus, a Shakespeare; and that it posed a question—one intensely critical at a time when primitive America was struggling toward civilized communion, when even congressmen openly brandished their horse pistols in the House, and out West every man toted judge, jury, and executioner on his hip. It was a question that touched the very heart of contemporary life: apart from self-protection under attack, do certain extreme provocations justify the injured in dealing death upon his injurer? And it was the wrestling with this problem of the "unwritten law" on the part of millions of Americans that gave the subsequent trial its aura of intense and nationwide excitement.

CHAPTER XVIII

"Gentlemen of the Jury——"

———◆———

Monday, april 4, 1859—10 a.m. . . . . A vast mob of morbid humanity blocks the street in front of Washington's drab, undersized City Hall. Within, the courtroom—dingy, cramped, dimly lighted, ill ventilated—already is choked with talesmen, lawyers, witnesses, reporters. Only fifty seats on bare benches remain for the accommodation of the curious. The doors roll back. A powerful body of police wrestles with the clamorous mob. Fifty panting, disheveled representatives of the public squeeze through. The doors are closed—but not before a number of young fellows, nimbly using packed heads for steppingstones, have managed to crawl through the windows. The disappointed crowd, men cursing, women tearfully gibbering, melts slowly away, with hoots and howls. The policemen straighten their uniforms, joke over missing buttons. The young men lounge, self-satisfied, on the window sills.

At 10:40 a.m. the prisoner enters. He is accompanied by the marshal and several friends. Well groomed, impeccably attired—black frock coat, gray striped trousers, choker collar and broad, black bow tie—he bears himself with dignity and ease.

A few minutes later the bailiff raps for order. Spectators, talesmen, lawyers, reporters scramble to their feet as a weazened little man, with the face of a peevish bat, takes his seat on the bench. The trial of the Hon. Daniel E. Sickles for the murder of Philip Barton Key has begun.

On one side of the judge stand two tiers of raised benches for the jury, and beside them the witness box. On the opposite side is the prisoner's dock—a low platform surrounded by rails and looking much like a calf pen. On the same side sit counsel for defense. Counsel for prosecution face the judge. Correspondents, growling at the fact that they are given no table and must write and sketch on their knees, scrunch on hard chairs about the clerk to the court.

The indictment is read. Formally questioned as to his plea, the prisoner responds in a firm tone: "Not guilty."

The task of obtaining a jury begins. Three days pass in tedious question and challenge. Two hundred talesmen are examined before twelve can be found who profess an open mind on the case at issue. The great majority of those dismissed confess strong prejudice in favor of the prisoner. A few, however, are aggressively unfavorable. One of these, passing out of the courtroom, is stopped by a dark-eyed, bushy-haired member of the audience. "Just now I heard you say something harsh of the prisoner, but let me ask you, if you had lost your wife, or had your daughter sacrificed, would you have been able to control your feelings and be governed by reason?" The talesman looks startled. "I don't know—but who is asking me this question?" The reply grates on tears. "I am the father of Mrs. Sickles." Touched, the talesman apologizes, admits that with the same provocation he, too, might have killed.

The fourth day. The battle begins. From the outset the contending forces appear bent upon a finish fight, but their strength is oddly ill-matched. On the one side stands a dull bull of a man, at one time a Baptist parson, recently assistant United States attorney, and just promoted by President Buchanan to the position formerly occupied by Philip Barton Key. His is a curious predicament. He is called to invoke justice upon the slayer of his former friend and chief. And, the ethics of office apart, he is not disposed to show mercy. At the same time he owes his appointment to the distinguished position of United States attorney for the District of Columbia to none other than the most intimate friend of the accused! And if the fact should tend to soften his thunders, he must confront the equally cogent fact that, from obscurity, he has suddenly been lifted to the status of a champion of the law in a case that has become a national, even an international, *cause célèbre*. Under the circumstances, Robert Ould of the full, heavy face, thick shoulders, decides to do what he always has done, rely on good, old-fashioned Biblical honesty and go to his work with a sledge hammer. Inspecting the defense, however, he, possibly, is consoled by the thought that, do what he may to acquit himself to the world and in his own eyes as a vigorous prosecutor, his most forthright efforts, most crushing tirades, will fail to put the noose about the prisoner's neck. He has reason for the thought. At his side his lone assistant sits—already unhappily aware of defeat—the acid, unstable, if brilliant, pleader, J. M. Carlisle, representing the deceased's relatives. But across the way it is a different story. There sits the most powerful battery of legal talent the old courtroom has yet witnessed: James T. Brady, master strategist of the New York bar, intimidatingly erudite on points of law, suave to the opposition, deferential to the judge, overwhelming before the jury; Edwin McM. Stanton, leader of the Maryland bar, with the massive head and flowing beard of some patriarch of Israel, stentorian in eloquence—always astutely aiming at some weak hinge in his opponent's armor; John Graham, Brady's only rival—given to adorning his driving logic with dramatic appeals, Latin quotations, recitations from Shakespeare worthy of Booth; and, for the lesser work of cross-examination of talesman and witness, the three prominent Washington lawyers, Ratcliffe, Chilton, Magruder, and the foremost figure of the Alabama bar, Congressman Phillips. And, looking them over, Prosecutor Ould prepares for dramatic battle, honorable defeat. Amid the breathless attention of judge, jurors, audience, he rises. Ponderously, powerfully, in blackest terms, he draws a gruesome picture of the killing, then presents the issue:

The prisoner at the bar came to the carnival of blood fully prepared. He was a walking magazine. . . . I say this not to influence your minds against him, but as an illustration of the common law: that homicide with a deadly weapon, perpetrated by a party who has all the advantage on his side and with all the circumstances of deliberate cruelty and vindictiveness, is murder, *no matter what the antecedent provocation in the case.*

Citing copiously from Wharton's *Criminal Law* he strives to make twelve simple, rather vacant-minded men—grocers, clerks, butchers, mechanics—realize the majestic tradition of the common law in relation to murder:

Its maxims are based on common sense and common justice. . . . All its features are essentially humane. . . . These principles owe their entire strength, and their veracity, to their humanity—not a maudlin, sickly, sentimental humanity, but one that is God-fearing, and to men loving. . . . Society, gentlemen, has its cries, no less than the common prisoner. . . . The jury that sends its deliverance to the offender whose stains are not washed off by the evidence in the trial, is itself morally derelict to the high obligations which humanity alone imposes upon it. . . . Innovation, even in its wildest moment, has never yet suggested the propriety of allowing *revenge as either a justification or a palliation of the crime of murder*. . . . The common law has a most sacred regard for human life, so sacred that even the rankest criminal—he who has assumed to himself the functions of judge, jury, and executioner—is himself given by law the privilege of a fair and impartial trial. It gives to Daniel E. Sickles, the prisoner at the bar, not only what he denied his victim, namely, an impartial jury, an upright judge, but until he is proven guilty, it clothes him in the spotless robes of innocence. . . . I charge you, gentlemen of the jury, by the duty that you owe to yourselves, to your God and to your country, to smite the red hand of violence everywhere by your verdict.

Follows the examination of nine persons who, in more or less fragmentary fashion, far or near, witnessed the killing of Key. The repetitious repicturing of the scene goes hard with the prisoner. Frequently he leans his head on his hand, closes his eyes, wishes he could close his ears.

Amid a decidedly unresponsive atmosphere, J. M. Carlisle, conducting the examination, resumes his seat. The prosecution rests its case.

It is now the turn of counsel for defense. They are smiling and confident. The fact that two hundred dismissed talesmen—underscoring the general attitude of the press—just have exhibited marked sympathy with the accused gives them good hope for victory. Also the case presents a superb occasion for the grandiloquent exhibitionism so dear to their hearts—and the heart of the Fifties! Nevertheless they have left nothing to chance. Their strategy has been planned to a finish. Obviously they have but one plea: the fact that the accused committed his crime under the excitement of extreme provocation. And, to make the most of this, they have agreed among themselves to: (1) turn the tables on the prosecution, place the dead Key on trial, and twist the case into a stupendous arraignment of adultery; (2) use this emotional appeal to fire the jury with the indignant conviction that the accused was fully justified in his action; (3) stress evidence to show that—*justified or not*—the homicide was committed under the impact of such grief and rage and jealousy as rendered the accused temporarily insane, and to cite precedent to show that such a state of mind has been accepted in law as precluding moral responsibility. Viewing their strategy, they feel that they have an unbreakable defense; but they also know that juries have been known to spoil the best-laid plans. And so each in turn, called to address the Court, gives of his utmost. And while each one follows the formula of defense agreed upon, each one devotes himself to some special point of attack.

Saturday morning, April 9, John Graham opens for the defense. After a few unctuous phrases expressing his friendship for the prisoner and a few scriptural and classic quotations thrown in for effect, he suddenly bites into his subject and in a few sentences delivers the whole theory of the defense:

A few weeks since the body of a human being was found in the throes of death in one of the streets of your city. It proved to be the body of a confirmed and habitual adulterer. . . . Had he observed the solemn precept, "Remember the Sabbath day to keep it holy," he might, at this day, have formed one of the living. But the injured father and husband beholds him and rushes on him in the moment of his guilt, and under the influence of a frenzy *executes on him a judgment which was as just as it was summary.*

The issue which you are here to decide is whether this act renders its author amenable to the laws of the land. In the decision of that issue, gentlemen of the jury, you have a deep and solemn interest. You are here to fix the price of the marriage bed . . . you are here to decide whether the defender of the marriage bed is a murderer.

Reciting Othello's speech above the sleeping Desdemona, he inveighs against the adulterer as the supreme criminal, piling up quotation upon quotation from the Old Testament and the Roman law to show that in wiser days his punishment invariably was death—and in Judea, death by stoning, that the whole community might take part in the execution. He points out that in these days it is far otherwise. The law makes no provision for any such punishment of adultery. The protection of the home is left to the vigilance and force of the husband. Deceived and wronged, he has no recourse but his good right arm—or a paltry suit for damages! And here he pours biting scorn on the idea that "the adulterer who stands ready to foot the bill shall stand cleared of all human and divine accountability!"

Then in great detail he recounts the history of the relationship between the deceased and the wife of the accused, minutely describing the events of the last three days leading to the tragedy. He dwells upon the sincere and consistent friendship the prisoner had shown toward the man who had violated his confidence.

We will show you that all the influence Mr. Sickles could wield to secure his friend the elevated position of prosecutor at the bar of this court was thrown into the scale. . . . He sent him clients, even engaged him as his own counsel.

Arraigning Key as one who had "sunk to the lowest depths of baseness" in betraying such friendship, he points out:

Mr. Sickles is a man in public life. He is compelled to trust the purity of his wife; he is compelled often and for considerable periods to be away from his family mansion, and to leave his wife to the guardianship of her own chastity. Mr. Key visits the house in the guise of a friend and shows her those attentions which gallantry is ordinarily supposed to prompt, but which in his case were the foundation on which the adulterer sought to rear his destructive power.

With Teresa he is gentle: "She is youthful, susceptible to flattery, too inexperienced to realize fully her responsibilities." Then, denouncing Key's gestures of indignation over Beekman's insinuations, he cries:

See the cunning of this man! When he is charged with treacherous designs towards Mr. Sickles, he declares proudly, "It is the highest affront which can be offered me, and whoever asserts it must meet me on the field of honor, at the very point of the pistol." Thus he cuts off with threats those who might report his conduct to Mr. Sickles; and that is why, for a period of nearly one year—although no doubt he was in the practice of almost daily treachery upon his friend—Mr. Sickles never harbored a thought of suspicion against him. . . .

Graphically he depicts the prisoner's suffering upon realization of his wife's unfaithfulness, and finds in the very ferocity of his attack upon Key convincing evidence that he committed it without premeditation and in a state of frenzy beyond reason and responsibility. Clinching the argument, he cites a number of precedents— one of them created by Judge Crawford himself, in this court—to show that previous juries have not hesitated to vote for acquittal in cases of homicide incited by obviously cruel provocation. In conclusion he once more excoriates the idea that mere payment of damages can be regarded as appropriate punishment for the adulterer, or any sum of money, however large, be compensation for a ruined home. His voice rings out so that it is caught by the crowd in the street: "In God's name repudiate that principle from your bosom!" Exhausted, he sinks into his seat. He has talked for two days.

Monday, April 18. Judge Crawford renders a critically important decision—one which, so far as the common law of homicide is concerned, establishes a precedent often invoked but never before distinctly defined. Under it, all testimony serving to show the existence of "an adulterous relation between the deceased and the wife of the accused," is declared admissible evidence. It is, of course, an acknowledgment that the Court is prepared to take full cognizance of that evidence in his final instructions to the jury.

The defense rejoices and calls for witnesses—and first for Samuel F. Butterworth. Ould objects. As the foremost witness of the homicide, Butterworth, of course, can be subpoenaed only by the prosecution. But Ould refuses to summon him and also refuses explanation of his action. "I do this for reasons which I shall keep locked within my own breast, but which, I have no doubt, are well known to counsel for defense." A mysterious remark! Butterworth long ago has fled—where, no one knows—leaving behind him a cautiously worded statement of his position as the loyal friend of the accused, counseling him against rash action, and as the surprised and accidental spectator of the ensuing attack upon Key! Why does Ould refuse to summon him? Is it because Butterworth's attitude and actions make him virtually *particeps criminis* in the case? But why make a mystery of a perfectly valid reason? Or has Ould more knowledge of Butterworth's relation to the tragedy —from the first warning to the final shot—than he cares to divulge? Who can tell? History merely records that the principal witness to the most sensational case of manslaughter in Washington annals never was called to the stand.

And now—to the exquisite torture of the prisoner—there unfolds, in piecemeal, the story of the tragic liaison as viewed through the prurient eyes of Dark Town and belowstairs. The witnesses revel in their momentary prominence, eagerly make the most of it. Mrs. Nancy Brown arouses laughter by her frankness. Mrs. Seeley is officiously detailed. Bridget Duffy is saucily alert, loquacious; coachman John Thompson is mordant; his successor, Cooney, talkative and sly. Very different is the comprehensive, sympathetic testimony of Wooldridge and Octavia Ridgeley picturing the incidents immediately preceding the tragedy. Then Walker takes the stand, giving a vivid account of the final scene at Stockton Mansion. Hitherto Dan has remained tense, frozen, staring straight before him. But now, as his own agony is reviewed before him, his "more than human grief," he breaks down, and, in a state of collapse, has to be assisted from the courtroom by his father and Manny Hart.

Friday, April 22. Nineteenth day of the trial. After a week of examination and cross-examination, counsel for defense exhaust their witnesses, and court adjourns. Throughout the trial Hart has hovered over Dan with unwearying solicitude; but now, forced to return to New York, he must bid him good-by. It is a hard moment for both. Dan has no great concern for the outcome of his trial. He is assured of the rightness of his action, has confidence in his counsel, and stands prepared to face what may come; but this last week of crucifying testimony has worn his nerves very thin. He wrings Hart's hand spasmodically and a moment later sinks back in his chair, fainting. And the jailer—who has come to regard him as a Scottish clansman might his chieftain—must put an arm about him and half carry him back to the room where flowers and Dandy, the good Dr. Haley, and solicitous friends await him.

Saturday, April 23. Despite one of the most violent gales in Washington's history, the courtroom again is crowded and a wearied jury listens with vast relief as the judge declares, "The testimony is closed on both sides." With unusual brevity prosecution give their opinions on the law applicable to the case.

Then Edwin McM. Stanton, thickset, bushy-bearded, begoggled, rises to reply for the defense. His manner, calm, precise, logical, suggests, to those who know him, the storm to come:

The law exempts from punishment the man who kills another in self-protection, or in defense of his household against thief and robber. But the law also will excuse or justify the taking of life under other circumstances. The most important of this class of justifiable homicide is that which is committed in defense of the family chastity, the sanctity of the marriage bed, the matron's honor, the virgin's purity. For, gentlemen, these are possessions held to be more valuable and estimable than the property or life of any man.

After a scathing indictment of Key, he proceeds:

The evidence in the case shows both the nature and extent of the injury inflicted upon the accused and the frenzy in which he executed judgment upon the offender. In view of this evidence, it is the contention of the defense that the prisoner stands exonerated of any crime. . . .

Reciting law and precedent in support of his position, Stanton then lets the bare bones of his argument stand and enters upon a magniloquent indictment of adultery as the greatest of social crimes, one that all ancient civilizations held punishable by death. Toward the close his voice rises to a roar. He is a prophet of Israel, rebuking wickedness in high places:

Lawless love is short-lived as it is criminal, and the neighbor's wife, so hotly pursued, is speedily supplanted by some fresh object of desire, and then the wretched victim is sure to be cast off into common prostitution and swept through a miserable life and a horrible death to the gates of hell unless a husband's arms shall save her.

His voice turns stentorian, ragged with fierce emotion:

Who, seeing this thing, would not exclaim to the unhappy husband, "Hasten, hasten, to save the mother of your child! Although she be lost as wife, rescue her from the horrid adulterer! *And may the Lord who watches over the home and family guide the bullet and direct the stroke!*"

At the last word, the overkeyed tension of the courtroom snaps. The wild uproar defies retraint. Heavily Stanton resumes his seat and for some minutes thereafter industriously mops glistening brow, streaming eye.

April 23, the twentieth day of the trial. James T. Brady begins his closing address. For a while he astutely argues points of law, then proceeds to out-Stanton Stanton in an effort to stampede the jury into quick and unanimous decision. Celebrated for his hypnotic oratory, here he is at his most hypnotic:

The whole world, your honor, has its eye on this case; and I cannot help saying that when all of us shall have passed away, and when each shall have taken his chamber in the silent halls of death, the name of everyone associated with this trial will endure so long as the earth shall exist. . . .

The whole world, I say, is watching the course of these proceedings and the nature of the judgment; and I believe I know what kind of a pulsation stirs the heart of the world. I think I know, if the earth could be resolved into an animate creature, could have a heart, a soul, and a tongue, how it would rise up in the infinity of space and pronounce its judgment on the features of this transaction. . . .

If Philip Barton Key's noble father, Francis Scott Key, inculcated in lines imperishable the duty of the American people to protect their homes against the invasion of a foe, how does it become less a solemn duty of the American citizen to protect his home against the traitor who, stealing into his embraces under the pretext of friendship, inflicts a deadly wound on his happiness and aims also at his honor? . . .

When Daniel Sickles realized how he had been betrayed, all the emotions of his nature changed into a single impulse; every throb of his heart brought distinctly before him the sense of his great injuries; every drop of his blood was burdened with a sense of his shame; he was crushed by an inextinguishable agony in the loss of his wife, in the dishonor that had come upon his child, in the knowledge that the future—which had opened to him so full of brilliancy—had been enshrouded in eternal gloom by one who, contrariwise, should have invoked from the eternal God his greatest effulgence on the path of his friend. . . .

Then, with dramatic abandon, he points at the prisoner.

Look, your honor, at Daniel E. Sickles! Look at Teresa, that was his wife. Look at the woman whom I knew in her girlhood, in her innocence, and for whom I pray the merciful interposition of Heaven! Look at Dan Sickles, and look at that poor girl—for although the mother of a child, she still is a girl and, as such, amenable to the influence of a master of seduction. And look at that young child, standing between its father and its mother, equally influenced by the great laws of the Creator to go toward either, and destined to leave one. . . . Look at that case and say whether you may break into the sanctuary of a man's heart, rifle the treasures of his home, betray his confidence, outrage his hospitality, bring shame upon him, leave him almost hopeless—a wanderer in the world. . . . If, under these circumstances, Dan Sickles had done less than became a man, then despite our deep and abiding friendship in the past, I would have been willing to see him die the most ignominious death before I would venture a prayer in his behalf.

For three hours Brady's voice has filled the courtroom. On the last words, shattered by his own emotions, he sinks into his chair and for some time remains bowed, his face in his hands as if in prayer.

Ould, closing for the prosecution, begins by dryly remarking that he completely agrees with the defense in their denunciation of adultery, but he wishes to point out that the question before the court is not one of adultery but of murder. Briefly he enunciates the doctrine that a woman's chastity lies in her own keeping, concluding pontifically:

The very moment you invoke the law of force for the protection of female honor, that moment you sacrifice female honor. If it must be protected by the sword, the knife, and the pistol, it stands unworthy of protection. Unless it be that God-ennobling nobility in and of itself, and unless it exists of itself and for itself, it is unworthy to be cherished or known.

So far as argument and oratory are concerned, the battle is over. Amid a silence vibrant with expectancy, Judge Crawford delivers his instructions with a dry, pedantic carefulness. At one-thirty the jury retires. As the door closes upon it, the tension breaks. All restraint is thrown off. Everyone leaps to his feet in an outburst of excited talk. In vain Judge Crawford, half smiling, half frowning, lifts a deprecating hand. In a body Dan's friends crowd about him with cheering assurances: "The jury will be back in five minutes. . . . There can be but one verdict. . . . It is all over but the shouting." Among them, beside the counsel for defense, there are the local ministers, Dr. Haley, Dr. Sunderland, Reverend F. C. Branberry; a contingent of New York Democrats, including DeWitt Graham, Captain Wiley, Nathaniel Lane, Thomas H. Brown, Henry Acker, George W. Brega; and a half-score of Washingtonians, notably Thomas H. McBlair, John Savage, John F. Coyle, William H. Donohue, Mayor Berritt, and Alderman Mohun. Dan responds like a man drained of emotion, without concern for the outcome. For him the ordeal is over.

But as the minutes pass and no jury appears, the atmosphere of the courtroom grows taut with suspense. There are those that predict a hung jury if another half-hour goes by. As the hands of the clock veer to two-thirty, comes a bedlam of speculation.

Meanwhile in the jury room a curious little drama is being played out. There twelve perplexed men are wrestling with a decision that —after listening to the fulminations of prosecution and defense— looms before them searchingly as the decision between the punishment, perhaps the life, of a man tortured to violence and the sanction of murderous vengeance without the law. Seven at once are for acquittal, three hesitate, two are completely opposed. Mr. Arnold, the foreman, struggles—against illness—to bring about an unanimous verdict. The first to give way is a young fellow named Knight. He has solaced his fellow jurors' long exile with his performances upon the violin and is looked upon as flighty and good-natured; but as a "Know-Nothing" he hates Tammany, is very prejudiced against the accused. Hopkins, the wag of the party, finally overwhelms him. "If I'd been Sickles, I'd not only have used a pistol and a Derringer on that fellow; I'd have turned a howitzer on him—and so would you!" The fiddler grins and gives up. Two more doubtful ones, after much conscientious argument, follow suit. John McDermott, a stubborn, righteous Presbyterian, is harder to convince. But finally, under the urgings of Arnold and the ten for acquittal, he, too, grudgingly surrenders. Eleven pairs of eyes are on the last juror. James Weaver, a gentle-faced old man, has taken little part in the discussion. Once he has left the table to kneel in a corner and pray. Now he has no reply, hardly seems to listen to the torrent of argument focused upon him. Presently he again leaves the group and kneels down in a corner. A complete hush falls upon the room. Minutes pass. Then the twelfth juror rises, comes back to the table. His voice is peaceful and assured: "Mr. Arnold, I have my answer. Let the prisoner go free."

As the jury files into court, on the stroke of three, riot breaks loose. With cries of, "Here they come! Here they come!" many of the audience are climbing up on the benches to catch a glimpse of the jurors' faces. There are protesting shouts, "Down in front—sit down!" The clerk raps for order, howling, "Silence in the court!" It is no use. Not until Judge Crawford, trying to make himself heard, orders the clerk to call the names of the jurors, is order restored. One by one the names are called. The stillness is electric. Then the jury stands up.

Clerk: "Daniel E. Sickles, stand up and look to the jury."

With a commanding fearlessness Dan rises, faces the men who hold his fate in their hands.

Clerk: "How say you, gentlemen, have you agreed to your verdict?"

Mr. Arnold: "We have."

Clerk: "How say you? Do you find the prisoner at the bar guilty or not guilty?"

Mr. Arnold: "Not guilty!"

The long-expected words explode a roaring, tumultuous "Hurrah! Hurrah! Hurrah!" Crashing through the open windows, the cheer is taken up by the vast throng outside awaiting the verdict. And while, in the street, men toss their hats in the air, women wildly wave their handkerchiefs, within the court it is a scene of mad jubilation. Some halloo, others weep, and a number leap into the dock and hug the prisoner hysterically. Counsel for defense show various reactions. Brady goes white, slumps in his chair, shaking with nervous relief. Stanton heaves his great bulk into a jig. Phillips covers his face with his hands and weeps like a child. The rollicking Magruder storms around, slapping everyone on the back, shouting, "Isn't it glorious, glorious?" Ould bows his head. "I thought it would be so." The only unhappy person present is Jailer King. He cannot bear to lose his favorite prisoner and is inconsolable.

Throughout the storm Stanton is trumpeting to the judge, "I move that Mr. Sickles be discharged from custody. . . . In the name of Mr. Sickles and his counsel, I desire to return thanks to the jury." Judge Crawford, the only person who seems to retain his wits, replies calmly, "Mr. Stanton, the verdict is not yet recorded."

Rapping for order, the clerk addresses the jury: "Your record is, gentlemen, that you find Daniel E. Sickles 'Not Guilty'?" The jury nods affirmatively.

Mr. Stanton: "I now move that Mr. Sickles be discharged as prisoner."

Judge Crawford: "The Court so orders."

Again the frantic joy breaks loose. Captain Wiley, climbing over the dock, seizes Dan in his arms and kisses him. Everyone is trying to shake his hand or hug him. Dan's eyes are wet but show no elation; he seems to be looking beyond the moment—to something that yet must be done. He is free—but what of Teresa?

CHAPTER XIX

"The Fearful Story of My Heart"

Bridle your virtue,
  Tether the tongue;
Pity the fair vine
  Blighted so young!
Why not the tomb?
  Sad, shattered life;
Think of her doom—
  Widow, yet wife!

Tears like sad rivers
  Roll through all time;
He, his heart-torrent
  Poured for its crime.
Billows of sod
  Swell o'er his rest;
Pleading with God—
  There let him rest!

Still to another
  Life is as death;
Home and its idol
  Gone with a breath!
Blood on his hands,
  Stain on his bed:
Pity them all—
  Living and dead!

> *Thou whose life-current*
>   *Flows calm and quiet,*
> *Whose love and whose passion*
>   *Never ran riot,*
> *Judge not too harshly;*
>   *Few fall by design;*
> *Pray for the erring—*
>   *Their fate may be thine!**

What of Teresa?

At first she returned, with Laura, as a paying guest to the home of her parents close to New York's Central Park. Only two of her letters—one written pending, the other during, the trial—remain to attest her wretched status, confusion of soul. And as in all our life the trivial and the tragic never are far apart, so here in these letters —with their racing, graceful penmanship almost obliterated by tears —the mention of petty yet pressing matters of daily living as a "fallen" daughter in a curmudgeon household is strewn between with sentences struck from a girl's Gethsemane. In them she appears the chastened child—her tragic first taste of passion blasted—reaching back in terrified contrition to her "dear, dear Dan." She has no reproach. She has laid her dead away in wordless atonement. But to live at all she must have home and husband—or the symbol of them—for Laura. Desperately she struggles to recover them. Exactly one month from the tragedy she is writing:

Good morning, dear, dear Dan—Mr. Fields has just left. He brought me a kind, good letter from you. Thank you many times for all your kind expressions and God bless you for the mercy and prayers you offer up for me. Do not ask if I never think over the events of the past month. Yesterday, at each hour by the clock, I thought, "One month ago this day, at this hour, such and such things were going on in our once happy home." That fearful Saturday night! No one has any idea what I suffered. If I could have foreseen the scenes of the following day I would have braved all dangers, all things, to have prevented them. Oh that Manny Hart could have been with us! . . .

I have been out of the house but three times since I came home; and you know how much exercise I have been in the habit of taking. . . .

*"Judge Not," by C. H. Webb, *Harper's Weekly*, March 12, 1859.

Last night I walked with Manny Hart; but my body trembled, my legs seemed to give way under me and my heart beat violently.

The verses you send me are very beautiful. I will keep them always, and I thank you sincerely for them. . . . Perhaps I spoke hastily of George Wooldridge. I promise you not to mention his name, Wiley's or Butterworth's again in any of my letters unless necessary. One thing I will assure you of, and that is that I did *not* tell Mr. Butterworth to mind his own business or something to that effect. . . . Mr. Butterworth, I think, only needed encouragement from me to flirt. I may be mistaken, but I doubt it. But let all suppositions be forgotten and unthought of—the reality is bad enough without suspecting or supposing things.* . . .

No, dear Dan, I cannot say you ever denied me what was necessary, and you gave me many things I did not deserve—everyone knows this. . . . I shall commence a pair of slippers for you in a few days, my dear Dan. I will not stop working on them until they are finished. Will you wear them for me? Or would you dislike to wear again anything that I have made? . . .

Can I say or do anything for you that you have not spoken of—if so, write me. Do not be angry at anything I have written you. I swear that I have not written a word to cause you pain. . . . Write when you can, and think and feel as leniently as possible of me and my unhappy position. God bless you for the two kisses you send me—and with God's help and my own determination to be good, true and faithful to you and myself hereafter, those kisses shall never leave my lips while *I* am called *wife* and *you husband*. I swear it by Laura. . . . God bless you, pray for me, and believe in the sincerity and gratitude of—

TERESA

A few days later, in the midst of the trial, she writes:

I cannot tell you, dear, dear Dan, how *much* pleasure your letter written yesterday gave me. I am so glad the flowers were acceptable. You are not wrong in supposing that I was pained at your silence, and equally pained at receiving the letter you sent me. You know, Dan, I *never* affect to love or dislike a person—and I am, in a certain way, as frank as any breathing creature. You say if I can hate those whom you love and who love you then it is vain for you to appeal to me again on such a subject. Dear Dan, it would be as impossible for me to love those who hate me and have injured me, have called me every vile name, as I believe it would be to have you love me again or ever wipe out the past. I enclose a letter written last night. I send it to show you how I felt about all you said. *It tells the fearful story of my heart.* . . .

*Did Teresa suspect the identity behind the initials R. P. G.?

You say that any object you have loved remains dear to you. Do I now stand upon a footing with the other women I know you have loved? I have long felt like asking you what your love affairs have been—love of the heart, or love of their superior qualities such as you have often informed me I did not possess, or attraction of face and form, or an infatuation? If during the first years we were married my good conduct did not keep you true to me, can I suppose for a moment the last year has? *Ask your own heart who sinned first, and then tell me, if you will.*

Socially exiled, shunned even by humble neighbors, compelled to keep the house by day or face the sneers and hoots of such street trash as recognized her, cut off from her cherished riding and walking, cooped up with a loving but overemotional mother, a penurious, egocentric father, Teresa, torn between grief for the dead, contrition for the living, began to fail. . . . With a compassion newborn out of his own suffering, Dan came to her rescue. He still loved her—quite poignantly; and he could bear neither her bitter humiliation nor the implacable attitude of all but a few toward her. In a gesture as hopeless as it was chivalrous, he boldly restored her to wifehood. Stockton Mansion stood shuttered. Never again could Teresa return to Washington. But, with her parents for guardians, he made her once more the mistress of Bloomingdale. . . .

It was an action utterly out of kilter with an age that neatly divided women into "sainted mothers," "pure virgins," and "fallen women." In Washington it created a state of scandalized shock. Not a few of those who had condoned the killing of Key found this fresh outrage more than they could stand. Gossip thrummed; old acquaintances looked the other way. Commonly it was predicted that Sickles had ruined himself socially, politically. In confusion, the *Globe* mumbled that he must have "succumbed to the pressure of most unwise counsels." As was his way in all things, Dan Sickles met the situation head on. In an open letter to the press, vibrant with deep anger, tinged with searching irony, yet noble in tone, temperate in phrase, he crushed all cavilings:

My reconciliation with my wife was my own act, done without consultation with any relative, connection, friend or advisor. Whatever blame, if any, belongs to the step, should fall alone upon me. *I am prepared to defend what I have done, before the only tribunal I recognize as having the slightest claim to jurisdiction over the subject—my own conscience and the bar of Heaven. I am not aware of any statute or code of morals* which makes it infamous to forgive a woman; nor is it usual to make our domestic life *a* subject of consultation with friends, no matter how near and dear to us. *And I cannot allow even all the world combined to dictate to me the repudiation of my wife, when I think it right to forgive her and restore her to my confidence and protection.** If I ever failed to comprehend the utterly desolate position of an offending though penitent woman—the hopeless future, with its dark possibilities of danger, to which she is doomed when proscribed as an outcast—I can now see plainly enough, in the almost universal howl of denunciation with which she is followed to my threshold, the misery and peril from which I have rescued the mother of my child. And although it is very sad for me to incur the blame of friends and the reproaches of many wise and good people, I shall strive to prove to all who may feel an interest in me, that, if I am the first man who has ventured to say to the world an erring wife and mother may be forgiven and redeemed, in spite of all the obstacles in my path, the good results of this example shall entitle it to the imitation of the generous and the commendation of the just. There are many who think that an act of duty, proceeding solely from affections which can only be comprehended in the heart of a husband and a father, is to be fatal to my professional, political, and social standing. If this be so, then so be it.

The restoration, of course, was only a gesture of protection—a warning to the world, "Tether the tongue!" It could be nothing more. Never could the relationship itself be restored. Teresa was still "widow yet wife." Dan's contacts with her necessarily remained infrequent, painful. Always between these two stood a ghostly figure. Despite every good intention, the gesture failed to accomplish its purpose. Teresa was unable to rally, no longer had any will to live. Often her food lay untouched. Sleepless, she took refuge in opiates. The habit grew. Torpor seemed preferable to the torment of thought. She sank slowly from frailty to invalidism. Presently tuberculosis set in. But her vital young body was loath to give up. It was eight years before, "enclosed in a handsome rosewood casket," it was borne by ten pallbearers, including four major generals of the Union Army and James T. Brady, and placed on a catafalque "surrounded by brilliant tapers" before the high altar of St. Joseph's amid the solemnities of Requiem High Mass.

*The italics are my own. They need no apology.—AUTHOR.

PART FOUR: "ARMS AND THE MAN"

CHAPTER XX

Chasm Agape

———◆———

THE DEATH OF THE tragic, cherry-coated huntsman of the Gwin ball coincided curiously with the sudden decline of Washington's hitherto gay social life. Six months later Congress reconvened amid an atmosphere bleak with foreboding. From Maryland to New Mexico the southern half of the continent was splitting away from the northern half politically, spiritually, with the horrible, creeping acceleration of a landslip. The chasm gaped across the capital, cut jagged fissures between mansion and mansion, ripped neighboring haunts and homes apart, clove the House with unbridgeable yawn.

No longer were more than formal courtesies exchanged between the opposing representatives of a riven people. Social life dwindled to the forced gaieties of anxious, isolated groups as matron and debutante, forsaking dinners, dances, at-homes, clustered daily in the Senate gallery, to follow, parched with excitement, the furious debates on the floor below.

John Brown, forsooth, with his fatuous foray, had keyed the situation to a hair-trigger tension; and while the North took the Bible-thumping old desperado to its bosom, fired silly salutes in his honor, enthroned him its patron saint-at-arms, the South shivered before the specter of an impending slave revolt urged on by abolitionist fanatics dedicated to putting her—like another Haiti—to the torch of some black Napoleon. Such was the tindery temper of the time that while the slender, shambling Seward continued to rasp his doctrine of "the irrepressible conflict," and the tempestuous Yancey summoned the Alabama chivalry "to the trial by sword," many a Kansas farmer drove to market with his muzzle-loader in the crotch of his whip arm; and many a congressman and senator, both northern and southern, took to buckling on his pistols beneath his frock coat before leaving home for the Capitol.

To one man, at least, this banishment of the old amenities before the hot winds of hate came as a boon. Where social activities had virtually ceased to exist, the fact that Stockton Mansion stood silent passed almost unnoticed. And at a moment when a brawny, expanding young commonwealth found itself threatened with havoc and mutilation, few could sustain interest in last season's scandal. Eight months is long in the public memory. Also a masterful magic lurks in the sense of inner sanction. Never for one moment had Dan Sickles doubted the authority of himself, either in his vengeance or in his pathetic effort to resurrect a desolated marriage. And, from the day of his release, he walked among men with the composure of one who had cast up accounts with himself and reckoned the score, undisturbed by any concern with public audit. The result was that before the close of the session of '59 he could write to his friend, William A. Seaver, managing editor of the New York *Tribune*, "All the stuff you see printed to the effect that people here give me the cold shoulder is bosh. On the contrary, ninety-nine out of a hundred are more cordial than ever; and many take pains to be very cordial." A defensive overstatement, possibly.

Nevertheless—unobserved by those around him, for he kept a firm front—the blood on his hands, the wrench in his heart had wrought a deep change in Dan Sickles. Two things had been taken from him: his one ambition, his one love. Bent tenaciously toward the White House, he had blasted its doors shut forever. Pursuing women as so much game, he yet had so fastened the inmost fibers of himself about one girlish figure that never again would he have the heart to seek a mate, and—except for one brief mockery of marriage, loveless and luckless—he would live out the remaining fifty years of his life alone. And thus when, in November 1859, he stood up before the House to review the national crisis, he was already in another arc of himself. Henceforth, although nominally a northern Democrat, he would ride alone, an independent rather than a party man; one who now, for better or worse, had taken America to wife.

A significant prelude to his memorable speech, "On the State of the Union," delivered fourteen months later—on the eve of his enlistment in the Union Army, this address of November 1859, "On the Relations between the North and the South," is both an authoritative refutation of a number of popular delusions on the subject and a notable example of the vigor with which Dan Sickles strove against northern ignorance in general, New England prejudice in particular, for the preservation of the Compact between the States—until the South herself, in the bombardment of Fort Sumter, blasted that Compact to powder.

Widely reported, and even more widely circulated in pamphlet reprint, it was an utterance well calculated to exert a steadying influence on the mounting agitation; for here, if Sickles still speaks as a Democrat, an advocate of states' rights, it is as an exponent of historic fact and constitutional principles rather than as a partisan. "Many of my fellow congressmen," he wrote Seaver, "thought my speech overbold; but," he adds characteristically, "nothing so disarms the crowd as a little pluck."

Opening on a plea for an informed attitude toward our own history and a respect for agreements entered into, he proceeds to take sharp issue with a northern opponent. Methodically he takes up, one by one, the "bold and grave charges of the gentleman from Pennsylvania" to the effect that the South was the first to fracture the Missouri Compromise and that it gained slave representation, the Fugitive Slave Law, exemption from taxes upon export, and a longer lease of life for the slave trade as a series of concessions extorted from the Constitutional Assembly. In demolishing rebuttal he points out that the North, in accepting California into the Union without slavery, itself first had violated the Compromise; that "slave representation" was a northern measure conceived to impose a due proportion of taxation upon the South; that the Fugitive Slave Law "had not one dissenting vote"; that the taxation of exports was prohibited by the Constitution and never had found an advocate in this country; that the "slave traffic—then, if not since, as much a branch of eastern, as of southern, trade—was prolonged by the votes of three northern states!"

Then, taking his stand upon the constitutional right of each state to decide its own policy in regard to slavery, as expressed in the Kansas-Nebraska Act, he urges Congress to endorse this principle before it is too late, "for we are in the presence of the most serious danger that ever has menaced the Confederacy." Earnestly he summons to view the close economic interdependence between the agricultural South and the industrial North. Impressive in its restrained eloquence is his conclusion—forecasting the dark results of Disunion:

The blow would fall with crushing effect upon the masses—upon those whose welfare and happiness depend upon steady employment and good wages. And, therefore, sir, it is to the poor that I look to maintain this Union—to those who have little else beside a home and a country. If civil war comes, they will have to fight the battles. If trade and manufacture are to be paralyzed, it is the laboring classes who will suffer the deprivations, the anguish of want. Is it wise to overturn all the foundations of our prosperity and bring unnumbered calamities upon the happy and thriving communities of the North, for the purpose of gratifying prejudices against slavery and slaveholders? Is it worth while to carry northern supremacy in the Union to that point which destroys the prize for which the struggle is waged? Do you thereby attain the end—the suppression of slave labor—which the philanthropist seeks? No, far from it! If we force the slave states out of the Union, we, by that act, extend slavery from the Rio Grande to the Pacific, and the Caribbean Sea, and to all the West India Islands. Cuba soon would belong to the Southern Confederation. England would cede to it Jamaica and its dependencies in return for the stipulations of a liberal commercial treaty; and Mexico would be an easy conquest. The result would be the extension of the institution of African slavery over a larger territory than the world has yet seen, and the establishment of a republic whose command of the great staple products would enable it to dictate its own terms to commercial and manufacturing nations. The progress of the Northern Confederacy could only be in the direction of Canada. The West would not hesitate long in choosing between the Mississippi and the Erie Canal as its avenue to the Atlantic. The North then becomes a nation of traders without customers—a manufacturing population competing with the cheap labor of Europe, buying its breadstuffs and provisions from the West and its cotton from the South—with no exports unless it could undersell British, French, and German products. No longer would it be an integral and controlling portion of one of the greatest powers on earth, but would yield up a future of which the glory and grandeur could only be portrayed by one who "first exhausted worlds and then imagined new." The North, the practical, prosperous, happy North, would be doomed by the statesmen who now rule its politics and its destiny to give up all it has achieved and, in a separate confederation, accept the rank of an inferior power—

the parallel of Holland; and to make all these unavailing sacrifices without securing the least benefit to the Negro race for whom they are hazarded.

It was Sickles's last effort to bridge the chasm—soon to be choked with the bodies of battling men.

CHAPTER XXI

"The Union Is Imperishable!"

━━━━━◆━━━━━

The fateful sixties . . . decade of red death and bitter rebirth dawning to the beat of distant drum. Slavocrat and Free Soiler gather to their tents. . . .

The hitherto regnant South—mothering nine Presidents, queening it over Cabinet and Congress, dominating the Army, leading the social cotillion—suddenly loses her pride of place in the national household. Her recent failure to keep Kansas a slave state, coupled with the admission of Minnesota and Oregon as free states, has cost her the balance of power. At the same time the onsweeping Republican party, by its avowed determination to confine slavery within its present borders, quenches forever her hope of regaining supremacy by the capture of new states gestating in the womb of the West.

A virtually separate country, homogeneous in territory, culture, economy, the South now sees herself not merely relegated to a secondary, and rapidly diminishing, role within the Union, but delivered over to the control of a master more alien to her than France or England: the truculent, prodigiously developing, industrial North.

So the issue stands in the eyes of the southern chieftains, grouped around the cold, doctrinaire Davis, swashbuckling Yancey and Wigfall, valiant, invalid Clay, crafty Slidell. As were Washington, Jefferson, Madison before them, these men are tenacious slavocrats meshed in their patriarchal web of life with its woof of landed pride, feudal tradition; its warp of white floss, ebony muscle. Sorry solace to them that this northern master proposes no interference with their regime where it already exists. They know that the gesture is but delayed sentence of death. If the admission of the new free states to the Union has sapped their political power, the excessive culture of tobacco and cotton likewise has sapped vast areas of their soil. And, in their present predicament, what they most urgently need is precisely what they now are denied: new fertile territories for a double crop, more bales for the wharves, more representatives for the House. And, beyond this immediate curtailment, never for a moment are they allowed to forget the furor of abolitionist crusaders pledged to the extinction of chattel slavery throughout the Union, and—unthinkable madness to these seigneurs!—the elevation of the black man to the rights and dignities of American citizenship.

There remains, of course, a perfectly common-sense solution to the southern impasse. And at least one southerner perceives it. Painstakingly, in his critique, The Impending Crisis, *the North Carolinian economist, Hinton Rowan Helper, marshals fact and figure to prove to his fellow citizens that chattel slavery already has become an unprofitable anachronism, doomed by its own inefficiency, its proven inability to pay dividends on an ever increasing capital investment; and that the plantation gentry, by freeing their slaves and simply hiring them as day laborers at a bare subsistence wage, could exact from them more diligent service, increase production, decrease costs, shunt off a vast load of burdensome responsibility toward the young, the aged, the infirm—and thus bring themselves abreast of the modern, industrial age. But the southern response to such a gospel is, quite naturally, an auto-da-fé for the book and a threat of tar and feathers for the author. The paternalistic planter knows well the plight of New England's sweated millhands, Boston's moldering unemployed. And not while he has breath and powder will he forsake all his traditions, set his "people" adrift to be hired and fired, and otherwise left to beg, steal, or rot while he himself writes off a heavy flesh-and-blood investment, already mortgaged at the bank! The mere suggestion smells of treachery, stirs him to red rage.*

The slave states, in truth, already have agreed among themselves that their only recourse is withdrawal from the Union into a solid Confederation of their own. In their view there is no alternative—

unless, perchance, they may win to power again in the coming election. At the moment, as a matter of fact, a defeat of the Republicans is by no means an unwarrantable hope. The Democrats still hold a majority in the House. United on a single platform, the party elements, North and South, even now might enforce their will upon the Union. They might—but not for long! The causes of severance lie too deep for that. As Lincoln clearly divines, the conflict over slavery is but the surface indication that the Union cannot long endure half archaic, half modern; half servile-agrarian, half industrial-capitalist.

No political reprieve for the South, however, is forthcoming. In the confusion and turmoil of the hour, the Democrats fall into wrangling factions. The extremists, in fact, determined now upon bullets rather than ballots, and realizing that the election of a "Black Republican" is all that is needed to rouse every cotton state behind them, deliberately set out to split the party ranks. Refusing co-operation with other elements, they bolt the Charleston convention and nominate John C. Breckinridge on an uncompromising pro-slavery platform. As a result the "popular sovereignty" men nominate Stephen A. Douglas, while a third aggregation, vaguely advocating "obedience to the laws and adherence to the Constitution," nominates John Bell, of Tennessee. And so by grace of a political plot—ironic, prophetic—Abraham Lincoln, winning the Republican nomination against Seward's bitter competition, comes to his tragic triumph as President-elect—with but forty per cent of the total vote!

In vain the Chicago platform pledges non-interference with slavery within its present borders; in vain Lincoln avows himself concerned only with "the preservation of the Union—with slavery or without." The little gang of secessionist conspirators banquet together in private glee. Under their tutelage the press, flaring scare headlines, thunders doom. And a dismayed South sees only a "Black Republican" in the White House; and behind him, towering spectral in the northern sky, the giant fist of Abolition. In hot haste South Carolina secedes and calls upon her sister states to fall in beside her.

Such was the national situation when, January 16, 1861, twenty-seven days after the secession of North Carolina, Dan Sickles rose to speak before an anxious House organized in Committee of the Whole to consider the decidedly dubious "State of the Union."

In those twenty-seven days much had happened. Mississippi, Florida, Alabama, Georgia, and—save for the final formalities—Louisiana and Texas also had seceded, and—contrary to their vaunted right and avowed intent—by no means peacefully. In every one of these states the authorities had laid violent hands on the federal arsenals, forts, navy yards, customhouses within their borders; and Charleston bravados, seizing the batteries of Fort Moultrie, had opened fire upon the unarmed government transport, *Star of the West*, bearing supplies to Fort Sumter. In swift consequence, something else had happened—an angry, powerfully decisive change in the hearts and minds of millions of northern men hitherto confident of a peaceable adjustment with the South.

To Dan Sickles the sudden belligerence of the seceding states came as a profound shock. Peaceful secession he regarded as the lawful, if lamentable, last recourse of sovereign states denied their due privilege within the Federation. But this unprovoked, deliberate attack upon forts and possessions flying the Stars and Stripes caused him to cry, "Sir, that was an act of war—naked, unmitigated war! Had such an offense been perpetrated by any foreign power, it would have roused every man in this nation." And if his speech in protest came as the very voice of a dismayed and indignant North, it was yet more than that—a masterly orientation of the whole dispute, a searching indictment of both the intransigent Republican and the violent Secessionist, and the first proclamation of the dread decision soon to be thrust upon the minds of northern men from Maine to California. Noblest prose is the peroration proclaiming his own stand:

Whatever may be the issue of existing complications, the Republic of the United States is imperishable. It will survive all the dangers which now assail it. It will vindicate the faith in humanity upon which it reposes. It will fulfill its destiny in the development of an ameliorated system of institutions and laws which recognize the equality of all the citizens composing the Commonwealth.

It is my prayer that these disastrous events may go no further; that the day-spring from on High may visit us and guide our feet into the way of peace. But whatever may be the issue of events—whether happily, by conciliation and justice to the South, we may find an honorable and fraternal solution of our difficulties; or whether, unhappily, we blindly drift into alienation, war, and irrevocable separation—the great commercial interests of this country require, the destiny of American civilization demands, that the political and territorial control of this continent, from the mouth of the Hudson to the mouth of the Mississippi, from the Atlantic to the Pacific seas, shall remain where it now is—in the hands of the Government of the United States. In all the partisan issues between the South and the Republican party, the people of the city of New York are with the South; but when the South makes an untenable issue with our country, when the flag of the Union is insulted, when the fortified places provided for the common defense are assaulted and seized, when the South abandons its northern friends for English and French alliances, *then the loyal and patriotic population of that imperial city—and I speak as certainly for them as for myself—stand unanimous for the Union.*

CHAPTER XXII

Armies in Haste

THE "LAME DUCK" SESSION of '61 limped along—none ever more limply! While Secession flamed, lighting the folds of a strange new "Stars and Bars" in the southern sky, and planter-politicians, with grandiloquent farewells, quit the Capitol to feed the flames, Congress squatted, both lame and maimed, before the conflagration, making no more than feeble garden-hose gestures toward it.

At the same time every department of the Administration floundered in a mesh of proslavery treachery and sabotage. Secretary of War Floyd, playing sedulous ape to his predecessor in office, Jefferson Davis, had been busily transferring huge amounts of arms and ammunition from northern arsenals to southern caches. The last shipload at sea, he had looted the Treasury of $800,000 in bonds and absconded to Virginia—there to receive a wild welcome for his "patriotic" services. By similar tactics the Navy also had been put out of commission, its vessels dismantled or secreted in foreign ports. Vice-President John C. Breckinridge, Assistant Secretary of State William H. Trescot, and former Secretary of Treasury Cobb already had crossed the Potomac, followed by troops of army and navy officers eager to apply West Point and Annapolis training to the business of destroying the Union. And Secretary of the Interior Jacob Thompson, in the act of signing his resignation, had turned aside to scratch out a code telegram to the mayor of Charleston apprising him that the *Star of the West* was about to be dispatched to the relief of Fort Sumter!

And what was true of the higher officials was equally true of the lower. Clerks, indebted for their jobs to southern patronage, constituted themselves, with great gusto, an amateur secret service. "Secesh" militia secretly drilled in government warehouses. And if, for the most part, the great southern families already had departed, the wives and daughters of those that remained, and enterprising widows such as the notorious Mrs. Greenhow, set themselves, with wit, charm, and wine, to seduce officers, congressmen and ministers still loyal to the Administration, or milk them of secret military information later to cost lakes of northern blood.

In the White House an "Old Public Functionary," as Buchanan liked to dub himself, already shrunk into the "lean and slippered pantaloon" stage of performance, wrapped himself in a drab dressing gown and, head askew, left eye aslew, prayed at his desk for the day when the Railsplitter would release him from grievous responsibility and the cares of an office "no longer fit for a gentleman." Bound by ties of personal affection and political fraternity to the small group of desperadoes who were now proposing to dispose of the Union, he sought merely to placate them, avoid an open rupture—and so end his term of office on a note of inglorious peace. It was a policy, of course, that bereft the nation of leadership in the supreme crisis of its history. Incidentally, it beguiled the Chief Executive on more than one occasion into dangerous compliance with southern demands.

From one of these blunders, the gravest, and from another, the silliest, it happened that it was only Dan Sickles who somehow, and at the last moment, managed to snatch him back—in the one case by a skylarking bit of strategy, in the other by an exhibition of plain sword rattling. If both episodes smack of comic opera, they illustrate, as perhaps could nothing else, the contrasting characters of the two men, the touch-and-go temper of the time.

When Major Anderson, commanding the decrepit Fort Moultrie on the shores of Charleston, moved his peacetime garrison of sixty men to the nearby and more defensible Fort Sumter, the secessionists became greatly agitated. Promptly a South Carolina delegation, including former Speaker of the House, Orr, and the former Assistant Secretary of State, William H. Trescot, waited upon Buchanan and demanded that the vigilant major be ordered to withdraw his garrison to its former position! Timidly bent upon peace at any price, Buchanan agreed. In vain, Edwin McM. Stanton, recently become Attorney General, and John A. Dix, the new Secretary of the Treasury, violently protested against his decision. Like most men of vacillating minds, Buchanan could be very stubborn—in the wrong place. And Dan Sickles knew it. When Stanton and Dix came to him, begging him to try to dissuade the President from vacating Sumter, he merely smiled. "It's no use, gentlemen. The more you pull at a balky mule the balkier he gets. I know Buchanan. You have to light a fire under his tail." After some thought, he added, "If you'll leave it to me, I think I can start a little fire in the right spot." He would say no more. And with that the two worried cabinet officers had to remain content.

That night Sickles entrained for Philadelphia, first telegraphing his friend, Daniel Dougherty, a leader of the Philadelphia bar and an intimate of the President, to meet him on his arrival. On the station platform next morning he rapidly outlined the problem to the astounded Dougherty—and the solution. "You know Buchanan, and that there is no way to reach him except through the force of public opinion. I want you to send a strong current of opinion from Philadelphia to the White House. First, have a national salute fired tomorrow morning in honor of the President's heroic determination to keep Major Anderson and his command at Fort Sumter. Then go to all the newspapers and ask the editors to print editorials glorifying the President for his patriotic resolution. Next interview the various bank presidents and ask each of them to send telegrams to the President praising him to the skies for his manly decision to keep Major Anderson at Fort Sumter. Give him a shower of telegrams—no matter how long!"*

With Irish alacrity, Dougherty promised to fulfill all instructions.

Again telegraphing ahead to friends to meet him on the platform, Sickles proceeded by the next train to Trenton, New Jersey, and

*His own words as reported in his speech to the Lincoln Fellowship, February 12, 1910.

promptly initiated a similar campaign. Then, again telegraphing friends to meet him, he pushed on to New York. There, in his home town, he lit a conflagration of editorials, started a pyrotechnic of telegrams—many of them from men powerful in Wall Street, and wound up by securing a one-hundred-gun salute at the Battery in honor of the President's "bold and decisive stand," as the *Herald* phrased it. Within twenty-four hours the press throughout the country was headlining the story and echoing the eastern plaudits. For the moment the colorless Buchanan emerged a national hero, his drab dressing gown transformed to a star-spangled toga.

When, five days after his hasty departure, Sickles returned to Washington, Stanton, meeting him, threw his arms about him in a characteristic bear hug. "Glorious, my boy, glorious! We've won! Anderson will stay! The Old Man is simply gloating over all those editorials and telegrams, to say nothing of the salutes! The delegation has been sent packing, and he's strutting around like a turkey cock!"*

Anticipating possible disorders at Lincoln's inauguration, General Winfield Scott, commander in chief, had mobilized a considerable force of regular troops in the capital; and, on the occasion of Washington's Birthday, Buchanan, without giving more than a routine nod to the matter, had agreed that they should march in the customary parade. But, catching wind of the arrangement, ex-President Tyler, the proslavery president of the farcical Peace Commission then in session, came hurrying to the White House to protest against "an offensive display of military force such as would be sure to wound the sensibilities of Maryland and Virginia." And Buchanan, always aiming to please a rebel, promptly cut the troops from the parade.

At the last moment, while fifty thousand Washingtonians and nearby country folk waited to see their army pass in all the splendor of plumed cavalry, thundering horse artillery, great snakes of marching men, bayonets glistening in the sun, Sickles happened to get word that the show was off, that the regulars had been ordered back to the barracks. Hotfoot he went in search of the President, finally traced him to the War Department. But the Old Public Functionary was closeted with Secretary of War Holt and had given orders that he should not be disturbed. Denied admission to the presidential presence, Sickles paced the anteroom and, in a voice calculated to

*Ibid.

pierce the solidest walls, proceeded to roar his indignation. A minute or two of this, and Buchanan timidly opened the door. Without ceremony Sickles stormed in. Before the ensuing blast, Holt merely bowed his head in his hands. He just had offered the President his resignation rather than consent to cancel the parade. But Buchanan, as usual, had been stubborn. Now, however, under the tornado of Sickles's eloquence—"the degradation of the national honor . . . the pusillanimous subjection of the executive power to a rebel . . . the outrageous insult to the memory of the man of Valley Forge . . . "—Buchanan quakingly discovered that he had thought it "a matter of no importance" and that, of course, the parade could proceed. Holt, vastly relieved, took the orders in person.

Buchanan, now suddenly terrified at his own temerity, endeavored to write a letter of apology to ex-President Tyler, explaining the reasons for his reversed decision. But the words would not come. Nervously he tore up sheet after sheet. Watching him sardonically, Sickles finally suggested, "Don't you think it might be just as well, Jim, for the President of the United States to postpone making an apology for exercising the powers of his office until an explanation is demanded?" Buchanan looked up at him in dazed approval. He had not thought of that!

The parade was late, but it went through to a hurricane of hurrahs —interpolated, here and there, however, with large layers of acid silence. For all the recent exodus of planter-politicians and their families, many southerners, many southern sympathizers, remained in Washington. They did not cheer.

Lincoln, apprised of a thoroughly organized plot to assassinate him as he passes through Baltimore, is compelled by his advisers to change his schedule and enter the capital by stealth and in disguise. Housed at Willard's Hotel, he endures days of crush and curiosity, but charms even his enemies by his easy, simple manners, his unfailing tact, amazing memory for persons, names. Presently, accompanied by Seward, he pays an informal visit to the House to greet its members, many of them already well known to him. Chivalrously he goes first to the Democratic side of the great rotunda. No man rises to welcome him. Suddenly Sickles leaps from his seat and grabs the arm of the young fellow member who sits beside him. "We're not seniors; and it's not our place to do it; but I can't stand this, Scott—

let's go to meet him!" Amid an electric hush the two come forward. Seward, who knows Sickles well—admires him as a tough opponent, a loyal friend—introduces him. Lincoln is wholly at ease. "Why, Mr. Sickles, from what I have heard of the doings at Tammany Hall, I expected you to be a giant of a man, big and broad-shouldered, tall as I am! But I would take you to be more a scholarly kind of fellow than the sachem—eh?" The chuckle is disarming. At once the two are friends. Shamefacedly the Democratic leaders—such as still hold their seats—come forward and are presented. Lincoln seems, as usual, to know something essential about each one, has always the ready, tactful word; but his gaze, over their heads, now and again seeks "a scholarly kind of fellow" returning to his seat. He is not the man to forget.

March 4. From the portico of the Capitol, while Seward holds his hat, and scar-faced Wigfall sneers in the background, Lincoln delivers his inaugural address. Here is no dalliance, no threat, but a grave, unblenching confrontment of fact. He will hold the forts and property of the United States Government. He will collect the duties and imposts. But beyond what is necessary for this he will use no force. "In your hands, my dissatisfied countrymen, and not in mine, is the momentous issue of civil war. The government will not assail you. You can have no conflict without yourselves being the aggressor. You have no oath registered in heaven to destroy the government, while I shall have the most solemn one to preserve, protect, and defend it. . . ."

In vain!

April 16, '61. Charleston rebels, busy for weeks planting gun emplacements at Forts Moultrie, Pinckney, Johnson, and Cummins—commanding Sumter on three sides—suddenly call upon Major Anderson to surrender. Met with a blunt refusal, they retort with a concentrated cannonade. The supply ships belatedly dispatched to relieve the starving garrison roll helplessly in heavy storm outside the bar, unable to enter the harbor. And before the gale abates, Sumter—rationless, crumpled, in flames—surrenders.

The War for the Disruption of the Union is on.

In the furor—as blatantly planned by the conspirators—reluctant Virginia is stampeded into secession. North Carolina, Tennessee, Alabama, Arkansas promptly follow.

Lincoln, man of peace, patiently endeavoring to avoid armed clash, *now realizes that the moment he long has foreseen, long dreaded, has come. He does not hesitate. If the Union must be reborn in blood—then in blood be it! Before the smoke has cleared from Sumter, he issues a call for seventy-five thousand volunteers. But not yet can he bring himself to believe that he faces one of the epochal wars of human history. He sets the term of service at ninety days! In Richmond, the new seat of the Confederate Government, the news of his action is received with a blast of derisive laughter. Seventy-five thousand raw northern militia—to subdue the southern chivalry in ninety days! The poor Yokel!*

But the North, like Lincoln himself, hitherto patient, confused, bent upon a peaceful issue, unwilling to strike the first blow, now had received the needful slap in the face; and like Lincoln it promptly stripped for the fight. On the instant in every city, town, hamlet, men stormed the recruiting stations, demanding to be mustered in. And among them—Dan Sickles. On the day of the President's call to arms he resigned his seat in Congress, took train to New York. There, first, he went before the Common Council—Tammanyites hitherto proponents of states' rights and the southern view—and in an impassioned speech swung them into passing a resolution, already prepared by himself, pledging the city to the unstinted support of the Union and the immediate appropriation of a million dollars for the organization and equipment of volunteer regiments in its defense. This done—and Chairman Frank Boole dispatched on his way to present the resolution in person to the President—he promptly enlisted as a private in Company B of the Seventy-first Battalion of the National Guard, under his friend, Colonel Vosburgh.

The battalion was under orders to embark at once for the defense of Washington. But Sickles was destined not to accompany it. The next morning, as he was entering his carriage to drive to the wharf, he was set upon by a group of his intimates, headed by Captain Wiley, begging him not to be a fool. Men were plentiful, organizing brains scarce; his business was to raise regiments, not shoulder a musket—so went their argument. The wrangle was long, for at the prospect of fight all the old Flemish baron blood in Sickles was awake. He was eager for action, glad to get away from politics, law, gossip, bitter memories. But finally his friends triumphed. And his coachman drove to the wharf alone—there to present Colonel Vosburgh a letter explaining that Private Sickles had been conscripted for other military duties. The same day—so fast were events moving—Sickles received from Governor Morgan, of New York, a commission to raise eight companies of volunteers. Overnight he found himself confronting the fantastic difficulties involved in recruiting the defenders of a Union that, for the moment, had neither uniform nor musket, ration nor roof to give them!

The South, secretly, long had been preparing for war. But the North, caught off guard—arsenals looted, navy dispersed, its officer personnel streaming across the Potomac, its tiny professional army of some sixteen thousand men scattered in frontier forts—was not merely unprepared, it was, in a military sense, simply destitute. But the technical difficulties involved in feeding, equipping, housing, training a sudden horde of men were, as Sickles soon discovered, nothing to the jurisdictional difficulties involved in recruiting them!

Although the right of Congress, delegated to the President, to raise troops in the national defense could not be questioned, the governors of the northern and western states had instantly assumed the right unto themselves. In their view the new army was not an independent national organization, but merely an expansion of the already existent state militia; and, from the first, they jealously fought to seize, and hold, control over all bodies of recruits raised within their borders. Their action, of course, was not prompted wholly by states'-rights ideology or by local pride. There was good grafting to be had in the distribution of supply contracts, valuable political patronage to be dispensed in the appointment of henchmen—no matter how grossly unqualified—to the command of the new regiments or to administrative posts created by the wartime emergency. And, for the most part, the governors were far more concerned with such matters than with putting a well-equipped and ably officered army in the field. What this system ultimately cost the North, history recites. And against it Sickles promptly rebelled and, with the tacit connivance of Lincoln, proceeded to conduct a one-man war upon it. From the first his innate military sense prompted him to demand a national army, raised under centralized federal control, free from local politics and peculations, and led by officers appointed and promoted solely on the basis of merit. For the moment, however, he had no recourse but to proceed to the organization of his eight companies under state directive. This quickly accomplished, to his surprise he received an order to raise forty companies and organize them in a brigade of five regiments. Such was his energy and popularity, and the general eagerness to enlist that in less than three weeks he had his brigade organized and mustered into the service of the state by officers of the governor's staff. At that moment, in reply to his request that the command of the new brigade be turned over to a regular army officer, he received an order from Governor Morgan to disband thirty-two of his companies—for the reason that "the interior counties might resent the raising of so large a force in New York City alone"!

Dumfounded, outraged, Sickles realized, at once, that his accomplishment had aroused the jealousy of Morgan's less successful henchmen. Nevertheless he summoned his men and, not without a sarcastic comment or two, read them the order to disband.

But the "Excelsior Brigade"—so named and officially registered by Sickles after the New York State motto—was not to be liquidated so easily! In twenty-one days its commander had gathered around him a body of picked men, hundreds of them known to him personally, men keen for fight, clear as to cause, proud of their name. Their loyalty was to him and the Union, not to any Albany politician! They listened respectfully to the reading of the order; then, after a moment of stupefied silence, they turned on him such a blast of protest that for some moments he could not make himself heard. That response was all that he needed. When, at last, some order was restored, his voice rang out, crisp with decision: "All right, boys, I see that we all feel the same way about this. Hold together for a day or two. I'm going to see the President and ask him to muster us in as United States Volunteers. If Albany doesn't want us, the Union does!"

And aware that now the battle was on, that to disband his brigade would be his first defeat, Sickles took train to Washington. Very clearly now he saw that it had to be settled, once and for all, whether the loyal states as a whole, or merely the separate states as parts, had authority to raise the national forces of defense; whether the President was truly commander in chief and the army a *national* army, or whether the organization of these men streaming from shop and mill and farm to the colors was to be manipulated by petty state politicians. A very pertinent question.

Lincoln received him with something more than his usual kindliness of manner. He had not forgotten that episode in the Capitol. Also he liked this handsome, stubborn-lipped, competent fellow, admired his independence, divined in him great possibilities. Tactfully, he had spread on his desk the specially printed copy of the New York City resolutions, for he knew very well who was responsible for them. And before he would talk of anything else he had to express his thanks: "Sickles, I have here on my table the resolutions passed by your Common Council appropriating a million dollars toward raising men for this war and promising to do all in the power of your authorities to support the government. When these resolutions were brought to me by Alderman Frank Boole and his associates of the committee, I felt my burden lighter. I felt that when men break party lines and take this patriotic stand for the government and the Union, all must turn out well in the end. When you see them, tell them from me they made my heart glad and I can only say God bless them!"*

Coming to the subject of his visit, Sickles was diplomatic. He was far too realistic in his thinking to suppose that offhand he could change the deeply entrenched state-militia system of recruiting the national army. But he had thought out a very practical plan of supplementing it and so, gradually, superseding it. His proposal was to establish on Staten Island a large training camp as a *reserve* depot for recruits for the whole army, volunteer and regular, where the men could be thoroughly trained in the various branches of the service and dispatched to the field as the need arose—simply to maintain the regiments at the front at their full strength. He argued that the state-militia system would have to be used for the initial enlistments; but that one or several well-organized, properly equipped training camps, competently officered under federal direction, could replenish these regiments much more efficiently than could a score or more of scattered state depots. This was the entering wedge of his argument. And so far it seemed simplest common sense. But there was more to come. His next suggestion was that out of the *surplus* of recruits there should be organized regiments of "United States Volunteers" enlisted for the duration under the exclusive direction and command of the War Department. And in conclusion he urged that "the power to raise armies granted to Congress by the Constitution conferred upon the federal government ample discretion to choose whatever

*His own words as reported in his speech to the Lincoln Fellowship, February 12, 1910.

manner and form of organizing the land and naval forces might be deemed most serviceable."*

Lincoln listened receptively to the crisp tones, rapid-fire reasoning, every now and again giving an approving nod, a thoughtful stare. Then, broodingly, he got up and paced about the room. "Sickles, I want your men, and I want you to command them; but we have no arms or equipments, and but little money to buy them, if they could be found. . . . How long can you keep your men together?"

The reply was prompt and assured: "I have my men quartered in private homes in the city and suburbs; but if I am formally authorized by the government to organize my brigade as United States Volunteers, I, personally, and from my own resources, will undertake their subsistence and equipment and hold the force subject to Your Excellency's orders."

Lincoln's face brightened, but he still seemed hesitant. "I like the idea of United States Volunteers, but do you see where it leads to? What will the governors say if I raise regiments without their having a hand in it? Let's hear what the Secretary of War has to say about it." And he reached for the page bell. When Cameron, quickly appearing, heard the plan, he not only approved it but proceeded to develop it, suggesting the establishment of a second reserve camp at Harrisburg. Growing enthusiastic, he went over to a large map on the wall and began pointing out other suitable locations. "We shall need all the men we can get, and now is the time to enlist them. By all means let us have three or four of these camps for our own recruits. From Staten Island, to begin with, they can be sent anywhere by sea, or from Harrisburg by rail, and there are several other points equally advantageous."

Lincoln now was thoroughly intrigued. "The subject of the various camps we will consider at a cabinet meeting. But meanwhile, Cameron, I'm going to ask you to give Sickles authority to raise five regiments as United States Volunteers, and we will see how this beginning ends."†

In high fettle Sickles returned to his men with the good news. Somewhat naïvely he imagined that the President's order would be executed by the simple procedure of mustering out his command from the service of the state of New York and mustering it into

*His own words as reported in his speech to the Lincoln Fellowship, February 12, 1910.

†Ibid.

the service of the United States. But he had not reckoned on the power of the political blockade! As soon as it was known that the President had decided to raise volunteers directly in the service of the United States, without the intervention of the governors and their coveted graft, there came such a blast from Albany, followed by such a howling storm of protest from the gubernatorial sanctums, North and West, that it shook the White House. For days Lincoln's desk was cluttered with abusive letters, indignant telegrams. Not a few governors came to Washington to protest in person. Lincoln, as usual, reasoned and told stories and waited to see whether this tempest would blow itself out. Finally, taking things a step at a time, he directed that, for the present, Sickles should be commissioned colonel of United States Volunteers and that his command should be mustered into the federal service, "leaving for further consideration the question of raising more troops in the same manner."

Sickles had established a bridgehead in his war for a national recruiting system. But he could not enlarge it. Promptly all the governors of the loyal states issued orders prohibiting any individual from attempting to raise volunteers except under state authorization. For two years they had their way. Subsequent to Gettysburg, however, their inability to furnish the necessary replenishments for Grant's campaigns compelled the War Department to adopt Sickles's plan. From that time all enlistment, volunteer or conscript, was conducted by provost marshals in charge of extensive interstate military districts and acting exclusively under the federal authority. Nevertheless, throughout the succeeding four years of war, Sickles's Excelsior Brigade remained—with the exception of a few colored regiments toward the close—the only volunteer force mustered as an original unit directly into the service of the United States.

But if the privilege of innovation had its charms, it also had its trials. Relying on Lincoln's word, Sickles removed his men to Staten Island and put them under canvas in a model camp. To do this he had to purchase out of his own funds, and wherever he could, tents, stores, equipment, uniforms, blankets, cots, arms, ammunition—all the paraphernalia required by a raw force of a thousand men; organize the supply, commissary, sanitation; and, with the aid of a few old drill sergeants, veterans of the Mexican War, such officer personnel as he could find, and three hundred antiquated muskets used in relays, train his men in the manual of arms and field evolutions. And all this against an opposition so solid that when, for example, on one occasion, he quartered some of his recruits—just arrived from upstate —in the New York armory for an hour's rest and the good hot breakfast he had arranged to be sent in to them from nearby restaurants, Governor Morgan ordered them turned out and would not let the tired, hungry fellows even touch their food!

Nevertheless, with his organizing ability and instinct for soldiering, Sickles soon was able to present his force in an exhibition of drill and field maneuver to admiring crowds at regular Sunday reviews.

But week after week went by—at a cost of several thousand dollars a day. Sickles's pocket soon sagged, but Sickles Sr., solidly approving, footed the bill. And still the Excelsior Brigade had no official existence. No longer state militia and not yet officially mustered in as United States Volunteers, it hung between heaven and earth, the private luxury and road to bankruptcy of one man with a vision. Meanwhile, as the opposition against it grew and the press daily predicted that Lincoln never would recognize it, the brigade itself was undergoing a change in personnel that made it as unique in composition as it already was in constitution—a change, incidentally, that actually saved its existence as a military unit.

In those feverish first weeks of recruiting—when it was generally believed that the South would be "whipped in ninety days," and thousands of lusty young fellows chafed to get to the front before the fighting was over, and political favorites, blossoming out in brigadier uniforms, were hectically endeavoring to bring their commands up to the required strength—desertions from one force to another, voluntary or bribed, were very common. And soon there developed that indigenous product, "the racket"—engaged in buying and selling volunteers as so much merchandise on the market. In consequence of its uncertain status, the growing doubt that it ever would be mustered into service, the Excelsior Brigade had suffered particularly heavy losses to other contingents about to go into action. To offset this depletion, Sickles had organized recruiting in neighboring states; and such was the popularity of the "United States Volunteers" idea that his ranks were always well replenished. But the fact that this amateur and innovator now was recruiting his brigade from all states brought a fresh outburst of wrath from the governors. The press took up the cry. A new campaign of detraction began; and soon the rumors were rife that Sickles had lost nearly all of his men and that Lincoln, at last, had definitely abandoned the whole enterprise.

The news brought Sickles hotfoot once more to Washington. Lincoln met him rather wistfully. "I hear that your brigade has gone all to pieces." Sickles smiled. "Not yet, Your Excellency!" Consulting some papers on his desk, Lincoln looked up, surprised. "But they tell me that you have lost most of your men. I hope this is not true. But I am still puzzled to see what I am to do with our United States Volunteers."

Sickles was ready with his answer. "It is true that I have lost a number of my men by desertion; but I have been able to replace them with recruits from a dozen other states. My numbers stand intact; and no man can say that I have been trespassing on the preserves of Governor Morgan."

A quick look of understanding came into Lincoln's eyes. For a moment or two he brooded over the matter, then rose decisively and came forward with outstretched hand. "Sickles, you're all right now. That last expedient of yours—recruiting from other states—has relieved me from embarrassment. Your organization is no longer local. Whatever may be said of the authority of the President to raise volunteers, you have put yourself outside the jurisdiction of any governor. You are raising United States troops from all parts of the Union. Hold your men together three days longer, and the mustering officer will come and take you all in out of the cold."*

At last triumphant, Sickles returned to his encampment, only to find that a whole company of his men just had deserted and were on their way to the ferry. With an armed troop he promptly pursued them and brought them back, putting the officers under arrest. When the racketeers—a fake "colonel" and two "lieutenants" who had sold the company to a political brigadier—arrived later to find out what had become of their merchandise, Sickles arrested them also. That same evening he haled the officers—sellers and sold—before a drumhead court-martial and had the six of them condemned to be shot at midnight.

On the stroke of twelve the prisoners were led out, lined up against a wall, blindfolded, and given fifteen minutes to prepare for death. Their wild pleas for mercy, their promises to expose, if par-

*His own words as reported in his speech to the Lincoln Fellowship, February 12, 1910.

doned, several other schemes afoot to entice away the Excelsior recruits, went unheeded. Colonel Sickles, smoking a cigar over the last New York *Sun* editorial describing the wreckage of his brigade, was not interested. The execution squad lined up. At the word of command, six rods rammed home a charge. "Ready!"—and six muskets leaped to aim. The pleas of the condemned died in a quavering. At that point the officer in charge stopped nonchalantly to open a letter Sickles had given him with orders to read it before he delivered the command to fire. The letter proved to be a reprieve, "until the sentence be approved by the President." Six shaken men staggered away from the wall, scarcely able to believe themselves still alive. It was the last attempt at raiding Sickles's command!

Three days later the Staten Island recruits were mustered directly into the federal service, regiment by regiment, as "United States Volunteers, The Excelsior Brigade, Colonel Daniel E. Sickles commanding." At once they were ordered by General Winfield Scott to proceed to the Shenandoah Valley. And the soldierly, smartly uniformed ex-congressman who rode at their head, as with bands blaring, flags flying, they marched in perfect parade form from the Battery landing up Fifth Avenue to Central Park—their overnight camping ground—was, undoubtedly, the most jubilant officer in the Union Army that day.

But "this upstart who would deprive the states of their right to raise volunteers" was not to be let off with a technical victory. The discomfited governors, particularly Morgan and his Albany henchmen, still pursued him and were to pursue him for many a day to come. The hounding took various forms: a demand that he pay $2,500 for the rent of the three hundred old muskets he had been compelled to draw from the state armory for the use of his men; a bitter struggle to thwart the commissioning of his officers; attempts, voucher by voucher, to block the War Department from reimbursing him for his tremendous outlay of some four hundred thousand dollars in organizing, equipping, and maintaining his brigade; and, finally, a determined campaign to deprive him of his command.

The matter of the vouchers turned up some illuminating sidelights on the exigencies attending the hasty manufacture of an army with empty treasury, bare magazines, looted arsenals. For instance, among the accounts Sickles presented to Quartermaster General Meigs was a small bill on an official form reading: "For one tent,

$500." In their efforts to discredit him his enemies already had spread wild tales of his extravagance in housing, equipping, accoutering his men. Here was proof of it! And, not surprisingly, the entire department blew up. "Five hundred dollars for a tent! An imperial marquee, if you please—for this rajah brigadier!" An explanation was demanded. Sickles calmly replied that, unable to draw sufficient tents from the army depot or obtain delivery on those he had ordered, he had been compelled to buy a disused circus tent from Barnum to shelter several hundred men already sickened by nights of sleeping in the open under heavy rain. With shrugs and raised eyebrows, the explanation was accepted. But soon there appeared another voucher even more alarming: "For baths and barbering 1,478 recruits . . . $147.80." This was too much. "So this pet, pampered brigade of Sickles luxuriates in baths and the attentions of the hairdresser—at the government's expense! A corps d'élite, indeed!" Again an explanation was demanded. The reply revealed something of the wretchedness that enlisted men had to endure while waiting for housing, clothing, equipment. For lack of better quarters, so it transpired, these recruits had been housed for weeks in the bare halls of the Assembly Rooms, 444 Broadway—without benefit of beds, blankets, even washtubs. And since few of them possessed a change of clothing or so much as a cake of soap, a razor, or a comb, their condition, at last, had become such as to arouse the wrath of the Board of Health. In the emergency, Sickles had engaged a cheap bathing house to shower and shave the poor devils at ten cents apiece. The voucher was accepted—and quickly filed away! The disbursing officers had hardly calmed down, however, when another outrageous little bill turned up: "To building one refrigerator at Camp Scott, $316. Ice for same, $211." Somehow news of this item reached the Albany *Gazette* and excited a fervent editorial, "Behold this amateur brigadier—proceeding on campaign with champagne and boned turkey on ice, and an eighteen horse truck to haul his monster on the march!" Once more the department queried Sickles, and once more his reply only served to show his practical good sense. He could draw fresh beef from the commissary depot in New York only twice a week—so ran his report. Consequently, in June, thousands of pounds of the unrefrigerated supply had been found unfit for use. As a simple measure of economy he had built a refrigerator capable of holding three or four days' supply and kept it well filled with ice; and in so doing, he had already saved its cost many times over. By that time the Quartermaster General's Department had come to view this "amateur brigadier" with a certain respect; and, in the upshot, all his vouchers were honored—except one quite considerable docket of them lost when two of his aides were drowned at the beginning of the Peninsular campaign.

If Sickles's success in establishing the principle of United States Volunteers proved circumscribed at the moment, it none the less foreshadowed what is now the accepted procedure in times of war emergency. Incidentally his brigade proved to be more characteristically "American"—which is to say, polyglot and interracial—than ever answered roll call; for it included in its ranks the sons of nearly every loyal state in the Union and specimens of nearly every nation on earth—including a doughty Chinaman killed at Gettysburg. But if it spoke a dozen tongues it marched and fought like one man. The very fact that it represented a cross section of a cosmopolite people gave it a special character and strength. And Sickles's bold, magnetic personality, his almost fanatical belief in this creation of his, the assiduous care he showed for its welfare in quarters, its efficiency in the field, endowed it with much of his own fighting verve. At Williamsburg, baptized in the blood of seven hundred men, it immediately established its reputation; at Fair Oaks, before Fredericksburg, in the fierce counterattack and rear-guard action at Chancellorsville, on the crucial "second day" at Gettysburg, it proved its surpassing spirit in attack, tenacity in defense, as a component of the famous Third Corps—Sickles's final command. Time and again it was selected to stopgap desperate predicaments. The figures tell the tale. From Bull Run to Appomattox, its total muster roll was 6,422 enlisted men—its total casualties, 3,028.

No less unique was the brigade's commander. An ardent friend of the South, he had joined the North in defense of the Union; a stout proponent of states' rights, he had defied the whole state-militia system in creating his United States Volunteers; steadfastly opposed to the appointment of any but regular army officers to positions of military responsibility, he soon found himself a major general—*the only one destitute of previous professional training;* and, finally, maintaining that amateurs and politicians were the curse of the Army, he completely disproved his own thesis by becoming—according to

that scientific and highly professional man of war, General Warren—
"one of the four great corps commanders" of the Union forces.

But for all his initial success, Sickles's efforts to persuade Lincoln
to establish federal recruiting as a government policy came too late.
Once surrendered to the state political machines, the power of the
Executive to raise troops was lost. And it was only by constant and
vigilant struggle that Sickles was able to preserve even his own small
organization intact, as a symbol of the principle he had sought to
maintain. But even as a symbol, the existence of a force of United
States Volunteers remained a menace to state patronage. And if it
could not be disbanded, then its name must be erased—so thought
Albany. In December 1861 Governor Morgan was able to bring
enough pressure to bear on the War Department to compel the in-
corporation of the Excelsior Brigade in the body of the New York
State troops. True, the brigade kept its unique composition, its
privilege of nationwide recruiting; but no longer were its regiments
known as the First, Second, Third, Fourth, Fifth United States Volunteers, but simply as the 70th, 71st, 72nd, 73rd, 74th New York
State troops. The hated name had been obliterated! That done, it followed naturally enough that Sickles would not be left long in enjoyment of his command.

Meanwhile the same political pettifogging had prevented the Excelsiors from participating in the festive advance, hysterical rout at
Bull Run. And, despite some picket and reconnaissance duty on the
Shenandoah and Lower Potomac, it had to wait some months for its
first brush with the enemy. Years afterward, in an address before the
Society of the Army of the Potomac, Sickles recalled that first
experience of his under fire:

It was early in 1862, before the Peninsular campaign began. General
McClellan was in Washington, and somehow he lost track of a portion
of the Confederate army. General Hooker, my commander, chose me to
make a reconnaissance in force and try to uncover the position of General
Longstreet. I took a thousand men of my brigade, and I picked them
myself, taking the huskiest and most reliable I could find.

We crossed the river from Maryland and made a march of some
twenty miles in the direction of Fredericksburg. At a place called Stafford
Court House we met the outpost of Longstreet's army—two regiments in
all. They outnumbered us two to one, and it was a hot fight. This was
the first time that I or any of my men had been under fire. I was sur-

prised when it was over and the Confederates had retired—evidently thinking we were the advance guard of a whole army. I was surprised that I had taken it so coolly. Mind you, I do not say this boastingly, but simply as a man reviewing his sensations under certain conditions.

But while Sickles had his face to the enemy, the politicians had been busy behind his back. Under Albany pressure the Senate Military Affairs Committee refused to confirm his commission as colonel, although for some months he had been performing all the functions of a brigadier general. And he was ousted from his command. In vain he volunteered to serve with his men in a subordinate capacity. Albany would have none of him. But not so Lincoln, Stanton, McClellan, Hooker! By their intervention, after three months of gnawing inaction, he was restored to his command—and now with his full rank of brigadier general. The ink still wet on his commission, he embarked for the James River, arriving just in time to lead his Excelsiors against Longstreet in the fiercely contested victory at Fair Oaks.

Throughout the following campaign that saw McClellan thrust cumbrously up the Peninsula from Fort Monroe, only to miscue each opportunity of crushing an enemy half his strength, and, finally, Richmond within his grasp, beat an absurd retreat, the Excelsior Brigade fought intrepidly, bled copiously. Over a thousand of the men who marched with Sickles did not come back, although he himself, always to the front in moments of crisis, came through unscratched. It was a grueling initiation. The Army of the Potomac not only had to face an alert enemy, brilliantly commanded and close to his own base, and endure the pusillanimities of a parade-ground general, but between mud and muddle its supply service frequently broke down and, for weeks at a time, officers and men fought on famished bellies. One good story of those lean days Sickles told in after years at—of all places!—a banquet:*

In the thick of the Peninsular campaign—at Malvern Hill, to be exact—I had occasion to employ a section of artillery, and hunting up my division commander, General Joe Hooker, I asked him if he could detach a couple of guns for use in my brigade.

"Fighting Joe," however, seemed to have his mind on something else. "Guns? Guns?" he snorted. "Oh, yes, you can have guns or anything else you want—if you'll only give me something to eat. I'm starving!"

*A speech before the Society of the Army of the Potomac, 1912.

I dug in my pockets and pulled out a chunk of hardtack and a small bag of brown sugar. Hooker stared at me in amazement. "If you'll tell me where you find sugar and hardtack, you can have four guns!—a whole damned battery!"

I said, "General, if you will send an orderly a few miles back along the road I just have come, he will find a broken-down wagon of the commissary train loaded with sugar and army biscuit. That's where I got this." Hooker bawled for his orderly—and I rode off with my guns!

The next morning the army had reached Harrison's Landing. It was July and terribly hot. But I was in high spirits—and for a very good reason! I hurried over to the Headquarters tent and found General Heintzelman, my corps commander, Generals Kearny, Hooker, and Warren and also my two very good friends, the French military attachés, the Comte de Paris and his brother, the Duc de Chartres, busy over maps and reports. "Gentlemen," I said, "would you do me the honor to lunch with me at my camp?"

Heintzelman squinted up from a chart he was studying. "None of your jokes, Sickles! You know you have nothing but sugar and biscuit."

Blandly I countered, "Come and see!" There were about twenty staff officers present, and raising my voice a little, I cried, "Gentlemen, lunch is laid and waiting—won't you do me the honor?"

Twenty pairs of incredulous eyes were staring at me. There was a general murmuring suggestive of what would be done to me if I were merely fooling with empty bellies. But, at last, hesitantly, the whole group followed me.

My camp happened to be pitched in a charming spot—a small grove by the riverbank, with a fine natural lawn. When my guests arrived they saw, to their wild surprise, a huge white cloth spread out on the turf, punctiliously set with white porcelain plates and dishes, napkins, polished knives and forks, wineglasses, and all the appointments of a luxurious dinner table.

"The rascal has robbed a hotel!" cried Hooker. Kearny was skeptical. "There are no hotels around here, General—that's plantation loot!"

At that moment, as I had given directions, my orderlies appeared bearing two large pails, one of purple, the other of amber, liquid—both garnished with lumps of ice, fresh strawberries, sliced oranges, pineapples, lemons—a most potent punch. Kearny seized one pail, Hooker the other, both dropping on their knees as if in adoration. And while the one grasped a chunk of ice and kissed it ceremoniously, the other squatted before his pail and drank from the brim like an Arab in the desert. Meanwhile my orderlies reappeared with great platters of roast turkey and chicken, steaming hams, rounds of beef, fresh vegetables and fruits, and even cranberry sauce!

Never was a man so bedeviled with questions as I was. But I remained mysterious. When Hooker cried, "But this is all a dream, Sickles," I replied, "It is, General—and I advise you to finish that turkey before you wake up!" But as first hunger was appeased and the good punch warmed us all, I confessed. "The truth is, gentlemen, that early this morning a steamboat arrived at the landing laden with every luxury from the northern markets for the sick and wounded of the army—a gift from that good angel of mercy, the Sanitary Commission. The agent in charge applied to me for wagons and men to transport the supplies to our hospital camps. And I promptly complied—requesting, however, that one wagonload be assigned to our famishing Headquarters Staff. My request was granted with a smile. And that wagonload was a royal one, you will grant! My orderlies did the rest. So, gentlemen, a toast: "The Sanitary Commission!"

CHAPTER XXIII

Muddle and Massacre

Over the White House hangs a huge sign: "Wanted—a General!" Lincoln has tried the conscientious but mediocre Irvin McDowell— only to be handed the disastrous rout at Bull Run. He has tried Mc-Clellan, "the hero of West Virginia"—only to be handed a handsomely organized army, a bloody and fruitless Peninsular campaign, and a masterly retreat before far inferior forces. And while, in the South, Farragut, the classic type of bold, ingenious naval commander, has captured New Orleans and opened the lower reaches of the Mississippi; and General Pope and Commodore Foote, in a parallel campaign, have opened its upper reaches; and Ulysses S. Grant—a dwarfish, tough, bellicose fellow recently returned to the Army from the paternal tanning yards—has seized Forts Henry and Donelson, and, by his all-but-lost victory at Shiloh, cleared western Tennessee of Confederate troops, the main attack on the forces of Lee and Longstreet, based on Richmond, has not advanced a foot.

Meanwhile the peevish academician, General H. W. Halleck, sits in Winfield Scott's chair as commander in chief and fights a desk war less with the enemy than with his own generals. In desperation Lincoln, finding no better man to hand, appoints Pope in McClellan's place and advises him to make a direct advance upon Richmond from Alexandria by the Manassas valley route. But if Pope is a good corps commander, he, too, is no general. Lee and Longstreet, Johnston, Stonewall Jackson and Jeb Stuart play hob with him; and his crushing defeat at Second Bull Run leaves the Army of the Potomac still on the Potomac, with still nothing to show for eighteen months of bloody struggle but a discouraging number of graves. Once more Lincoln turns back to McClellan and, in a letter of sober rebuke, sad counsel, reappoints him to his old command—just in time to counter Lee's bold march into Maryland. In the terrific struggle at Antietam, McClellan manages to check the enemy, but with his usual dilatoriness fails to pursue and rout him. Lee recrosses the Potomac in sight of Washington! Once more Lincoln changes generals. This time he turns to Burnside, a humble-minded man who pleads his unfitness for such a responsibility—and soon proves it!

Throughout the disastrous Manassas campaign under Pope, Sickles's Excelsiors had been continuously in action. At Bristoe, Groveton, Second Bull Run, Chantilly, they had fought stubbornly, suffered brutally. And the close of the campaign found them so shattered, depleted, exhausted, that when the army under the reappointed McClellan marched to meet Lee at Antietam, they were put on garrison duty at Alexandria to rest and recruit, and so—for the first time since they took the field—missed an important engagement. But two months later they rejoined the Third Corps in time to take part in the action before Fredericksburg.

On a score of bitterly fought fields Sickles had won the idolatry of his men. And his fellow commanders, such as Heintzelman, Hooker, Reynolds, Hancock, Kearny, Warren, Couch—West Pointers naturally inclined to be highly critical of a brigadier without a shred of military training—quickly had come to accept him as one of themselves. From the first, Lincoln, Stanton, McClellan had detected his fighting qualities. And when Burnside, before Fredericks-

burg, reorganized the Army of the Potomac, no one was surprised—
if certain Albany politicians were chagrined—to see Sickles promoted
to the command of the Second Division, Third Corps, in charge of
three brigades and a battery of artillery.

No new and untried division commander could have taken the
field under less auspicious circumstances than did Sickles at Fredericksburg. Lee at the moment lacked two of his most powerful
divisions—those of Johnston and Longstreet; and Burnside, with his
overwhelming temporary superiority in numbers, could have stormed
him out of his position in twenty-four hours. But the precious days
passed while Burnside dallied, fussing over a faddish and quite unnecessary reorganization of his army. When, at last, all was readied
for the advance, the pontoons required for the crossing of the
Rappahannock failed to arrive. Meanwhile Longstreet and Johnston,
with their heavily gunned divisions, had come up to reinforce the
Confederates. And on Marye's Heights—a ridge commanding the
whole field of operations—Lee was able to mass artillery wheel to
wheel. His effective strength, fire power, and dominating position
were such that any force attacking him across the river faced certain slaughter. Nonetheless, as soon as the pontoons arrived, Burnside
ordered the attack. Vainly his senior corps commanders, Stoneman,
Reynolds, Couch, Butterfield, Hooker, Wilcox, pleaded with him
not to hurl the army at the Heights but to make a rapid march west
and cross the river at its upper reaches. Hooker skirted close to
mutiny in the violence of his opposition. But Burnside, aware that
he already was under severe criticism for his delay, and realizing that
Lincoln had appointed him in the hope of obtaining prompt action,
refused to change his orders for an immediate assault. For the Army
of the Potomac it was once more a case of

> *Theirs not to reason why,*
> *Theirs but to do and die . . .*

But each corps commander knew what was coming. And it came
—massacre! The Union forces, storming Marye's Heights with mad
valor, were blasted at every lunge by Lee's massed artillery, entrenched infantry and, finally, driven back across the river. Sickles's
division, held in reserve until the last hours, came off with slight
casualties. Not so the assault troops. Before the action ended, more
than twelve thousand of them had been slaughtered or maimed to

no purpose by a general whose sole claim to fame lay in the cut of his whiskers!

In utter distress Lincoln came down to the Army Headquarters at Falmouth to observe the situation for himself. Before leaving he spent one entire day with Sickles—to somewhat distracting results.

Reviewing the Second Division assembled to do him honor, and returning the salutes of the men with an air of infinite sadness, Lincoln suddenly cried out, "Sickles, can you see an end to this dreadful business? It breaks my heart to think how many of these brave fellows—here and across the river—will perish before peace can be restored!" Sickles was as sick at heart over the recent massacre as Lincoln, but as a fighting man, a subordinate commander at that, he could not express his real thought. Instead, albeit a bit soberly, he countered with Macaulay's famous lines:

> And how can man die better
> Than facing fearful odds
> For the ashes of his fathers
> And the temples of his gods?

Meanwhile, at Headquarters, a group of officers—one, here and there, accompanied by his wife—had assembled in the hope of being presented to the President. And Lincoln, returning from the inspection, bravely endeavored to rouse himself to greet each one of them with some word of praise or remembrance. For once, however, his usual genial tact failed him. Suddenly Sickles, realizing that something must be done to break through the President's tragic mood, bethought himself of the ladies! Mischievously he went among them suggesting that they storm the Lincolnian heights, and each one convey her admiration in a kiss!

But those were not the days of promiscuous kissing. The ladies were bashful, argumentative: "It is not for us to begin that sort of thing. . . . How can five-foot-two kiss six-feet-four? . . . Besides, Mrs. Lincoln might seriously object . . ." Among them, however, was one adventuress, the Princess Salm-Salm, youthful and attractive wife of an Austrian nobleman commanding a Union regiment. She had known gay days in Vienna, had been recently at the court of Maximilian and Carlotta in Mexico, and was not disposed to regard a kiss too solemnly. Seeing that no one else seemed inclined to make a move, she volunteered to lead the charge; and by way of encouraging her followers, gave the President, not one, but several highly artistic kisses. On the instant cloud-capped Lincolnian heights caught the sun. Enviously the others sought to outdo the Princess. When it was all over, Lincoln was laughing and blithe as a boy . . . But, alas! Tad, his spoiled and adored brat, was watching. And when, next day, Mary Lincoln arrived, he eagerly recounted to her the kissing episode. Once more gloom descended. In Lincoln's tent a high-pitched voice was heard far into the night pouring psychopathic anathemas upon the faithlessness of men.

The next morning, while the whole staff over coffee covertly discussed the fact that Uncle Abe was "in hot water again," Sickles to his dismay found himself—of all men—ordered to escort the President back to Washington. He knew very well by now that Mary Todd would have preferred the devil for escort! But orders were orders. Dutifully he joined the President and his family at Aquia Creek and embarked with them for Washington. And with what was something more than tact, he managed to keep out of the way—until suppertime. Then, compelled to sit in a tiny cabin *vis-à-vis* with the outraged Mrs. Lincoln, he found himself subjected to a process of complete refrigeration. The First Lady would neither speak to him nor even look at him. Desperately Lincoln, exerting all his whimsy and quaint humor, told one good story after another. He might as well have been trying to amuse a tombstone. Suddenly, as though he had just remembered something, he turned to his unhappy military escort. "Sickles, until I came down this week to see the army, I never knew that you were such a pious man!"

Sickles looked puzzled. "I'm sure I don't merit the reputation, Mr. President—if I've gained it." Lincoln's gray eyes twinkled. "Oh, yes—they tell me you are the greatest psalmist in the army. In fact they say that you are more than a psalmist—they say you are a salm-salmist!"

Mary Todd tried to choke back her laughter. But it was no use. Lincoln had won.

CHAPTER XXIV

Defeat Grotesque

———— ◆ ————

Made tragically aware that Burnside was not the man to be entrusted with the Army of the Potomac, Lincoln looked about him long and thoughtfully. What he wanted was a man who would neither make masterly retreats nor let himself be completely out-maneuvered nor throw his men upon foredoomed massacre, but a man who would carry the fight to the enemy—with some respect for common sense and the rules of warfare. And in an unlucky moment his glance fell upon "Fighting Joe."

That General Joseph Hooker came by his sobriquet honestly enough cannot be questioned. Graduated from West Point in 1837, in the same class with Jubal A. Early, Confederate division commander; Chilton, Lee's chief of staff; and Sedgwick, commander of the Sixth Corps, Army of the Potomac, he had won three brevets for gallantry, as artillery and staff officer, in the Mexican War; and in the Peninsular campaign, his fighting qualities had brought him rapid promotion to the rank of major general. Unfortunately he was cursed with a very unstable temperament—one that today, probably, would be classified as "manic depressive." Oscillating—as this type tends to do—between pompous self-confidence and morbid gloom, he also exhibited in marked degree the customary associate symptoms of egotism, criticism of others, vanity, self-petting, irritability. Hitherto it does not appear that this psychological imbalance had proven an obstacle to Hooker's military efficiency. Within the limited scope of brigade, then division, then corps commander, he had shown himself keen and capable, if temperamental. It was only when given supreme command on a critical field that, suddenly, all checks and guides removed, his every defect loomed up with a tragic magnification, foreboding disaster. How Lincoln and Halleck came to choose such a man—over commanders of such character and distinction as Reynolds, Couch, Hancock, Meade—is hard to understand.

At first, however, the choice seemed not only wise but even brilliant.

With great energy Hooker, thrusting aside Burnside's cumbersome scheme of reorganization, proceeded to put the army in first-class fighting shape. At the same time, working in utmost secrecy with a few of his military confidants, he evolved a thoroughly scientific plan of campaign against Lee. It called for a frontal demonstration by three corps against Fredericksburg to cover, and coincide with, a sweeping flank movement of the remaining four corps across the upper reaches of the Rappahannock and Rapidan rivers—thus taking the enemy in reverse, crushing him between the jaws of a powerful pincer movement, while at the same time a heavy force of cavalry, sweeping far to the south, cut him off from his supply base at Richmond. To Hooker's corps commanders the plan came as an electrifying surprise. Hitherto they had not overestimated his abilities. But his strategy—if he could carry it through—seemed, at last, to have the true Napoleonic touch; and they set to their task of moving their masses of dogged veterans and huge wagon trains with the sense that, for once, a decisive victory lay within their grasp.

In the reorganization of his army, one of Hooker's first moves was to recommend Sickles for promotion to the command of the Third Corps with the rank of major general. The request was promptly complied with, and Sickles entered at once upon his new responsibilities—although political pettifogging once more held up the actual issue of his commission for several months. And so Private Sickles, without benefit of West Point, compelled to learn the business of handling fighting men as he went along, in two years had become Major General Sickles, one of the gallant little group of corps commanders who, first and last, remained the brain and backbone of the Army of the Potomac.

Incidentally, as so often happens with men torn by warfare from their civilian life, that year and a half of tough campaigning had wrought Congressman Sickles out of all likeness to his former self —a fact that Brady's camera portrait of him, taken before Fredericksburg, reveals with startling abruptness. Here is no longer the chin-tufted, dandified diplomat, the Washington fashionable, politician d'élite, epicurean master of Stockton Mansion; but a ragged-mustached fellow, rugged, sad, worn—looking rough, valiant, and dependable as an Irish wolfhound. So far, in truth—except in what might be called the "lucky victory" at Fair Oaks—Sickles had known little of glory, much of muck and blood and death, stubborn defense, bitter defeat, crass command. And just as he had received his initiation as brigadier general under the coxcomb McClellan, the puttering Pope, and his baptism as division commander under the dull, disastrous Burnside, so now he was to make his first essay as corps commander, savagely endeavoring to salvage an army delivered to rout, under the catastrophic Hooker!

With some excusable lapses in timing and co-ordination, Hooker executed his basic maneuver in forthright fashion. Leaving three corps—including Sickles's Third—to make a covering demonstration against Fredericksburg, he swept the main bulk of his army in a rapid march westward along the northern banks of the Rappahannock and its tributary Rapidan, and splitting them into a four-pronged fork, forded them at convenient shallows some miles apart, and, reuniting them, curled them around Lee's far-flung, thinly held defense lines on the southern banks. The concentration point was a lonely, massive old country house, known as Chancellorsville, standing in a broad clearing in "the Wilderness"—a heavily treed district bordering open country to the south—and adjacent to three roads paralleling the course of the Rappahannock. Having effected his concentration in good order, Hooker, deploying a defensive line along his southern front, the Plank Road—to guard his base and communications—dispatched powerful columns eastward, along the three main trails through the forest, in an assault upon Lee's army based upon Fredericksburg. His idea was to seize a ridge running at right angles to the Rappahannock on the eastern edge of the Wilderness that commanded Lee's position in the open country beyond, and, massing this with artillery, make it the base line of his attack. At the same time he had dispatched twelve thousand cavalry under Stoneman in a sweeping southeastern curve to raid Lee's communications with Richmond. And confident now that he had the enemy trapped and that Sedgwick, in command of the forces before Fredericksburg, needed no more than two corps for the projected covering demonstration, he ordered Sickles to bring his troops to Chancellorsville—following the nearest route already well trampled by the main flanking column.

No army that lived to convert imminent annihilation into brilliant victory was ever in a more desperate predicament than was the Confederate force before Fredericksburg at that moment. And no army, in military history, was ever more dependent on pure genius of generalship. Lee had little more than forty-five thousand effectives; for he had sent Longstreet with his division—a third of the Army—to guard the Peninsular seaboard. He had been caught off guard, brilliantly outmaneuvered and encircled; and he now faced a massive, heavily gunned offensive of 125,000 men advancing upon him simultaneously on both flanks, while, at the same time, his scouts apprised him that Union cavalry detachments were freely raiding his rear!

It was, in truth, the most critical moment of the entire Civil War. And had Hooker carried through as he had begun, there is no doubt that Appomattox would have been predated two years and vast, useless bloodshed saved. But conception is one thing—performance quite another!

That Hooker did not fail to appreciate his own achievement-in-the-making is shown by his grandiloquent announcement to the army upon taking up his headquarters at Chancellorsville: "The Twelfth, Second, and Fifth Corps have accomplished their task magnificently . . . the enemy now must ingloriously flee or come out from behind his defenses and give us battle on our own ground where certain destruction awaits him . . . the Rebel forces now are the legitimate property of the Army of the Potomac!" This before a shot had been fired! And Lincoln, head bowed upon his desk, waited for news. . . .

Hooker, of course, was positive that Lee, finding himself trapped, would retreat. But Lee did nothing of the kind. Instead he attacked. Thus when the Union columns had seized the ridge commanding the Confederate position from the west, they found themselves facing no retreat but a fierce onslaught. And at that moment Hooker suddenly, like an overinflated balloon, collapsed.

Much has been written to explain that collapse: Hooker was drunk; Hooker, aware of his tremendous responsibilities, denied himself his stout daily rations of Kentucky, and had caved in; and so forth—all of it beside the mark. The fact is that Hooker had great ability but small capacity, and, faced with crisis, this discrepancy between his ability to conceive and his capacity to perform un-

nerved him. As he afterward confessed, he "lost faith in Hooker"—
a typical manic-depressive reaction. And thus, tragically, at the very
moment when he had full command of the field, he crumpled and—
against the well-nigh mutinous protests of his advancing corps commanders, Couch, Hancock, Meade, and his staff artillery officer,
the brilliant and indefatigable Warren—ordered a retreat! From
the very strategic ridge he had planned as a base of assault, he cuddled
his army back into a purely defensive position helplessly entangled
in the Wilderness thickets—there to await whatever it might be
that Lee should choose to do to him! And Lee was not long in
choosing. He had the prime qualifications of a great, in contradis-
tinction to a merely good, general—he knew just when to completely
disregard all the accepted rules of warfare. And he also had the second qualification—he knew men. And it was these two qualifications
used in brilliant conjunction that had given him—against heavy
odds in numbers and matériel—the whip hand in the first two years of
the war. In each campaign—and often with daring disregard for
academic military science—he conformed his strategy to the psychology of the opposing Union general: by bravura tactics backed
by dangerously small forces frustrating the chickenhearted McClellan on the Peninsula; with dangerously divided forces outmaneu-
vering and carving up the slow-witted Pope in the Manassas Valley;
with dangerously inadequate equipment, crossing the Potomac, in
the hope of raising all Maryland behind him, and attacking the reappointed McClellan on his home ground—confident that, if foiled,
he would be permitted to withdraw at leisure; dangerously drawing
in his flanks at Fredericksburg, waiting for the dull Burnside to
bring his army to massacre in a frontal assault. He knew these men
and what could be expected of them—and what he dared risk with
them. Also he knew Hooker, the braggart and poseur, man of large
mouth, small fist, big beginnings, whitling endings.

But for the moment—when he first realized that Hooker had
taken him in reverse and had powerful forces poised on his western
flank—he thought that, for once, he had mistaken his man. Was
Blowhard then a general, after all? His strategy so far was brilliant,
but would he carry through? If, for an uneasy quarter of an hour,
Lee lost some faith in himself as psychologist, he suffered no loss of
faith in himself as commander. Making forehanded preparations for
a last-minute withdrawal upon Richmond, he promptly split his

pitiful force of less than forty-five thousand men in two and, leaving a fraction to hold off Sedgwick's menaced attack upon his right flank at Fredericksburg, threw his main force forward in an enveloping movement against Hooker's advance from the west. It was the instinctive response of first-class generalship to desperate predicament—this bold attack in full force, with preparations for orderly retreat.

But Lee had not misjudged his man. While his forward divisions under Anderson and McLaws were skirmishing smartly with the Union lines, his scouts came galloping in with the incredible report that, for no discernible reason, the enemy advance had suddenly changed into a hasty withdrawal. Instantly then Lee realized that Blowhard had blown himself out, that, expecting to meet an enemy flanked and in retreat, and meeting instead energetic attack, he had lost his nerve and now was committing himself to a defensive in the Wilderness thickets. There, Lee knew—from the nature of the ground with its tangle of scrub, few clearings, many swamps and ravines—Hooker's whole army would be helplessly entangled, the artillery without position, the cavalry almost useless, the infantry unable to maneuver except along a few narrow roads. And for him the problem at once became: how with forty-five thousand men—free to maneuver in the open behind a screen of woods—to carve up a headless, blindfold mass of seventy-five thousand men muffled in those same woods, while holding off another force of fifty thousand men to the east. He knew that Hooker had deployed a strong defensive line on his eastern front and that he would establish the remainder of his forces behind the long line of entrenchments facing south. This would be routine tactics. But what about the far flank of the Union line on the west? Would Hooker, facing advance from the east, also think to "refuse" his right flank and guard himself from the west? Probably not! In any case, with Sedgwick menacing his base and rear at Fredericksburg, there was no time for Lee to find out. Whatever action he took must be instant, backed by all the element of surprise.

That night Lee and Jackson held high council alone, over a tiny campfire near the Wilderness edge. And between them they evolved one of the most fantastically daring maneuvers in military history. With five thousand men left at Fredericksburg to hold off Sedgwick's menaced attack in the rear, Lee had but a scant forty thousand men wherewith to meet the entrenched seventy-five thousand men confronting him. Taking the line of uttermost risk, he once more split his force and, retaining only some twenty thousand troops to keep up a David-to-Goliath demonstration against the Union left and center, he dispatched Jackson with the remainder of his mobile force—amounting now actually to a little more than twenty-two thousand men—on a march clear across the whole Union front with a view to making an attack in force where Hooker would least expect it: on his western, and probably weakly defended, right flank. What made the maneuver so fantastic was not merely that Lee, by cutting his army into three parts widely separated by forest country, laid himself open to a double counterthrust through the gaps between his forces—an offensive that could have rolled him up on all sides in complete debacle—but that Jackson's flanking march must be made along a road that for half its length was parallel to the Union lines and separated from them by little more than a mile width of screening scrub land. The fact is that Lee and Jackson simply were betting on Hooker! Having seen him make a brilliant offensive gesture, then huddle back and cover up, they expected nothing more than a nervous defensive. And luck was with them. Of course, columns of troops, encumbered with artillery, baggage trains, ambulances, could not crawl all day along an enemy front within gunshot without presently being discovered. But at that moment when, half their march completed, they were at last discovered, it happened that the road they followed curved sharply southwest, clear away from the Union lines, thus giving them the appearance of being in full retreat.

Sickles, in command of the Third Corps on the Union center, apprised by scouts of an enemy movement across his front, immediately sent word to Hooker and rode forward in person to reconnoiter. Plainly the sight of the massive column marching southwest, back turned to the Union front, indicated the retreat of Lee's whole army. Excitedly he sent back a galloper with a report of the good news and asking leave to attack. Hooker, who had based all his strategy on the surmise that Lee, finding himself three-quarters surrounded, would quit the field, had a moment of renewed exaltation. He had been right after all! The Confederate demonstration on his left had been nothing more than a feint to cover the retreat of the whole army! Excitedly he gave Sickles orders to attack at once with two divisions of his corps—those of Birney and Whipple; and by way of supporting columns, sent him also Williams's division of the Second Corps and Bigelow's Brigade of the Twelfth Corps. At the same time he dispatched General Pleasonton, "the little cavalry commander," to place his four hundred horse and five batteries of field artillery at Sickles's command and go forward himself to assist in the necessary disposition of troops. This done, in a final burst of bombast he telegraphed Sedgwick "to cross the river and capture Fredericksburg and everything in it and vigorously pursue the enemy," adding, with magnificent idiocy, "We know that the enemy is fleeing, trying to save his trains. . . . Sickles' divisions are among them." This before Sickles had marched a yard. Then, as though the world once more were his, he was sending circular instructions to all his corps commanders to replenish their supplies of "forage, provisions, and ammunitions" and be prepared for a rapid pursuit march at dawn. So much for Hooker —while Jackson, circling back on a bold arc, was stealthily preparing to crash through the forest screen in a smashing surprise attack on the Union armies' heedless and unprepared western flank!

Before Sickles could throw his men into action, the main body of Jackson's column already had passed and was far to the south on its apparent path of retreat. Nothing but cavalry could reach it now. And had Stoneman's twelve thousand horse been present, instead of conducting an absurd nuisance raid far to the south, they, of themselves, could have cut it into helpless fragments, and brought the Lee-Jackson wild maneuver to its just military conclusion. As it was, all Sickles could do was to throw his infantry upon Jackson's rear guard. In a hot fight he routed them, took five hundred prisoners. But by that time the enemy column had completely disappeared.

Then it was that Sickles, hounding after the remnant of Jackson's troops on his right, became aware of Confederate forces still massed in position on his left—and suddenly realized that what he had been attacking was no army in retreat but the rear of a powerful flanking column bent on mischief to the west. Instantly he dispatched an aide to Hooker with the information and, requesting reinforcements, begged permission to change front and throw his force against the newly discovered enemy contingents. An hour earlier such a disruption of the Confederate maneuver well might have decided the day. Executed with Sickles's customary energy and co-ordinated with a simultaneous advance of the Union center (such as any commanding general worth his salt would have launched), it would have rolled up Lee's small "demonstration" force, leaving Jackson in mid-air, unsupported, to meet envelopment, massacre, or flight in face of an enemy four times his strength. But the suggestion came too late! Hooker had foreseen nothing, planned nothing; had left everything to luck and Lee. And before Sickles's aide could return with the impatiently awaited orders, suddenly, out of the already fading west, belched red uproar. Jackson, having completed his desperate sickle-shaped march, was bursting—through thickets that tattered and stripped his men—down upon the Union right flank. There the Eleventh Corps, largely German in composition, convinced that the Confederates were in retreat, had stacked their guns and were peacefully engaged in cooking and eating the evening meal. Howard, their commander, afterward claimed that he had received no specific orders from Hooker to be on the alert against a flank attack. Be that as it may, it seems incredible that a commander of his experience should have failed to carry out the routine procedure of protecting his flank with a substantial force facing west, or, in dense country, have failed to throw out an adequate picket line against possible surprise from a screened enemy. But he appears to have taken neither of these precautions—at least in any sufficient measure.

Approaching in three lines through a shroud of woods, at first stealthily as panthers, directed only by orders whispered from mouth to mouth, Jackson's men would have crept right in on the Union flank without need to fire a shot had it not been for the startled deer and quail and hare that fled before them—apprising the feasting Germans that "something was coming"! Then along a mile front burst the rebel yell. The rest was pandemonium, rout, massacre.

The power of a surprise flank offensive, of course, lies in the simple fact that masses of men formed to face an attack from one direction are helpless—until re-formed—to resist an attack from any other direction. And to re-form troops at dusk, in the midst of a forest, in face of a yelling, shooting onslaught—and soon a maddened mass of fugitives—was a virtual impossibility. The Eleventh Corps, hurled back upon the Twelfth Corps, threw it also into confusion and panic. And soon the whole Turnpike, running from Dowdall's Tavern on the west wing to Chancellorsville, the army center and headquarters, was choked with crazed men, thundering wagons, careening caissons, bellowing cattle, in mad stampede.

Instantly Sickles realized that the force he had been pursuing to the south already had swung about and was attacking from the west—before he could cut it off from its base by his countermove against Lee. Ordering his divisions under Birney and Whipple to reverse front, form column of line, and follow him, he galloped back with Pleasonton toward Chancellorsville. Coming up from the shallow valley where he had been engaged, he could see nothing of what was going on, but topping a low bare mound known as Hazel Grove—a mile or so southwest of Chancellorsville House and commanding a large clearing—he suddenly came upon a chaos of panic. Before him the whole terrain was a churning mass of animals and men in frenzied flight. Already the foul swamp on his right was bedded with floundering wagons, stalled artillery, choking fugitives, making a bloody bridge for the rout that poured over them.

Fortunately, it was right here that Pleasonton had parked his five batteries and, in a little well-screened hollow near by, posted his four hundred horse before cantering forward with a small escort to help Sickles organize his attack. But at that very moment the whole position was being overrun and rendered useless by the fleeing horde. At the same time down the Turnpike, a little to the right, and through the woods directly in front, scarcely two hundred yards away, the Rebels already were emerging, shooting, yelling in demoniac pursuit. Nothing but artillery could stop that advance. But before the guns, parked facing south, could be wheeled into position facing west, the field of fire must be cleared. And Sickles, with bitter decision, ordered Pleasonton's cavalry escort to charge the panic-stricken mob and drive them off to the right. But to wheel and realign twenty guns on rough terrain takes minutes—and minutes were few. It was plain that unless something could be done to check the oncoming Confederates, the guns would be taken before they could be served. And Sickles knew that his position, once captured, would enable the enemy to command the whole field of action and turn a routed wing into a routed army. The only help at hand was Pleasonton's cavalry in the little hollow behind him. And even while the escort was clearing the ground ahead and with slash of whips and shouts of men the guns were swinging into position, he ordered the troop into action. At the trumpet call "To horse!" four hundred lounging men were leaping to their saddles and, in three squadrons in column of four, were topping the mound at a canter. Hidden in their hollow, oblivious of what was taking place, believing the firing and uproar to come from the recent attack on the retreating Rebels, not even the officers, for a moment, realized what it was that was expected of them. But one glance at the havoc-strewn field before them, the dim forest spurting flame, and they knew. Pleasonton rode to meet Major Huey, in command. "We are flanked! The enemy is advancing in force down the Turnpike. You will charge them, cut your way through, then wheel right and try to reach our lines again if you can." At the same time Sickles was exchanging a rapid word with young Major Keenan, in charge of the first squadron—a man he much prized. "I am sorry to do this, Keenan, but it's our only chance." With a quick smile Keenan saluted. "I will do it!" Major Huey shrilled the order to advance. In perfect cavalry fashion, walking quietly a hundred paces, then trotting, then cantering, then bursting into a mad gallop, four hundred men charged an oncoming host of twenty-two thousand! At the point where the Turnpike, now crammed rank upon rank with Confederates, debouches into the open terrain before Chancellorsville, they crashed with slashing sabers into the head of the column. Falling like leaves, horse and man, before a blast of bullets, the first squadron yet managed to throw the enemy into an instant of confusion. The second and third squadrons, immediately behind, met momentarily empty guns and rode a thinning charge over ground cluttered with floundering horses, shattered men. Saved in part by dusk, audacity, surprise, the survivors then swerved off into the forest toward their own lines. For a moment the Rebels, scattering right and left, had thought that the whole Union cavalry was coming down on them. And, before they had recovered from their panic, Pleasonton had his guns in position and was raking their front with shrapnel aimed to ricochet into their ranks at a three-foot level. Nothing could stand against that murderous, searching fire. And the Rebels, halted in their berserk pursuit, wilted back into the shelter of the forest. The attack had been stalled. But at cost! In that Balaclava charge 121 men, including thirty officers, had ridden into the "jaws of hell," never to come back—among them the brave Keenan, found dead at dawn with thirteen bullets in his body.

Sickles's and Pleasonton's bloody check, backed by nightfall, brought a temporary lull to Jackson's onslaught, and thus gave Howard and Slocum an opportunity to re-form their shattered lines before Chancellorsville.

Meanwhile, under a full moon, the infantry divisions of Birney, Whipple, and Bigelow, wearied by their belated, if successful, attack on Jackson's rear guard, had followed their commander back to Hazel Grove—still the key point of the entire action. And now, for the third time that day, Sickles requested permission to attack. And, for the third time, Hooker, now completely dazed, acquiesced.

Twice on his own account Sickles had seized the initiative soundly and well and had been cheated only because he did not have the facts of the situation before him and had been compelled to improvise his own strategy on the spot without more than the passive consent of a collapsed commander. And now that, at last, he had the facts before him—a routed right wing, a powerful, triumphant enemy ambushed in thick woods waiting only for dawn to complete the disruption of the whole Union army—he was determined to take the initiative once more, and this time to good purpose, play back surprise, and, at the point of the bayonet, impale the Rebels where they lurked trusting to forest darkness. His men were weary, but also they were raw with disappointment and the sense of gross mishandling from Headquarters. In the way that troops will on the field of action, they already knew how Sickles had stopped the Rebel advance, had heard of Keenan's gallant charge, Pleasonton's murderous barrage. All right! Here was a fighter—and a fight! If, with nothing but cold steel, they had to rout out an enemy fortressed in black forest, they would go. The Rebs be damned! They had been told that Pleasonton's artillery would play over them and that Berry, of Slocum's corps, would support them on the right. And in they went.

General Williams, sitting in his saddle at the head of his reserve division of infantry and artillery at Hazel Grove, was in a position to observe the whole action; and in a letter to a friend a few days later gave unforgettable account of it:

A tremendous roll of infantry fire, mingled with yellings and shoutings almost diabolical and infernal, opened the conflict as Sickles' divisions went into the attack. For some time my infantry and artillery kept silent, and in the intervals of the musketry, I could distinctly hear the oaths of the rebel officers, evidently having hard work to keep their men from stampeding. In the meantime Sickles' artillery opened, firing over the heads of the charging infantry, and the din of arms and inhuman yellings and cursings redoubled. All at once, Berry's division, across the road on our right, opened in heavy volleys, and Knipe (commanding my right brigade) followed suit. Best (chief of artillery of the Twelfth Corps) began to thunder with his thirty-odd pieces. In front, and on the flanks, shell and shot were poured into these woods which were evidently crowded with rebel masses preparing for a morning attack. Along our front, and Sickles' flank, probably fifteen thousand or more musketry were belching an almost incessant stream of flame, while, from the elevation just in the rear of each line, from forty to fifty pieces of artillery kept up an uninterrupted roar, re-echoed from the woods with a redoubled uproar from the bursting shells which seemed to fill every part of them with fire and fury. Human language can give no idea of such a scene—such an infernal and yet sublime contemplation of sound and flame and smoke, and dreadful yells of rage, of pain, of triumph or of defiance. Suddenly, almost on the instant, the tumult is hushed, hardly a voice can be heard. One would almost suppose that the combatants were holding breath to listen for one another's movements. But the contest was not renewed.*

Commenting on these twelve hours of desperate struggle, Stine, in his *History of the Army of the Potomac* (pp. 353, 390), concludes, "If Sickles had not brought up his command in time to strike Jackson's right and rear, there is no telling where disaster to Hooker's army might have ended. . . . His subsequent night attack against Jackson was one of the most brilliant actions in military history." He might have added that from forenoon to midnight of that day Sickles had fought three different types of major engagement—a pursuit, a check, a counterattack—on two fronts, each one improvised, each one successful, and two of them executed amid conditions of pandemonium.

Ironically, it was not in the fury of that night of flame and slaughter, but in the lull of exhaustion and confusion succeeding it, that the Confederates suffered their severest loss. Jackson had ridden forward with his staff down the Plank Road to reconnoiter. With his usual daring he had crept almost to the Union lines. Suddenly came a burst of fire. He wheeled and galloped back with his escort.

*Quoted from *History of the Army of the Potomac* (pp. 355-56), by J. H. Stine.

But, as he neared the Confederate line, came another burst of fire. His own men, keyed to hysteria, had mistaken his troop for Union cavalry. Under that volley, twice repeated, but two or three of the escort came through unscathed. Jackson was mortally wounded. . . . Lingering, the pious, fanatical genius of the Rebel army passed the command of his division to its *beau sabreur*, the youthful, dandified, incomparable cavalry leader, "Jeb" Stuart. A few days later, clutching Lee's noble last-minute message, "I wish it had been myself rather than you," he raised himself, shouting orders in momentary delirium, then relaxed with a quiet smile and the loveliest *l'envoi* given human lips: "Let us pass over the river and rest under the shade of the trees."

Hooker already had lost his overwhelming advantage of surprise, even any semblance of a sound defensive—and more than ten thousand men. But Lee had lost much more. He had lost "Stonewall," the right arm of his power.

The next morning Sickles still held on to Hazel Grove. But Stuart, realizing that it was the key to the whole position, pressed him with desperate élan. Charge after charge was wiped out in bloody repulse; but still the Grays re-formed and came on. An eyewitness of the action (*Campfire and Battlefield*, p. 246) gives an amusing thumbnail sketch of Sickles at the moment, cool, sardonic, electric.

The corps colors were already advancing. General Sickles, smoking a cigar, was standing a few feet from the regiment about to attack, when a dismounted orderly hobbled up to him in a great state of excitement. "General, my horse has been killed." Came the calm reply, "Captain, the government will furnish you with another." Just at that moment a captured Rebel officer of high rank, passing on his way to the rear, recognized the general and, stepping aside, tried to open up a conversation with him:

"General, how do you do? I had the pleasure of meeting you in New York."

"Move that battery forward!"

"But General, I am quite sure that you——"

"The Brigade will advance!"

"General, don't you remember——?"

"Go to the rear, sir! I am about to attack!"

Sickles's ammunition was running dangerously low. Again and again he sent his aide, Major Tremaine, to Chancellorsville to beg

for one train of the many trains of shot and shell he knew lay idle
to the rear. But although the enemy was stalled, exhausted, and
Slocum, Humphreys, Hancock, and Couch by their own efforts
had improvised a contracted but still powerful front, Hooker already
had decided to abandon the field. And Sickles, facing a new onslaught with empty guns, received—instead of the idle ammunition
that would have saved the day—orders to retreat. . . .

Thus to surrender, without reason or necessity, a position that,
once in Stuart's hands, would enable him to join forces with Lee on
his right, rake the retreating Union army with his own massed
artillery, and in combined attack complete the rout already begun,
seemed to Sickles criminal madness. Turning the command over to
Pleasonton, he galloped off to Headquarters. As he drew rein at the
Chancellorsville mansion, he noticed that Hooker was on the balcony
above him, leaning broodily against one of its wooden pillars. Without waiting to dismount, and standing in his stirrups, Sickles had
just begun to shout his protest when, as ironic luck would have it,
a shell struck the pillar Hooker was using for spine and knocked
him unconscious. At once the rumor spread that he had been killed.
But he quickly recovered and a few minutes later mounted his horse
and rode among the troops to show that "Fighting Joe" was still in
action. It was his last gesture. Quickly he retired to a tent far to
the rear and took to bed. He was not really hurt—a bit bruised and
shaken, that was all. But the shock had completed his collapse. And
just as he had left the field at Antietam because of a slight foot
wound that interfered no whit with his riding, so now he quit
Chancellorsville—with nothing more than a bad bump! To Sickles he
peevishly reiterated his original order. He would send him no more
ammunition "since it only would fall into enemy hands"!

Hazel Grove, the strategic key to the whole field of battle, held
at terrible blood cost, still could have been used to mount a counterattack in overwhelming force—for Anderson's corps of forty thousand men had not yet fired a shot. And to hand it over to the enemy
as a gift was, for Sickles, the bitterest experience of his military career.
From that moment he knew that, for all his efforts, for all the
valiant struggle of Slocum, Couch, Meade, Hancock to retrieve the
field, the Union army faced once more—at the hands of hapless
command—shameful, inexcusable defeat. Hoarsely he ordered his
guns drawn off, his men to form column of march. And Stuart,

watching through field glasses scarcely a mile away, could not believe his eyes. "By the Eternal!—they're packing up and going home!" Within the hour, massing his own artillery where Sickles had planted his, he was blasting Chancellorsville to kindling, punishing the huddled, retreating Union center, and hilariously joining hands with Lee. In a solid arc now both forces prepared to drive the Yankees into the river in a final rout. But at that moment came word that Sedgwick had crossed the Rappahannock, taken Fredericksburg, and was coming down on the Confederate flank. Hooker with seventy-five thousand men in line of battle had called upon Sedgwick with twenty-five thousand men to come and save him! Under the circumstances Lee decided that before he could finish Hooker he had better brush Sedgwick out of the way. Deliberately he denuded his front of all but a skirmishing line and threw himself on this new danger. Sedgwick, expecting to meet Union troops, met instead a yelling line of Rebs in front, in flank, and soon in rear. With a perilously thin line Lee had surrounded him. Receiving no support, and guessing that Hooker must have met disaster, Sedgwick skillfully maneuvered his forsaken divisions northward to the river and, fighting a desperate rear-guard action, successfully forded them. Lee then turned back to dispose of the main Union force.

But Hooker, leaving Sedgwick to his fate, was not even waiting to be disposed of! Hastily he had called his corps commanders together to decide, of all things, whether to attack or retreat! In his simpleton's heart he believed that, in their present discouraged state, they would vote for retreat—and thus enable him to shift the onus of the final decision to their shoulders. There is little doubt that, even at that late hour, any one of them, given full command and the use of the entire force—including Anderson's forty thousand idle, chafing men—could have turned and thrashed Lee's exhausted little army. And they knew it. But Hooker, lounging on his cot, nursing his bruises, showed no sign of relinquishing command. Nevertheless Meade and Howard voted for attack. Reynolds, not yet having been engaged, felt that he could not vote either way. Slocum's attitude was foreknown; he had proven himself able to hold Jackson's right wing amid all the frenzy of rout—but he was on active service with his line and could not be present. Couch, the senior corps commander, reserved his decision. "Before I give my voice, I first wish to know what the plan of operations will be and who will command." Hooker promptly sat up. "I shall decide the plan of operations—and I shall command them." Couch was coldly decisive. "In that case, General, I vote for immediate retreat across the river." Pretending not to notice the biting tone, content that he had the senior commander for buffer, Hooker turned on Sickles. "And you?" Sick at heart, loathing the idea of retreat, but realizing that so long as the Army of the Potomac remained south of the Rappahannock under Hooker's command it simply would be served up for slaughter at Lee's hands, Sickles voted with Couch. Whereupon Hooker—for two days now wishing himself safely across the river—pretended to make the final decision himself and, turning to Couch, indicating the rear-guard positions he wished him to occupy, ordered an immediate retreat.

Thanks to the utter exhaustion of Lee's small force and the tireless, efficient Couch—twice wounded, his horse shot under him, but still carrying on—the Army of the Potomac, despite floodwaters, withdrew in good order and without undue loss. And with it recrossed forty thousand cursing reserves who had never been permitted to sight a Rebel, and miles of ammunition trains never unloaded; while from Marye's Heights to Dowdall's Tavern seventeen thousand men had been buried or cremated alive in the flaming woods, crippled or captured—in cruelest waste. Chancellorsville, opening in brilliant surprise, had ended in defeat grotesque.

CHAPTER XXV

Improvisation at Gettysburg

——————◆——————

JUNE 1863. Two years of rigorous campaigning and increasing responsibility had hammered Sickles into a seasoned commander. Under four disastrous generals he had been compelled to realize that the Army of the Potomac had been, still was, and probably always would be a "headless army"; and that, hitherto, it had been saved from annihilation only by the stubborn quality of its rank and file, the desperate efforts of its officer personnel. All of this, naturally, ordered his military thinking, caused him to conclude that in future actions he would have to do what he just had been forced to do—make the most of whatever opportunities appeared on his own front and trust that, once engaged, Headquarters would back him up. And it was in this state of mind that he crawled with the army —still under Hooker—back to Falmouth.

Lee, meanwhile, reinforced by Longstreet, already was creeping craftily westward and northward—up the Shenandoah Valley. With only half the force now at his command, he had administered the Union army its severest defeat in a long history of defeat. Now he rode right into the heart of the enemy country, circling for the kill! On the face of it that march of his, like his flanking foray at Chancellorsville, seemed a perilous gamble. While he had held, repulsed, or whipped the Army of the Potomac wherever the two had met in anything like full force, he never had been able to destroy it, cripple it, nor, more than momentarily, reduce its soon recruited fighting strength. And what he had been unable to accomplish on his own ground, close to his own base, with a whole population for spies, he now proposed to do on enemy ground, far from his own base, subject to imminent attack, flank and rear, amid a bitterly hostile people keen to play eyes and ears for his opponent.

But the adventure was not as mad as it looked. Never was a general so befriended by sheer terrain. On his rapid, hidden thrust across northern Virginia from Fredericksburg to Williamsport—where he forded the upper reaches of the Potomac—and thence north to Chambersburg, his temporary headquarters, he was shielded on his right flank successively by the Rappahannock and Shenandoah rivers, the Blue Ridge and the South mountains. And he was well into Pennsylvania before Hooker, squatting at Falmouth, became cognizant that the enemy he believed to be facing him across the river was already far behind his back! And just as Lee was shielded by terrain and knew how to make the most of it, so he was shielded by Lincoln's concern, Halleck's morbid anxiety, for the safety of Washington; and he knew how to make the most of that also. Well aware that the Army of the Potomac had no freedom to "seek out and destroy the enemy wherever he may be," but that it must always

work on a leash tied to the White House, he took the bold chance
that, in face of his invasion, it would be permitted neither to march
on his unprotected base at Richmond, nor cut his communications
at his Williamsport fording, nor make a flank attack upon him
through the South Mountain passes—his three supreme hazards—
but that Halleck would keep it hugged to an inner circle guarding
the capital. Which is exactly what happened! Hooker begged to be
allowed to march on Richmond. He was refused. Then, shifting
his forces northward to Edwards Ferry, and crossing the Potomac,
he begged to use the idle garrison of over ten thousand men at Harpers Ferry and, reinforcing them with two divisions, cut Lee's line
of communications to the rear. Again he was refused. And at that
he resigned. And George Gordon Meade, a well-balanced, if by no
means brilliant, commander, suddenly found himself, at Lincoln's
behest, charged with the responsibility of meeting the supreme crisis
of the war—under precisely the same restrictions.

Thus, shielded by terrain and the Administration psychology,
Lee was enabled to proceed almost at leisure up the Shenandoah and
Cumberland valleys, debouch through Chester Gap, and spread his
forces in a broad arc clear across Pennsylvania as far as Harrisburg
—an arc that parachute-wise had road-strings concentrating at
Gettysburg, within but three days' march due south to Washington!

In all of this—it may be noted parenthetically—Lee made but one
mistake. Curiously, as did Hooker at Chancellorsville, he denuded
himself of his cavalry—permitting "Jeb" Stuart to take his whole
body of horse off on a raid behind the enemy's rear, thus depriving
himself of the means of ascertaining with any certainty Meade's intentions. Thus, in the upshot, he virtually blundered upon the advance left wing of the Union army and had no recourse but to give
battle on unfavorable ground not of his own choosing.

But carefully as Lee had calculated the protective factors in his
favor, and dangerously self-confident as he had become, it may be
doubted if he would have undertaken his invasion had it not been
for a series of bitter compulsions. He needed shoes for his barefoot
army; and these could be had only in the North. Also he needed
food, fodder, horses—long stripped from war-trampled Virginia but
abounding in the rich farmlands of Pennsylvania. But more than
that, the South was running out of everything except courage. Its
ports blockaded, the whole Mississippi—save only beleaguered Vicks-

burg—in the hands of the enemy, it faced economic collapse unless a quick decision could be reached. Moreover, one more victory—and this time on northern soil menacing the capital—could be counted upon to produce two feverishly desired results: it would encourage the already strong northern peace party to demand a cessation of hostilities and an agreement with the South; and—supreme consideration!—it might well precipitate the long-pending recognition of the Confederacy by England and France, thus paving the way for British aid, at least, in breaking the Union blockade. Added to this there was the possibility that the campaign, whether successful or not, might drive Halleck to withdraw a stout portion of Grant's troops from before doomed Vicksburg in order to safeguard Washington.

Such, in brief, was the intricate mesh of reasons, from footgear to power politics, which launched Lee on the most unorthodox military adventure of his career. He did not know that in the ranks of the Union army lurked a corps commander as much given to the bold and unorthodox as himself! He did not reckon that Sickles, who had balked his *grand coup* at Chancellorsville with a swiftly improvised change of front, would balk him again in much the same manner at Gettysburg!

No more than Lee did Meade deliberately choose Gettysburg as a field of battle. The one already had decided to make his stand at Cashtown, some twenty miles to the west of it. There, backed by the South Mountain, with Chester Gap—a perfectly protected path of supply and retreat—immediately in his rear, he felt he would have a practically impregnable position. The other had selected the south bank of Pipe Creek, a sound defensive line covering Baltimore and Washington, about thirty miles to the south. But the gods decreed that a strong detachment of Confederates foraging for shoes at Gettysburg should come into collision there with a Union cavalry reconnaissance in force, under Buford. The engagement, once begun, rapidly sucked increasing support from both sides; and, before the day was over, the two armies—of some eighty-five thousand Blues and seventy-five thousand Grays—were converging in full force upon what had been, but a few hours before, a sleepy, obscure little village.

Gettysburg, with its ten intersecting cross-country roads, was an admirable concentration point for either army; and to prevent the enemy from using it for this purpose, Meade already had ordered

Reynolds, commanding the Union left wing, to push forward and occupy it with his own First Corps and place the other two corps under his command—Howard's Eleventh and Sickles's Third—at nearby points to protect his flank and rear. Thus Buford, aware of Reynolds' rapid approach, fought fiercely to hold the town against his arrival. Meanwhile, however, the far-flung Confederate forces, alarmed by the news of the growing battle, were also pouring toward Gettysburg—from York in the east, Harrisburg and Carlisle in the north, Cashtown on the west. Reynolds, arriving on the field, found Buford making a last stand; and, quickly realizing that his own troops were greatly outnumbered, and in immediate danger of being flanked, sent a call for help to Sickles, his nearest subordinate commander.

Sickles, with his Third Corps, had been posted at Emmitsburg, some ten miles to the southwest, with special orders from Meade to examine its suitability for a battleground and to hold it against a possible flank movement of the enemy. But an emergency summons from a ranking officer such as Reynolds could not be ignored. There was no time to consult Meade—many miles to the rear. Leaving two brigades to hold Emmitsburg, Sickles immediately putting his men on the march, dispatched a galloper to Meade reporting his action and requesting that definite orders of approval or recall be sent to him en route. Meade, realizing now that the battle was joined, instantly approved Sickles's action, sent the remaining two brigades forward, and commanding Howard, with his Eleventh Corps, and Hancock, with the Fifth, to follow in support, issued general orders for the whole army to advance and concentrate at Gettysburg. At the same time, and with a like rapidity, Lee, cheated of his chosen position at Cashtown, was marshaling all his forces to the same field —bent upon decisive battle.

During those last hours of July 1, 1863, in one of the bloodiest and bitterest engagements of the war, Buford's three thousand horse, supported by the First and Eleventh corps, outnumbered and overpowered, were driven back to Cemetery Ridge, a fairly steep hogback running some five miles south from the edge of Gettysburg. The battle had opened inauspiciously for the North. But only technically could the tenacious, if broken, resistance of Buford, Reynolds, Howard, and their men be regarded as a defeat. Actually it was a valuable, although costly, holding action—giving time for the main body of the Union army to arrive on the field.

Already it was dusk. The exhausted Confederates, fearing the presence of powerful Union reinforcements on their front, desisted from further attack. Reynolds had been killed early in the action. And Hancock, now in command, instantly appreciating the strategic advantages of Cemetery Ridge, proceeded to reorganize the shattered troops and set them to throwing up earthworks along its rocky five-mile length; while every hour throughout the night, up the Emmitsburg Road, the Taneytown Road, and Baltimore Pike came the dust-muffled tramp of heavy columns, the growl of artillery caissons, ammunition trains, supply wagons, as the Army of the Potomac wheeled into position. At midnight Meade arrived and under the pale glare of a full moon hastily examined the ground and the disposition of the troops. Across the narrow valley to the west, on wooded Seminary Ridge—the twin of Cemetery—the Confederates also were massing, felling trees, erecting abatis. And Lee, with Longstreet at his side, was riding from point to point, giving last orders. Tomorrow—the grapple!

Dawn of the fateful Second Day at Gettysburg revealed the fact that the position hurriedly occupied by the Union army during the night, was—for all its eleventh-hour adoption—one remarkably well adapted to the defensive battle Meade proposed. Protected on its southern extremity by two rugged, boulder-strewn mounds—the one, Big Round Top, some three hundred feet high, too precipitous for any military purpose, yet still an obstacle to the enemy; the other, Little Round Top, just north of the first and a hundred feet lower, a key position for infantry and light artillery—it ran thence three miles northward along the gradually rising crest of Cemetery Ridge, and finally curled back upon itself on the steep, half-moon, wooded height known as Culp's Hill. Thus, following the natural contours of the country, it presented a striking resemblance to a fishhook. And while this comparison from a bird's-eye view has become customary, it seems to have escaped notice hitherto that the Union horizon line viewed from the Confederate side presented precisely the same appearance. Lay a fishhook flat, and you have the one; stand it on its side, only butt and barb touching the table, and you have the other. The high curve of the barb would be

Culp's Hill; the shank, the down-sloping crest of Cemetery Ridge; the butt—supposing it to be a rather pronounced knob—would be Little Round Top. But while this position, with its well-buttressed flanks and short interior line, was decidedly strong, it had one very weak spot: the lowest section of the "shank" just before it joined the "butt." Here the ground was not only low but swampy, thicketed, ill defined, lacking in artillery positions, and cut up by small ravines obstructive to troop movements. Moreover, it was commanded—a mile to the west—by high ground where a stone-walled enclosure (the Peach Orchard) offered the enemy excellent emplacement for his own batteries. For while Lee's line—deployed along Seminary Ridge parallel to Cemetery Ridge, thence down through Gettysburg and around the base of Culp's Hill—closely conformed to Meade's "fishhook" line of defense, the terrain it occupied exhibited a quite contrary order of elevation. And thus while its lowest point, the Village, confronted the peak of the Union position (Culp's Hill), its highest point—the southern region of Seminary Ridge marked by the Peach Orchard—dominated the lowest point on the Union front. And, as luck would have it, this depressed sector was the one given Sickles to hold.

It happened that Geary had occupied this same sector for a few hours the previous night with his Second Division of Slocum's Twelfth Corps. Meade's instructions to Sickles, therefore, were to establish his troops along the vacated line. But Geary had left no line, had been given no time—before he was ordered to the right—to do more than bivouac "in position," and had withdrawn long before the Third Corps began to arrive on the ground. Sickles thus was left in considerable doubt as to the exact location and extent of his sector, and had to appeal to Meade for more specific directions. But, apart from a glimpse by moonlight, Meade had found no opportunity to inspect his left. Consequently his instructions were explicit enough as to "line of front" but delivered without any actual cognizance of the ground to be occupied. Indicating the Round Tops as marking the terminus of the Union left, he ordered Sickles to cover them and extend his troops due north until he contacted Hancock's Second Corps on Cemetery Ridge—in other words to protect the "butt" and lower part of the "shank" in the already well-defined "fishhook" line.

But, examining the position allotted him, Sickles quickly became aware not only that, for the most part, it ran through a broken, tangled swale but that he had by no means enough troops to cover it; that if he connected with Hancock on his right, he could not man the vitally important crest of Little Round Top on his left. He thus faced the disturbing fact that, until Sykes with the Fifth Corps—assigned to his support—could reinforce him, he would have to leave one flank or the other unprotected, "in air." And he drew small comfort from the knowledge that Sykes, at the moment, was thirty miles away! And scarcely had he dispatched a report of his situation to Meade when he was shocked to discover that, by some blunder at Headquarters, Buford's cavalry, stationed hitherto just behind Little Round Top to guard his sector—and thus the whole Union left—against an encircling movement from the south, had been withdrawn, sent back to base at Westminster far to the rear, *and had not been replaced!*

Sickles was now thoroughly concerned. He had been long enough at war to know that—down in a hole, commanded from the front, unprotected on his left, unsupported to his rear, and without troops enough to fill out his line—he stood at the mercy of the enemy. But what troubled him most was the realization that, should the Confederates—repeating Jackson's trick at Chancellorsville—crash in on his left flank, he would find himself, like Howard, helplessly aligned the wrong way; and that once his depleted Third Corps was enveloped, crushed, the whole Union line, taken in reverse, would go with it. Was it then to be Chancellorsville again? . . . Determined to put his predicament before Meade in person, he galloped off to Headquarters.

But he might have saved himself the trouble. Meade, completely convinced that the major attack would be launched against Culp's Hill, was too intensely preoccupied with strengthening his right to spare much thought for his left. . . . Cavalry protection? Yes—it had been ordered; but the squadrons assigned were some hours' march away. As to reinforcements—Sykes, with his Fifth Corps, was coming up, and, in due time, would provide them. For the present no others were available. And when Sickles, arguing in terms of *tactics*, requested permission to advance his troops from their present low, jumbled position to more defensible ground on his front and left, he was met with refusal based upon the hoary maxim of *strategy* which decrees that, in adopting a battle line, a commander must consider the whole as paramount to the parts, in other words "take the fat with the lean." It was the old clash between the well-tested general rule and the new particular case. Both men were right, the one tactically and realistically, the other strategically and theoretically. But it would have required a dispassionate executive intelligence—such as Meade did not possess—to combine both views to definite advantage.

Once more Sickles found himself, in face of the enemy, thrust upon his own devices. Believing—Meade to the contrary—that the onslaught would come on the left, and lacking cavalry for reconnaissance, he instructed General Birney, commanding his First Division, to advance a line of pickets along the Emmitsburg Road paralleling his front a mile to the west and throw out a skirmish line three hundred yards beyond. This "feeler" of his soon elicited a brisk fire from the woods on the southwest; and, strongly suspecting now that a considerable force was creeping around his flank, he dispatched General Berdan with a hundred United States Sharpshooters supported by the Third Main Infantry, to smoke it out.

Penetrating the forest screen, Berdan soon contacted enemy pickets and, in a sharp action, drove them in, to discover, as Sickles had surmised he would, a heavy enemy column stealthily circling toward the Union left. Dispatching an aide with the news, he gave orders to his men to fan out in line of fire. Instantly he had realized that the column must be delayed; and he knew that the only way to delay it was to engage it, throw it into confusion, make it believe itself beset by a powerful force.

It was a few score against thousands. But the Sharpshooters were virtuosi. Carefully selected, specially trained, many of them experienced Indian fighters, they were the keenest scouts, deadliest shots, cagiest crew at an ambush, in the Union army. Berdan knew he could trust them, the Third Main, too—self-reliant fellows, reared to hunting and a hardy life. And, in an action of pure, devoted bravado, he attacked. The sudden rapidly repeated blast of the Sharpshooters' new breechloaders threw the whole column into panic. Amid a haphazard crash of return fire, blurt of bugles, bawlings of officers, the Confederates, convinced that they were being flanked in force, first wavered, then rallied, and finally re-forming their line, advanced to the charge. Crushed back almost to the

Emmitsburg Road, Berdan, to the last stretch of daring, held them in play. Then, before they could discover their mistake, he skillfully withdrew. He had lost sixty of his men, but he had sprung the enemy's surprise, thrown a dangerous flanking maneuver off balance, given his commander time to prepare against it.

Sickles, meanwhile, had been carefully examining the rising ground on his left. Not yet had he received Berdan's report, but he scarcely needed it. A flanking assault from that direction was something that he now fully anticipated, and he already was preparing to counter it by a quick change of front. He knew that—Meade notwithstanding—he had no alternative if he would meet it from *commanding ground and face to face*, instead of *down in a hole aligned the wrong way*. What he sought, therefore, was a higher line of defense hinged on his present position and at right angles to it, so that, in a crisis, he could swing out his low westward-facing line—as one would swing open a gate—to a high southward-facing line, and thus meet the attack from uphill and head on. And it was not long before he had found what he sought—or, at least, a reasonable resemblance to it.

A few hundred yards away on his immediate left, and divided from Big Round Top by a swampy ravine (Plum Run), stood a grotesque, hundred-foot-high pile of boulders (Devil's Den)—good cover for an enemy attack but, by the same token, a good hinge for a defensive line. Thence northwesterly ran a low ridge, bare at first, but soon wooded—where it bordered a broad, upsloping clearing (the Wheat Field)—as far as the elevated ground on his front. Here the Emmitsburg Road—connecting the northern end of the Union position on Cemetery Ridge with the southern end of the Confederate parallel position on Seminary Ridge in a long, shallow diagonal—passed out of sight into enemy territory. And at this point stood the stone-walled Peach Orchard, the very spot from which he momentarily expected to be shelled—a vantage ground for the guns of either side.

Here, he decided, was his true fighting position. And if, for the present, he must remain where he had been put—facing west—he was determined that, at the first hint of assault from the south, he would swing out his whole line on the hinge of Devil's Den, deploying it along the partially wooded ridge as far as the Peach Orchard, and there "refuse" (bend back) the scanty remnant of his corps along the Emmitsburg Road. His proposed new emergency front, therefore, presented a broad spearhead with a long flange and a short flange: the long flange aligned against the expected major attack from the south; the short flange a temporary protection against encirclement from the west. Truly, by thus turning a sump into a salient, he would lose contact with Hancock on his right and Little Round Top on his left, and so leave both flanks dangerously "in air." But in his present position one flank would have to be left to luck anyhow; and here, aligned the wrong way, he could do little but await massacre. In his proposed position he at least could confront the onset, surprise, baffle, and—with luck—hold it until reinforcements could be massed to his support. Once more, therefore, he rode off to the little farmhouse on the Taneytown Road. There energetically he outlined his whole predicament, in view of a possible, and highly probable, enemy assault on his flank; and indicating the change of front required to meet it, he requested Meade to view the ground for himself and judge which of the two lines, the present or the proposed, offered the better chance of defense.

But Meade, still anticipating imminent attack on his right, skeptical of Sickles's fears for the left, and reluctant to make any alterations in what he deemed sound military dispositions, expressed himself as unable to leave Headquarters and his telegraph at such a critical moment. Sickles then begged that General Warren, that topographical chief—and general good genius—of the Headquarters staff, be allowed to examine his position and give his opinion. This, too, was refused. Finally, yielding to Sickles's insistence that he must have some advice, Meade delegated General Hunt, artillery chief of staff, to make the desired inspection.

Hunt, however, proved cautious and noncommittal. Agreeing that, especially in a lack of artillery positions, Sickles's sector was unsatisfactory, he contented himself with pointing out that the suggested new front, while offering definite advantages, was too long for the Third Corps to cover if Little Round Top was to be properly protected. And, unwilling to assume responsibility for authorizing any change in the established line, he rode off.

Sickles sat brooding in his saddle. His uncanny prescience was gnawing on him. Deep in himself he knew that Lee was outsmarting Meade, that the major attack would come not against the almost impregnable Union right but against his own decrepit left, that the new high line he had chosen was the only possible line of defense, and that if he did not occupy it now, *the enemy soon would!*

Berdan, seeking to penetrate the enemy's movements, had been out of communication for some time. Now suddenly his aide, astride a mare soapy with sweat and froth, came in with the scribbled report: "A powerful enemy column moving around your flank. . . . I am attacking." Sickles slid the note into his pouch and without a moment's hesitation ordered his corps to form line of march. Down the line the bugles were sounding, "Fall in!" And within a matter of minutes—while Hancock's men on Cemetery Ridge, sensing the situation, cheered uproariously—the Third Corps, in perfect division formation, colors flying, bayonets glinting in the brazen glare, the blue flag of the Excelsior Brigade leading the parade, marched up out of their sump hole and proceeded to deploy, in echelon, along their new upland position from Devil's Den to the Peach Orchard, and thence northward a space along the Emmitsburg Road. And on the instant, depressed, grouching men were larking, jubilant. Here they saw that, at least, they had elbow room, vista, shade, breeze, a chance to breathe—and to face fighting whatever the enemy had to offer.

Made, as they were, at driving speed, the dispositions yet took time; and it was already three o'clock before the last man and gun were in place. To Humphreys, a division commander with an exuberant delight in battle, Sickles assigned the protection of his right flank, with Carr's brigade aligned along the Emmitsburg Road supported by Brewster's Excelsiors. Graham's brigade, backed by thirty pieces of field artillery, he stationed at the peak of the salient—the Peach Orchard. Thence the ridge he had chosen for his main line of defense bent obtusely back toward Devil's Den. This mile-long sector he assigned to his senior commander, Birney, with his brigades of De Trobriand and Ward—the one occupying the wooded portion of the ridge, the other the bare portion. In support of this line he deployed Burling's brigade across the Wheat Field to the rear, at the same time planting twenty-six guns behind De Trobriand, two atop the Den, and four commanding Plum Run.

The movement had been made not a moment too soon. Scarcely had it been completed than an outburst of skirmish fire along the southwestern arc announced that the long-expected flanking on-slaught was about to break.

What had happened in the interval makes a curious piece of military history. Lee, at first, had concluded, rightly enough, that the Union left was anchored on the Round Tops. But mistaking Sickles's pickets at the Peach Orchard for an occupation in force, he sharply revised his judgment. Knowing Meade to be a strict academician, he could not conceive of him thrusting out an impudent and perilous salient on his flank; and, without a flicker of doubt, he assumed that the whole Union line had been advanced from Cemetery Ridge to the vicinity of the Emmitsburg Road and now terminated at the Peach Orchard. His flanking maneuver, therefore, was projected to envelope that point. And, consequently, his orders to Longstreet—commanding the movement—were to "attack by echelon up the Emmitsburg Road." Had his assumption been correct, this plan of attack would have paralleled, and might well have repeated, Jackson's coup at Chancellorsville. A broad line of troops marching north on both sides of the Emmitsburg Road would have curled around the Union position supposed to be aligned along it. And a simultaneous assault, front and rear, by successively advancing echelons would have proceeded to roll up the whole line from south to north. And, as a matter of fact, so convinced was Lee—seven miles away!—that this was the actual enemy position that not the most urgent, if belated, reports to the contrary from the scene of action—first from Longstreet, then from Ewell, leading the Confederate right wing—could induce him to change his original orders. Thus, in the supreme struggle of the Civil War, both generals completely misapprehended the situation confronting them; and, in the upshot, both had to be saved from the full toll of their errors by the last-minute directives—and technical disobedience—of their subordinate commanders. No more than Sickles could persuade Meade to see that an attack was impending on the left, not on the right, could Longstreet make Lee credit his too late discovery that the Union flank rested not on the Peach Orchard but on Little Round Top and Devil's Den a mile to the east!

By three o'clock a crescendo of skirmish fire to the southwest gave warning that Longstreet's massive corps was advancing on a wide front on either side of the Emmitsburg Road toward the Peach Orchard. Sickles, tense, galvanic, riding his lines, had every man nerved for the onset. But it was precisely at this moment that Meade, still blindly preoccupied with his right, chose to summon a conference of corps commanders at his headquarters. Sickles, pleading that he was in face of the enemy, requested to be excused, but was peremptorily refused. And, turning over his command to Birney, he galloped off. As he whirled up to the porch of the little farmhouse where Meade was conferring with Warren, Hunt, and Doubleday, chief of staff, the thunder of cannonading burst out behind him. Surprised, Meade sprang to his feet. "What is that, sir?" Sickles, without dismounting, saluted grimly. "I am under attack, General." It was a bad moment for Meade. The amateur had outguessed him. His own elaborate preparations on the right had gone for naught. And warned and warned again, he had given but one moonlit glance to his left. But he wasted no words. "You are excused from dismounting. Return to your command, sir. I will follow you."

Coming up on the "spearhead" at a gallop, Warren at his side, Meade appeared amazed at Sickles's dispositions—and this despite the fact that they had been under discussion all morning and had been made nearly two hours before! Stung by the belated criticism, Sickles countered coldly, "I will withdraw to my original position, if that is what you prefer, General." A burst of shrapnel overhead pointed the answer. "It is too late, sir—those people won't let you!"

In consternation Meade saw that, with the enemy coming down in full force, Sickles's salient stood wholly "in air," that its long flange facing the immediate assault failed to cover Little Round Top on the left, and that its short flange along the Emmitsburg Road failed, by half a mile, to connect with Hancock on Cemetery Ridge. Sickles knew it as well as Meade. And he also knew that if a tithe of the attention given to the right had been given to the left, those gaps would not be there. But there was no time—as yet—for recriminations. And if Meade had shown himself mistaken in his judgment, he now showed himself competent and decisive in emergency. Ordering Warren to seize upon any reserves he could find and instantly man Little Round Top, he proceeded to strip his whole line —even dangerously denuding his right—in vigorous effort to support Sickles's spearhead. But these measures, hastily improvised and uncoordinated as they were, failed tragically of the efficacy they would have had, taken an hour earlier.

At the same time Longstreet, equally suffering from misapprehension at Headquarters, and balked by Sickles's massing of troops across his supposedly open path between the Peach Orchard and Devil's Den, found himself compelled to extend his line eastward and concentrate his assault on Little Round Top—the true Union left. As important to Federal as to Confederate, and seized by the one only a minute before the other, this insignificant hump of rock turned on the instant to a human abattoir. Clotted with frenzied men grappling over boulders slimed with blood, it flew the Stars and Stripes, at last, only after Blue and Gray lay thick upon it as its own stones, and three Union leaders of the fight—Vincent, Weed, and the gallant young O'Rourke—had fallen on its crest.

Failing to capture Little Round Top, Longstreet fiercely pressed his attack along the line from Devil's Den to the Peach Orchard; and soon, also, along the Emmitsburg Road. By six o'clock—the sun dipping, a smoke-hazed ball in the west—the spearhead had been clutched and driven in from both sides.

Many efforts have been made to describe that delirious death struggle; but none has ever pretended to succeed. Suffice it to say that Sickles's reinforced salient, unbroken for the past three vital, valiant hours, finally collapsed in a coiling chaos of fight-maddened men and, foot by foot, was slowly crushed in—leaving six thousand wounded and dead upon the field.

But that most frightful affray of the Civil War was also its deciding crisis. When the salient had been flattened back into its original position—now massively reinforced—Lee already was defeated. The Confederate army had spent its strength—and gained nothing. The Union line simply had been hammered into impregnable solidity; and no soldier in gray—except as a prisoner—had set foot within it. The *grand coup* on the left had failed; and a minor attack on the right, momentarily successful, failed a few hours later. Gettysburg had one more day—and Pickett's sacrificial, foredoomed charge on the center. And not for two years would come Appomattox. But those five fierce hours of battering against Sickles's spearhead had broken the peak of the Rebel power, forecast its final destruction.

Throughout the action Sickles, riding back and forth along his front in a cold flame of excitement, had come through unscathed. But returning for a moment to his headquarters, the Throstle farmhouse in mid-field, he was struck by shrapnel—his right leg splintered from thigh to ankle. Fearing the effect the news might have upon his men, his orderlies rushed him to the rear. There, stoically smoking a cigar while he waited for the surgeon, he demanded to be kept informed of every development on the battle front. Within the hour his leg was amputated; and two days later he was dispatched to the base hospital in Washington. As his stretcher was borne from the train to the waiting ambulance, the curious crowd noted the imperturbable calm of this man who had made Lafayette Square echo to his cries of grief and rage. But the same Sickles who had slain Key and defied public opinion; and now—putting his own instincts ahead of orders—had thrown out his protective salient and compelled the whole Army of the Potomac to support him, still knew he was right! En route he had received news that the Union line held. Lee was in retreat! And his sense of inner sanction could not have been more complete had he foreknown that in later years three authoritative voices would sound his vindication: that the brilliant British military critic, Captain Cecil Battine, would write, ". . . the new position acted like a breakwater upon which the fury of the attack spent itself, and by the delay enabled all the Federal troops to come into line";* that Jesse Bowman Young, an eyewitness, and, thereafter, a lifetime student of the battle, would sum up his exhaustive investigation on this point with the declaration, "Longstreet's blow, falling upon the Third Army Corps, in its original position . . . could not have been warded off or withstood; it would have made a hole clean through the line to the Taneytown Road";† and, finally, that his defeated opponent, the chivalrous Longstreet, would write to him, "I believe that it is now conceded that the advanced position at the Peach Orchard, taken by your corps and under your orders, saved that battlefield to the Union cause. It was the sorest and saddest reflection of my life for many years; but today I can say with sincerest emotion that it was and is the best that could have come to us all, North and South. . . . As a Northern veteran once remarked to me, 'General Sickles can well afford to leave a leg on that field!' "‡

*The Crisis of the Confederacy, p. 216.
†The Battle of Gettysburg, p. 226.
‡Published in Lee and Longstreet at High Tide, by Helen D. Longstreet.

PART FIVE: HIGH TRUST AND INTRIGUE

CHAPTER XXVI

General on Crutches

———❖———

IT WAS THE SUNDAY after Gettysburg. In his Washington quarters—the first floor of a private residence on F Street—Sickles lay on a stretcher. The orderlies who just had carried him in had departed. His colored valet had bathed and shaved him. And now, clad in white drill, save for the bandaged stump, his head supported by several pillows, he was smoking a cigar—now and again biting hard on it against some unusually sharp twinge—and discussing the recent battle with two of his staff officers, Captain Fry and Lieutenant Colonel James F. Rusling, his chief quartermaster. "He was in much pain and distress at times," reported Rusling, "and weak from loss of blood, but calm and collected and with the same iron will and clearness of intellect that always characterized him."*

Suddenly the clatter of cavalry without. The orderly at the door announced, "His Excellency, the President." The prankish face of young Tad appeared, and behind him an ungainly apparition—Lincoln, a rail-thin six-foot-four clad in ill-fitting black broadcloth topped by a silk stovepipe hat, his trousers thrust into high riding boots complete with heavy spurs. He had just heard of Sickles's arrival and had immediately come to visit him—cantering in with his escort from the presidential summer residence, the Soldiers' Home.

Lincoln and Sickles, by James Fowler Rusling, a pamphlet published by the Third Army Corps Reunion, 1910, and based upon the author's letter to his wife written immediately after the ensuing episode.

According to Rusling, "the meeting between the two men was cordial —and pathetic. It was easy to see that they held each other in high esteem." Solicitously Lincoln inquired about Sickles's wound, how it happened, when, where, concluding, "And what do the doctors say about you now, General?" Sickles's tone was quiet, controlled. "They tell me that my condition is serious, and that I had better put my affairs in order at once." But Lincoln, raising a great hand as if to stop the words in mid-air, would have none of it. "General, listen—I am in a prophetic mood today; and I prophesy that you will soon be up and about, and that you'll live to do many an important service for your country yet."* The cheery, deeply assured tone, the shrewd challenge to the onward view, instantly relaxed Sickles. The grim tension faded from his face. Nor did it return. From that moment he seems never to have doubted either his firm recovery or his future career. Six months later, as able on one leg as he ever had been on two, he was to prove Lincoln a true prophet—and a sound psychologist.

Lincoln, who had been standing in sympathetic concern, now sat down, and, crossing his prodigious arms and legs, began to question the general as to all phases of the encounter at Gettysburg. Distressed by the appalling Union casualties, he inquired anxiously what measures were being taken to care for the wounded of both sides. And finally, stressing the magnitude of the victory, he voiced the fervent hope that Meade would follow it up, strike Lee swiftly, and bring the war to an end. On this point Sickles, careful to avoid criticism of a superior, was diplomatically evasive. But for the rest, prone on his stretcher, puffing leisurely at his cigar, he answered Lincoln freely and in great detail. Wrote Rusling, "He discussed the battle and its probable consequences with a lucidity and ability remarkable for one in his condition. . . . Occasionally he would wince with pain, and call sharply to his valet to wet his fevered wound. But he never dropped his cigar, nor lost the thread of the discussion."

Then, from the questioned, Sickles presently turned questioner. "I suppose, Mr. President, Washington was pretty close to panic while we were battling up there? You had reason enough—God knows. It certainly was nip and tuck with us."

Lincoln nodded gravely. "Yes, I suppose we were a little rattled

*Here and throughout this episode the conversation is quoted from Rusling's report.

now and then. There was talk of the city being captured. The Cabinet ordered a gunboat, and went so far as to send away some of the archives. They even wanted me to go along. But I said, 'No, gentlemen, I'm not going aboard any gunboat. We're going to win at Gettysburg.' . . . No, General, I had no fears about Gettysburg."

In his astonishment Sickles half sat up. "But how was that, Mr. President?"

Lincoln looked at him very steadily. "I will try to tell you, but I don't want you to speak of it. People might laugh, you know. But the fact of the matter is, in the pinch of the battle up there, when we had sent General Meade all the soldiers we could rake and scrape, and yet everything seemed going wrong, I went into my room one morning and locked the door, and got down on my knees, and prayed God Almighty for victory at Gettysburg. I told Him this was His country, and our war His war, and that we could not stand another Fredericksburg or Chancellorsville. And then and there I made a solemn vow that if He would stand by you boys at Gettysburg, I would stand by Him. I prayed, 'Oh God, have mercy upon me and my afflicted people! Our burdens and sorrows are greater than we can bear! Come now and help us, or we must all perish! And Thou canst not afford to have us perish! We are Thy chosen people, the last best hope of the human race!' . . . I don't know how it was and I can't explain it—I'm not a 'meeting man,' you know —but somehow or other a sweet comfort crept into my soul that God Almighty had taken the whole business up there into His own hands, and that things would come out all right at Gettysburg. And He did stand by you boys there, and now I will stand by Him. No, General, I had no fears for Gettysburg, and that is why."

For a moment or two the room was quite still. Then Sickles spoke. "Mr. President, what do you think about Vicksburg? How are things going there?"

Lincoln appeared soberly cheerful. "I don't quite know. Grant is still pegging away. And I rather think, as we used to say out in Illinois, he 'will make a spoon or spoil a horn' before he gets through. Some of our senators and congressmen think him slow, want me to remove him. But I like Grant. He doesn't bother me for reinforcements all the time like some of our other generals. He takes what soldiers we can give him, and does the best he can with what he has. Yes, I confess, I like General Grant. There is a great deal to him, first and last. And Heaven helping me, unless something happens more than I know now, I mean to stand by Grant a good while yet. He fights, he fights!"

"So then you have no fears today about Vicksburg either, Mr. President?"

"Well, no, I can't say I have." Lincoln spoke slowly. "The fact is I have been praying over Vicksburg also. I have told Almighty God how much we need the Mississippi, and how it ought to 'flow unvexed to the sea,' and how its great valley ought to be free forever. I have done the very best I could to help Grant and all the rest of our generals—though some of them don't think so. And now it is kind of borne in on me that somehow or other we are going to win at Vicksburg, too. I cannot tell how soon. But I believe we will."

Unknown to the President, his, of course, was a prophecy already fulfilled. Vicksburg had fallen July 4; and at that moment a Union gunboat was churning up the Mississippi to Cairo with the news. Curious coincidence that, on the birthday of Independence, Lee should retreat and Vicksburg fall!

Taking summer quarters at Lake George, Sickles made rapid recovery. Five months later he was again in Washington seeking active service. The ingenious, knee-action artificial leg constructed to his order by New York experts failed to satisfy him, and, except on special occasions, he preferred to use crutches. But there was little of the cripple in his stance and demeanor. He stood as straight on one leg as formerly on two and manipulated his crutches with unobtrusive dexterity. Nor had he long to wait for a call upon his services.

The previous year Lincoln had issued his Proclamation of Emancipation—well calculated to weaken the South economically, strengthen the North morally. Now in December 1863 he essayed a stroke of pure psychological warfare, and in his third message to Congress delivered his famous Amnesty Proclamation offering pardon and restitution of citizenship to all Rebels—other than the higher officers of the Confederate forces—who should swear allegiance to the Union and the Constitution; and the restoration of statehood to any member of the Confederacy able to certify that ten per cent of its voting population had registered the required oath. For some ten weeks he awaited southern reaction to his gesture of reconciliation. None came. And, dubious now as to the effectiveness of his two great experiments in non-military warfare, he commissioned Sickles to make a confidential tour of all southern ports in northern hands and investigate the results of both.

It was a day or two before his departure for the South that Sickles first met Grant. The occasion was a levee at the White House. Recently placed in supreme command of Union military operations, Grant had been summoned to Washington to receive his commission as lieutenant general. It was his first visit to the capital, his first appearance at a high social function; and blushing as furiously as a bashful boy he stood beside Lincoln and Stanton at the south end of the great East Room, jerkily shaking the cordial hands extended to him as the long reception line filed past him. As Sickles came up and was introduced by his old friend Stanton—now Secretary of War—he quipped genially, "Besieged by friends, even you must surrender, General!" Quipped Grant smartly, "You're right, sir—I've no arms left!" The next day the two met again casually at Willard's, drifted off to Grant's suite for a chat. Their mutual admiration of Lincoln was an immediate bond, but simply as men—diverse as they were in everything but fighting spirit—they liked each other. And by the time they had refought Vicksburg and Gettysburg over a bottle of Kentucky's best, they had established a comradeship destined to link them in official life for many years to come. Incidentally, circumstances soon put that comradeship to a tough test. Prior to Grant's arrival in Washington, it happened that Stanton, Halleck, and Meade had drawn up plans for the complete reorganization of the Army of the Potomac. Among the many changes decided upon was the consolidation of the twice-decimated Third Corps with the Second. It was an unnecessary and cruelly tactless act; for the Third had a brilliant record, an unsurpassed *esprit de corps,* and to obliterate its identity was to strike at the soldierly pride of thousands of veteran campaigners. The moment Sickles caught wind of the matter, he sought out Grant, begged him to protest against the absorption of his old command. Grant, however, felt compelled to refuse. Regretfully he explained that, in accordance with his general practice of committing as much executive power as possible to his subordinates, he had entrusted all matters of administration to Meade, and that it would be likely to cause ill-feeling if he meddled with the reorganization of the army—and, especially at a moment when he himself had but just assumed his new functions as lieutenant general. Noticing that inadvertently his request was proving embarrassing to Grant, Sickles gracefully withdrew it. And the two parted cordially—the one to accompany the Army of the Potomac, the other to proceed upon his confidential mission.

That Lincoln expected no very encouraging report from Sickles's tour of investigation seems certain. But that he needed the information, felt that Sickles was the right man to obtain it, and welcomed the opportunity to launch him on his new career with one of those "important services" he had prophesied for him, also seems certain. Curiously, his letter of instructions to Sickles remains the only documentary record of the assignment:

EXECUTIVE MANSION
Washington, Feb. 15, 1864.

MAJOR-GENERAL SICKLES:

I wish you to make a tour for me (particularly for observation) by way of Cairo and New Orleans, and returning by the Gulf and Ocean. All Military and Naval officers are to facilitate you with suitable transportation, and by conferring with you, and imparting, so far as they can, the information herein indicated, but you are not to command any of them. You will call at Memphis, Helena, Vicksburg, New Orleans, Pensacola, Key West, Charleston Harbor, and such intermediate points as you may think important. Please ascertain at each place what is being done, if anything, for reconstruction—how the Amnesty Proclamation works, if at all—what practical hitches, if any, there are about it—whether deserters come in from the enemy, what number has come in at each point since the Amnesty—what deserters report generally, and particularly whether and to what extent the Amnesty is known within the Rebel lines. Also learn what you can as to the colored people—how they get along as soldiers, as laborers, or in service, on leased plantations, and as hired laborers with their old master if there be such cases. Also learn what you can about the colored people within the Rebel lines. Also get any other information you may consider interesting, and, from time to time, send me what you may deem important to be known here at once. And be ready to make a general report on your return.

Yours truly,
A. LINCOLN.

Save for one routine dispatch, dated May 3, 1864, from U.S. gunboat *Fairy*, at Memphis, there appears to be no record of Sickles's reports to the President. Probably their not too enthusiastic tenor made publication politically inexpedient. Possibly they were buried in Lincoln's private files. But that Sickles had conducted his survey in a highly competent fashion is indicated by the fact that a year later Lincoln assigned him a far more complex confidential mission to revolution-torn Colombia.

His investigations completed and reported, Sickles, chafing against his long absence from the field, now formally applied to the War Department for active service. His physical disability, of course, was against him. And he was by no means *persona grata* with either Halleck or Meade. But both Stanton and Grant felt that his military experience could be used to good purpose; and, as a result, in May '64 he was assigned to duty as inspector general with Sherman's army. Present on the firing line at Resaca, Kennesaw Mountain, and the battle of Atlanta, for six months he endured the heat, malaria, hardship of that blistering campaign. Then, in November, his health—not yet sufficiently established for such an ordeal—suddenly broke; and with the rollicking strains of "Marching Through Georgia" ringing in his ears, he took indefinite leave of absence and returned to Washington.

CHAPTER XXVII

Mysterious Mission

LATE IN JANUARY '65 Sickles, now fully recovered, was on board a steamer bound for Panama. Again he had been entrusted with a confidential mission—and one, this time, apparently so fraught with the possibility of international repercussions that its precise nature has remained a State Department secret to the present day. That Sickles acted both as the special envoy of Lincoln himself and as the secret agent for Secretary of State Seward, is evident. But what his instructions were, what objectives they concerned, with what success or lack of success they were pursued, can only be surmised. And while the history of the period, and an examination of the routine

State Department records relative to United States relations with Colombia at the time, suggest a fair field of speculation on these points, the fact remains that only a fraction of the documentary record concerning them has been made available to the public. From the very first the State Department, doubtless for reasons of public policy, clamped the padlock on the Seward-Sickles correspondence. And the Lincoln-Sickles correspondence was padlocked by Robert Lincoln, even against the State Department itself, when, exercising his legal privilege immediately after his father's death, he sealed the presidential files for fifty years and, at the expiration of that period, resealed them for a like term! Under these circumstances it would appear that the full story of the Colombia mission cannot be revealed officially before 1965—and possibly not even then.

However, using what clues are at hand, it is not impossible to detect the outlines, at least, of some of the plans and purposes that may well have been involved in this mysterious diplomatic adventure.

Ostensibly Sickles was sent to Panama to obtain permission for the transit of United States troops across the Isthmus—a favor that had been denied the French. So far as this matter is concerned, the outlines are fairly clear. Panama, at that time, was simply a constituent state of the Republic of Colombia. The governor, therefore, rightly enough, professed himself without authority to grant the required permission and referred Sickles to the President. It was a twelve-day journey by steamboat, canoe, and horseback to the Colombian capital of Santa Fé de Bogotá, crannied high in the Andean Alps. And Sickles's letter to Seward describing this picturesque bit of travel is on file, together with one or two other letters recounting his inconclusive conferences with the President, and the official and popular acclaim he himself received, as American envoy, when the news of Appomattox arrived. But all that appears here is that while President Murillo and his Cabinet desired cordial relations with the United States, they considered that, in view of the insurgent activities then menacing Panama, the presence of foreign troops on the Isthmus might result in regrettable complications. And there the record fails; and there the matter seems to have rested.

But that this phase of Sickles's mission was put forward both as a sop to public curiosity and as a testing ground for negotiations far too important and delicate for publication at the time, seems certain.

In the first case Seward, an exponent of the newborn industrial imperialism, had become intensely preoccupied with the possibility of an American-built, American-owned Panama Canal. And although it would be fifteen years before Ferdinand de Lesseps would land his men and machines on the Isthmus and essay the digging of the Great Ditch on behalf of France, it was known in Washington that his engineers already had made tentative secret surveys of the project and that Louis Napoleon, not satisfied with the military occupation of Mexico, had proceeded to bring pressure to bear on Colombia to permit his troops to "cross" the Isthmus. Under the circumstances Seward naturally felt that decisive countermeasures were in order. And it is rather more than likely that in the chaotic condition of Colombian politics he discerned an opportunity to induce Panama— always simmering with insurrection and secessionist talk—to declare itself an independent republic; and by the promise of American recognition, American gold, secure its pledge at birth to the cession of the whole Isthmus zone to the United States Government. But Seward was ahead of his time. It would be thirty-eight years before Theodore Roosevelt, under curiously similar circumstances, and by quaintly similar means, was to land Isthmus and Canal in the American lap!

Seward's expansionist dreams, however, were by no means limited to the Panama Canal. For some years he had been cogitating a gigantic project—nothing less than the extension of the Monroe Doctrine to the economic sphere. The establishment of American monopoly control over all the more valuable raw resources of the southern continent, to the virtual exclusion of European competition, was his aim. And as a first step toward this he had conceived the idea that it would be sound business for the United States Treasury to assume the foreign indebtedness of such Latin-American republics as had fallen into bad standing with their European creditors. His first attempt to put this policy in practice had crashed in failure. In the fall of '61, Juarez—facing destruction of Mexico's newly established constitutional regime at the hands of a fake debt-collecting invasion by the joint forces of England, France and Spain—had appealed to the United States Government to assume for five years the delinquent interest owed to these Powers. And with Lincoln's consent, Seward, seizing his chance, had taken charge of negotiations. But his proposal in reply had revealed all too crudely his real intent. In it he had declared that the United States would assume the payment of the interest on Mexico's three per cent consolidated debt—a matter of some sixty-two million pesos—for a term of five years "on the condition that the Mexican Government undertakes to pay to the United States for the reimbursement of the money loaned an interest of *six per cent*, warranting such payment with specific retention upon *all public lands and upon the mines in the different Mexican states of Lower California, Chihuahua, Sonora, and Sinaloa, these mortgaged properties to fall under the absolute domain of the United States* at the end of the term of six years counted since the signing of this treaty, if the said reimbursement has not taken place during that term." And Juarez, rather than put all Mexico's most valuable assets in Seward's "carpetbag," had chosen to face invasion—as by far the lesser of the two evils.

On that occasion Seward had overreached himself. But the field of future experiment was still wide. Stubborn and shrewd as he was, it may be doubted if he relinquished his dear design or failed to learn from his first rebuff. And it is not unlikely that Sickles bore in his portfolio a similar, if more dulcet, proposition to debt-entangled Colombia as an opening wedge in the financial invasion of her sister republics.

At the same time Lincoln, dubious as to the future of the emancipated Negroes in the South, had been brooding the idea of establishing them in a home of their own, a new Liberia—but one close at hand. And after much probing about, he had become convinced that the fertile, virgin valleys of New Granada on the western slopes of the Colombian Andes would prove a location highly suitable for the purpose. The project was as subtle in concept as it was beneficent in motive. For while Lincoln contemplated no such absurdity as a mass transplanting of the freedmen, he knew that the mere existence of such a homeland would inspire them with a new sense of dignity and security, and, by the same token, gently force the southern planter to accord them such fair wages and considerate treatment as would entice them to stay on their jobs! Obviously it was an undertaking that the least premature exposure could have aborted. The South, of course, would be bitterly opposed to it—and must be kept in the dark for the present. And an unpredictable—and probably divided—Colombian opinion must be sounded in secret before any further steps were taken. The instability of a "republic" that had never been more than the arena of successive insurrections and mili-

tary dictatorships demanded that—unless the Negro colonists were
to be sold into a new and worse bondage—the proposed Liberia
must be established as a leased concession under the protection and
control of the United States Government. And while the Colombian
business element might be disposed to accept this arrangement for
the sake of its impetus to the state's agricultural development, the
politicos, shorn of their chance to exploit it, would be likely enough
to raise the cry of "Texas!" and damn it as an attempt to create
"incidents" leading to American military occupation and annexation.
And if Lincoln's "promised land" were ever to become more than a
promise, the negotiations on this touchy point would have to be
conducted not only behind the scenes but with extraordinary finesse.

The principal danger to these large dreams, needless to say, lay
in the tempestuous flux and flow of Colombian politics. To obtain,
therefore, a keen, close, impartial view of the politico-military scene
was a prime necessity to the planners in Washington. And there can
be little doubt that such a survey formed an integral part of the
mission entrusted to Sickles—one that as a soldier of prestige dealing
with a caste self-consciously military, as an astute politician dealing
with politicians, and as a diplomat able to speak fluent Spanish to
gentlemen devoid of English, he was well equipped to conduct.

That some very illuminating papers concerning Seward's ambi-
tious schemes, Lincoln's benevolent project, might have been found
in Sickles's dispatch bag is a warrantable surmise.

But Washington society, lacking any real data in the matter, had
its own surmise; and it was the current gossip of the more malicious
that Lincoln, in his quietly devious way, had deliberately assigned
Sickles a mythical mission for personal reasons not unrelated to the
White House boudoir. It had happened, early in '61, that a certain
Henry Wikoff, a fascinating but shady international adventurer,
Washington correspondent—and secret agent—for James Gordon
Bennett's New York *Herald*, and known to be assiduous in his attentions to Mary Todd, had telegraphed his paper a substantial portion
of Lincoln's first Inaugural Address prior to its delivery. Outraged,
the House Judiciary Committee had started an investigation into the
origin of the leak. Summoned for questioning, Wikoff had refused to
divulge the source of his information and had been jailed for contempt. Public suspicion had pointed to Mary Todd as his accomplice.
And Sickles, to save Lincoln further embarrassment, had energeti-

cally intervened and had forced John Watt, the White House head gardener—a thievish, disreputable fellow, but much in Mary Todd's favor—to declare that he had seen the text of the speech by accident on the President's library table and had retailed it to Wikoff from memory! That little drama—starring Mary Todd as a First Lady given to strange infatuations and the amorous General Dan Sickles as her confidant and champion—had not been forgotten. And now when, newly arrayed in battle glory, the general had returned to Washington—and conquests of another kind—his frequent visits to the White House had revived the buzz of speculation. Manifestly, with one leg, he now was more fatal to the feminine than ever he had been with two. And in delicious anticipation the drawing rooms awaited the explosion of a fresh scandal. . . .

But what the drawing rooms did not know, or preferred not to know, was that Sickles, ruthless with women, was scrupulous with a friend; and that his hours at the White House were spent not in the boudoir but in the library—deep in conference with Lincoln over the plans for the "New Liberia."

As a matter of fact it was upon one of these visits that Sickles had offended the First Lady past forgiveness. Pausing at the drawing room to pay his respects to her, he had found her entertaining her foster sister Emilie—widow of the Confederate general, Hedin Helm! The sight had touched off all his fierce allegiance to the harried President, the still-battling Union. And unsparingly he had rebuked her for daring to place her family ties above the obligations of her position. Deliberately, knowingly, he had struck Mary Todd on her most sensitive nerve—her much criticized devotion to her southern relatives. And from that moment, so far from enjoying her favor, he had become to her the most detested of her husband's detested friends!

All things considered—and assuming the foregoing speculations to be somewhere near the mark—it is small wonder that all but a few of the documents in this curious chapter of American diplomacy still remain tightly bound in their original ribbons, unbreakably sealed.

But whatever might have been his secret business in Colombia, Sickles had but short time to accomplish it. Prompted by the belated news of Lee's surrender, he was returning to the coast to put his dispatches aboard a gunboat and obtain the last reports from the capital, when, at La Honda, an Indian runner brought him a canvas-bound package. Within it was a black-edged official envelope. One glance at the enclosed black-edged letter told him that it had been six weeks in transit. Stunned, he stared at it. Lincoln assassinated! Seward wounded! . . . He was summoned home.

CHAPTER XXVIII

Struggling with Chaos

———◆———

THE WAR now belonged to history, Lincoln "to the ages." The heroic epoch had passed. And before the last taps had sounded, the era of capitalistic expansion had seized the stage. Abnormally stimulated by the demands of the Grand Army, northern industry had grown fat. The vast new accumulations of capital, in turn, cropped a new craze for speculative enterprise, and with it what proved to be an enduring dynasty of financial buccaneers proficient in stripping the public purse by ruthless market manipulations and in suborning courts, legislatures, and the avenues of public information and opinion in favor of their schemes to reduce white labor below the level of the prewar black and gain monopoly control of the national resources. For nearly seventy years the regime of "The Plunderbund"—as it came to be known—pocked with political putrescence at home, "dollar diplomacy" abroad, gargantuan thieveries, hysterical speculations, booms, panics, glutted markets, catastrophic disemployment, delirious wealth, crawling destitution, ravaged forests, swollen slums, was to career along its path of havoc until, like a stricken dragon (every bank in the country closed!), it drooped a slobbering head in the lap of the first President of the United States to base his domestic policy on the proposition that a political democracy must set itself to the progressive realization of economic democracy or suffer itself to be destroyed by economic dementia.

A new age had been born—symbolized by a Republican-dominated Congress far more concerned with capturing the black vote, crippling the South and exploiting it as a lucrative field for graft and bureaucratic jobholding, than with any reconsolidation of the Union. Against this crowd of little men avid for loot and safe vengeance, Andrew Johnson—President by tragic chance—stood well-nigh alone.

Himself an unprivileged son of Tennessee, Johnson, from the first, set himself to carry out Lincoln's policy toward the erstwhile Rebel states and, in the spirit of "let bygones be bygones," restore them to the national family circle with the least possible delay. But it was a policy that probably not even Lincoln himself—for all his tact, patience, persuasive eloquence—could have hoped to pursue in the face of a Congress so little touched by grace or good will. And Johnson was no Lincoln. Honest he was, and right-minded. But years of struggle to overcome the poverty, illiteracy, social contempt that were the lot of southern "po' white trash" had bred in him a defiant determination fatal to the wise handling of a House wholly at odds with his views. First taught the alphabet by his schoolmistress bride, he had risen by his own efforts from patching rustic pants to a place among the four or five ranking senators of his time. The battle had taught him but one answer to opposition—fight! And now as President, with all that was brave and upright in his heart, but also with all that was crude, tactless, uncouth in his breeding, he met defiant congressional measures with even more defiant vetoes—always overruled. By a single vote escaping vindictive impeachment, he was to complete his term with little to show for his bitter bout but his three ever expanding Amnesty Proclamations—virtually the only expression of his policy permitted him.

In the fall of 1865 Grant, as commander in chief of the Army of Occupation, divided the southern states into five military departments, placing each under the control of a military governor, aided by post commanders and supported by such troops as he deemed necessary for the maintenance of public order pending the reconstitution of civil government. Among the major generals selected for the new administrative task, Sickles was the only one among his confreres—Meade, Halleck, Pope, and Sheridan—with a background experience in diplomacy, politics, law. To him, therefore, Grant gave the most difficult assignment: the Department of South Carolina—

credited with the touchiest temper and possessing the largest and most backward Negro population of any state in the Union—and, the following year, under the Reconstitution Act passed by Congress, added North Carolina also to his charge.

The duties of a military governor were only slightly military—so slightly, in fact, that Sickles, disdaining a show of force, rapidly dismissed all but two of the regiments placed at his disposal, thus reducing his command to one soldier for every thirty-three square miles! For the rest, he found himself called upon to exercise a fantastic complex of functions—legislative, judicial, executive. In part they involved: the supervision of the liberated Negroes in their new status as hired hands of their former masters, and the regulation of their right to use common carriers such as railways, streetcars, steamboats; the organization of the new system of free labor in agricultural communities; the establishment of poorhouses and hospitals for sick and infirm ex-slaves—hitherto a traditional charge of their owners; the proclamation of stay laws to protect a mass of helpless small debtors, white and black, from sheriff's sale; the establishment and administration of quarantine and sanitary regulations against yellow fever and cholera—both menacing southern cities in '66 and '67; the organization and supervision of provost courts for the settlement of disputes ordinarily within the jurisdiction of the civil courts; the distribution of rations to a starving population, white and colored, in almost every county; and, finally, the re-establishment of civil government by registration of all citizens entitled to the vote—including the enfranchised Negro; and the superintendence of the elections required by Congress as a prerequisite to the restoration of a rebel state to representation in House and Senate.

It was a pretty large order—too much for any one man, particularly a northern general, to fill without provoking criticism. Sickles, realizing this, laid down for himself three principles of policy in the task ahead: order must be maintained and the law enforced; consideration must be shown to southern sensibilities; immediate relief must be provided for the distressed elements of the population, and every encouragement given to the normal resumption of business and agriculture. Grant, visiting with Sickles at Raleigh, warmly approved these principles; and their famous all-night conference ended in a mutual understanding never afterward beclouded. And that thenceforth—despite some characteristic flashes of anger, impatience, impetuosity—Sickles strove consistently to promote the prosperity of the state and the welfare of impoverished aristocrat, debt-ridden poor white, bewildered Negro alike, is writ in the record of his acts, in his popularity among the depressed classes, and in the high, if belated, praise accorded him, at last, even by planter and banker—his most persistent critics.

Sickles, needless to say, firmly believed that the presence of an impartial authority in the South—in the form of a temporary military administration—was as essential to the protection of the white population as to the welfare of the black; that, lacking it, the two races almost inevitably would drift into an antagonism and bloody clash fatal to the tranquillity required for the reconstitution of civil government. In this, of course, he reflected the northern view as expressed in Congress. But, as a matter of fact, while holding himself constitutionally responsible to congressional directive, he was far from sharing the congressional attitude. Many distinguished southerners had been, and still were, his friends. A soldier, he wished no vengeance. He left that to civilians. On the other hand, he was deeply concerned with the problem of the Negro and the poor white. Between the creditor class, his social friends, and the debtor class, white and black, his mournful charge, tact bade him steer a fine, if determined, line. To the one he gave all due consideration; to the other he gave Order No. 10.

The issuance of the famous Order was at once the most important, the most socially beneficial, and the most abused, action of Sickles's administration. Devised to alleviate at one stroke a vast amount of distress among wage earners and small property owners, white and colored, it abolished imprisonment for debt; established a year's stay of execution on all causes of action arising during the war; suspended, for a like period, all sheriff's sales on judgments recovered prior to December 19, 1860—save by the debtor's consent; exempted a homestead of twenty acres, and personal property in the amount of five hundred dollars, from levy or sale for any debt; prohibited infliction of the death penalty for burglary and horse stealing; absolutely forbade whipping for any cause; declared the carrying of concealed weapons a crime; and, finally, conceded the pardoning power to the civil governor of the state.

Although framed as a general measure of relief to a festering situation, the Order, of course, was aimed specifically at the recent invasion of northern "carpetbaggers" then gluttonishly engaged in buying up delinquent claims and using them to despoil already desperate families of hut and corn patch, mule and plow and cradle. On these locust gentry, Order No. 10 descended with an obliterating thud. To their howls were added the loud protests of the business and plantation element. The ban on enforced collections pleased the one no better than the loss of the whip pleased the other. The intransigent Charleston press, assailing Sickles as a "dictator" and "despot," opened a determined campaign to have Johnson remove him from office. But so obvious were the salutary effects of Order No. 10 that his critics soon found themselves compelled to concentrate their complaints against him on such minor grievances as inevitably arose out of the confusion of authorities. And of that there was plenty!

In the first case, from Washington poured contradictory orders from a President and a Congress locked in a struggle to abort each other's reconstruction policies. The abolition of whipping is a good instance in point. Sickles decreed it; Congress authorized it; Johnson forbade it; Sickles enforced it; federal courts overruled it; state officials ignored it—and so forth.

But this was only the beginning! Grant held that the authority of a military governor over his department was paramount—subject only to Congress and to himself as commanding general. And so Sickles viewed it. But there were also four other bodies of authority or quasi-authority in the field—each jealous of its own actual or supposed spheres of control. These included the state and local officials, judicial and executive, under the aegis of a civil governor: two cabinets, one radical, the other conservative—so antagonistic to each other that they refused to sit together and, consequently, had to be consulted separately: the federal courts—determined to brook no interference with their prerogatives; and, finally, the Freedmen's Bureau—established by Lincoln, given amplified powers by Congress, and charged with a wide range of duties appertaining to the rights and welfare of the emancipated Negroes. As a result, Sickles, coming upon a sick scene as emergency surgeon, could do practically nothing without cutting through one or other of these already conflicting zones of state and federal authority—to the great indignation of the officials concerned. Nevertheless he proceeded upon his course; and in subsequent orders reinforced No. 10 by abolishing distraint for the collection of rent; prohibiting common carriers from making any distinction in their treatment of patrons by reason of race, color, or previous servitude; forbidding the commercial production of spirituous liquors; declaring all persons assessed for taxes eligible as jurors without regard to race or color; and prescribing that sheriffs, chiefs of police, city and town marshals must obey the orders of the military provost marshals.

However, if these new edicts raised a fresh sizzle of criticism, they also brought their lowly meed of praise. In April '67 the freedmen of the Charleston district, gathering spontaneously in thousands before the executive mansion on Charlotte Street, proceeded to serenade the author of Order No. 10 in a chorus of song—that ended in mighty uproar when at last his becrutched uniformed figure appeared on the balcony. Surprised and stirred, Sickles thanked them in a little speech well matching the spirit of his administration:

. . . You are now citizens of the Republic. And you must try to vindicate the hopes of your friends and repel the forebodings of the skeptical by proving yourselves worthy of the privilege to which you have been admitted. . . . Whenever any large additions have been made to the voters of a state, the same apprehensions have been expressed that are now heard with reference to yourselves. . . . Let me advise you as a friend to preserve at all times the utmost moderation of language, temper, and conduct. Avoid everything like violence or impatience. . . . Whatever seriously impairs the interest of one race must result seriously to the other. . . . Without a happy, prosperous, and contented laboring class, society lacks an essential element of strength. . . . I promise you that every man in the Carolinas entitled to a voice in the decision of the great questions to be passed upon under my supervision shall have a fair chance to act his part without let or hindrance from anyone.

Three months later, when a delegation of freedmen called upon him by appointment to thank him more formally for his many services in their behalf, and especially for his recent active promotion of schools for Negroes, he spoke more at length—and now for the record. While counseling and encouraging his colored friends, he used the occasion to shoot a few sarcastic shafts—over their heads— at the critics who had prophesied nothing but calamitous results from his policy toward them.

By midsummer of '67 Johnson had become estranged from Congress to a degree unparalleled in White House history. And, naturally enough, he had come to view with mounting disfavor the military governors entrusted by Grant with the direction of congressional reconstruction policies in the South. If that disfavor was shared by Halleck, Meade, Pope, Sheridan, it fell particularly upon Sickles. That "one-man legislature"—as Greeley dubbed him—presented a curious and irksome problem to the White House. While siding, on constitutional grounds, with Congress against the President, he yet had conducted his administration much in the spirit of Lincoln himself; and had dramatized both attitudes by daring to enforce the abolition of the whipping post—in the teeth of both the federal courts and a special presidential order. That something had to be done about him was evident. Johnson could not dismiss him without locking horns with Grant. He therefore tried diplomacy, offered the recalcitrant General: first the collectorship of New York, then the post of minister to the Netherlands. But Sickles, at Grant's urging, resolved to stay where he was. Foiled in his attempts at seduction, Johnson decided to try castigation. Angrily he invoked the services of Attorney General Stanberry to issue an opinion declaring Sickles guilty of illegal and unconstitutional procedure in the conduct of his office, a censure that, according to the Charleston correspondent of the New York *Times*, "dropped like a bomb on the city."

The same day Sickles, in consultation with Grant, wrote out his resignation, and demanded a congressional investigation of his administration. Grant, outraged, forwarded the document himself. It was a bold counterstroke—shrewd as it was unexpected. Too late Johnson realized that the demanded investigation only could redound to Sickles's prestige and popularity and diminish what was left of his own. Outwitted, he refused the resignation—and bided his time. Remarked the New York *Times*, "a vindication for General Sickles!"

To Johnson, as their champion, the southern states always had looked for sympathy in their complaints against the congressional reconstruction policies in general and the military administration in particular. And Johnson's endorsement of Sickles—negative though it might be—was not without its effect upon the die-hards. This—combined with the unblenching attitude of Sickles himself, the beneficial results of his emergency measures in terms of general tranquillity, restored confidence, and a remarkable increase of agricultural production—finally turned the tide of criticism against him into a flow of general appreciation. But the Executive axe was on the grindstone!

By supporting his friend and appointee, Grant for the first time had placed himself in open opposition to the White House. And seeing now nothing to lose in that direction, Johnson, the following September, summarily dismissed both Sickles and Sheridan. And rumor had it that he only narrowly was dissuaded from dismissing Pope likewise.

Ironically, Johnson based his action against Sickles, not on any charge of oppressing the people of the Carolinas, but on a charge of interfering—in a whipping case—with the authority of the federal courts! And with equal irony, it was from the camp of his former critics, "the leading citizens" of Charleston headed by James L. Orr, the civil governor of South Carolina, that Sickles received—at a farewell banquet give in his honor—a conclusive verdict of vindication and praise upon his administration. Said the governor:

He has made even the burdens of the military government upon the people of South Carolina as light as it is possible to make them under the circumstances. He has secured to all their rights and attended to, and advanced, their material prosperity. By his orders he has developed the resources of the state, secured to labor, fair wages, and to the producer protection. . . . Under his administration the laws of Congress pertaining to Reconstruction have been faithfully and honestly administered, and he has left nothing for his successor to do but see that a fair and just election is held by the people. . . . The crop of '67 was the largest and most valuable gathered in South Carolina in a decade, and that result was due in large measure to the aid afforded by General Sickles in settling the difficulties arising out of the Act of Emancipation.

Johnson's dismissal of Sickles and Sheridan, of course. was not only a personal revenge and a smart slap at Congress. It was a mailed glove tossed at the commanding general. And Grant was not slow to pick it up. When the two ex-governors arrived in Washington he welcomed them ostentatiously with a reception and banquet attended by the highest officers of the Army and Navy and the ranking members of the Diplomatic Corps!

The following night—and not at all to Grant's dissatisfaction— the two generals were made the recipients of a military serenade at Willard's Hotel. But what started out to be a musical tribute on the part of the garrison regiments of the Grand Army, and of the various local political associations, both white and colored, soon turned into a mass demonstration of welcome such as Washington had seldom seen. According to the genteel report of the *Globe,* "The balconies of Willard's were filled to overflowing with ladies and gentlemen of the foremost circles; and even the corridors leading from the generals' quarters to the parlors were lined with enthusiastic admirers who showered bouquets upon them as they passed by to receive the compliments of the assemblage in the street." Phil Sheridan, responding to the tumult of cheers, answered with a few brief clichés and withdrew. Not so Sickles. When he appeared, supported on his crutches, what was tumult became a tornado; and his response was no this-is-the-happiest-hour-of-my-life kind of thing but a spirited, and uproariously applauded, defense of the temporary military administration in the South in its constitutional legality, human necessity, and good result.

But naturally enough it was in New York, his home town, that Sickles was to receive his most vociferous acclaim. There thousands of veterans of his Excelsior Brigade and famed Third Corps united with War Democrats and sons of Tammany to organize a monstrous ovation in his honor. For five hours, despite a light rain, the Brevoort House, his hotel, was beset, in typical American fashion, by a rocket-illuminated mass of hero-worshiping humanity mingling cheers with the blare of bands and stirred to fresh bursts ever and again by the invasion of marching, bemedaled battalions come to salute the Chief.

In Washington, sensing his moment, Sickles had spoken for the record. Now, with the same infallible timing, he spoke briefly—simply as a soldier to former comrades in arms.

Still a Republican in practice, if still a Democrat in theory, Sickles now threw all his energies into promoting Grant's candidacy for President. For months he literally "stumped" the country, north, south, east, and west, rallying the vote as much perhaps by his crutches, his personal prestige and popularity as by his knack of combining polished speech, cogent argument with an instinctive touch upon the pulse of the crowd. And Grant, swept into office in November '68 by a huge majority over his opponent, Horatio Seymour, governor of New York, was not unmindful of the aid. Almost his first act as President was to promote Sickles from his previous position on the retired list as colonel of the Forty-Fourth U.S. Infantry, to his full rank as major general—something that, as a decent recognition of the man who had stopped Jackson at Chancellorsville and baffled Longstreet at Gettysburg, he had long planned to do. Incidentally, the promotion was one of the highest honors accorded any commander of the Grand Army—whether Volunteer or West Pointer. But Grant did not stop there. He immediately offered to reinstate Sickles in his former post as military governor of the Carolinas. Sickles, however, declined on the grounds that his work there was done and that his successor, General Canby, was too good an administrator to be disturbed. Grant then suggested the post of minister to Mexico. Again Sickles declined. He knew the President's ill-timed ambition to annex Lower California to the United States, and he had no wish to be a party to it. Finally Grant offered him the most difficult diplomatic post in Europe, that of minister to Spain. Sickles instantly closed. He had one reason—Cuba!

*   *   *

TERESA B. SICKLES

Aged 31 years

Died Feb. 5, 1867

This morning a solemn High Mass of Requiem was offered for the repose of Mrs. Sickles, the wife of the distinguished Major-General, at St. Joseph's Church, Sixth Avenue. The sad occasion attracted an immense congregation to the sacred edifice to witness with devout attention the impressive ceremonies which called it forth. Every portion of the temple, from the porch to the sanctuary, was thronged long before the hour appointed for the services.

At half past ten o'clock, the remains were conveyed up the main aisle, and placed on a catafalque which was surrounded by brilliant tapers. They were followed by the pall bearers—Dr. John M. Carnochan, James T. Brady, Maj.-Gen. Gordon Granger, Maj.-Gen. A. Pleasonton, Gen. Henry E. Tremaine, Gen. K. Graham, Otto Gabriotti, John Krug, William H. Field, Edward Vermylie.

General Sickles and the parents of the deceased lady, Mr. and Mrs. Bagioli, occupied the pews near the altar. The venerable father of the General was also present.*

Early in the second year of his military governorship Sickles had been summoned home by the news that Teresa, slowly dying for eight years, had passed into a coma. Death had supervened before he could arrive.

*New York *Express*, February 5, 1867.

It was with grave misgivings that the thirteen-year-old Laura had been allowed to attend the funeral. In the dim church she had huddled in a corner of the pew—a thin, ghostly little figure, quivering with grief, vague shame, fierce childish anger against her father. The service ended, she had collapsed.

As soon as she had been well enough to travel, Sickles had taken Laura back with him to Charleston. There he had endeavored to place her in the fashionable academy conducted by Madam Tivane. Completely horrified at the suggestion, however, Madam had declared that she would close her school rather than accept the child of such heritage. A rival academy fortunately had proven less righteous. The headmistress, Mrs. Alston, a southerner of the blood, gladly had enrolled the delicate, lonely child, announcing that if the parents of any pupil objected they would be welcome to seek another school!

Baffled, feeling himself at a cruel disadvantage, Sickles had striven—and with an unfamiliar sense of awkwardness—to win his little daughter's confidence and affection. Too late! Frustrate, confused, perverse, she was not to be wooed. And as her repining slowly waned under the stimulus of new scenes and companions, she had developed a moody resistance broken with sudden bursts of temper. And Sickles, watching her anxiously, had been forced to admit to himself that if she inherited her mother's fragile dark beauty, she also inherited his own strong passions, headstrong will. Too busy, too inapt for the delicate work of reconstructing a tortured child psyche, he had petted her, pampered her, and—as with Teresa—had showered her with expensive, enticing gifts. But all his efforts to please had failed. His gifts were pushed aside, his sallies received without a smile. Nothing he could do could overcome her stubborn withdrawal. And hoping that time, growth, and an impersonal environment would soften her attitude toward him, he presently had placed her in a New Jersey academy in the care of his own parents. But in his heart he doubted if she ever would cease to blame him for her mother's desolation, her own blighted childhood. Already the little daughter he had adored had become a tragic phantom of the past.

CHAPTER XXIX

"The Yankee King of Spain"

Early in july 1869 Sickles was on the high seas—neaded toward Spain and eight fantastic years of high-tensioned diplomacy, international intrigue, royal amour. The main document in his dispatch bag, however, was again one that never would be made a matter of official record. Of his own adroit design, its purport was: Cuba for cash—cloaked in the offer of the United States Government to mediate between the Spanish authorities and the Island insurrectos.

That objective, persistently cherished since Ostend Manifesto days, at last seemed to him well-nigh within grasp.

Cuba just had flamed up in new insurrection—and now with a force predicating serious civil war.

Spain, after twenty years of misrule by an irresponsible queen counseled by a vicious camarilla, had upset the throne amid political chaos, national bankruptcy.

In those two facts Sickles had divined his long-awaited opportunity to add "the Pearl of the Antilles" to Columbia's crown; and they had constituted the main, if not the sole, reason for his promptly accepting the post of minister to Spain.

The proposal he took with him was, in substance, if not in form, no novelty to the Spanish authorities.

Long ago the thievish and conscienceless Maria Christina, Queen Regent of Spain during the infancy of her daughter, Isabella, had offered to swap Cuba—and the Philippines to boot—with Louis Philippe for a paltry twenty million reales; and had failed only because her agent, in utter shame, had refused to grant a demanded last-minute reduction in price! Aware of this, the United States Government twice had offered to purchase the unhappy island for a more respectable sum—on the last occasion, under President Pierce, for a hundred million dollars—and twice had been smartly rebuffed. Sickles, however, seems to have thought three a lucky number. In any case he knew that never had Spain such need as now to cash in on a colony that already had lost her more in ill repute and costly cruelty than she was ever likely to regain in pride or profit.

If the Escorial, occupied, always had been the seat of storm, now, unoccupied, it had become, in fact, the empty vortex of a cyclone. While the exiled Queen bored herself at Biarritz with the blandishments of her last lover—the Italian opera tenor, Mafori—the twin leaders of the recent revolt, General Prim, commander in chief, and Marshal Serrano, the interim Premier, were struggling to subdue the ever recurring rebellion of the Pretender, Don Carlos, in the north, and the revolt of the Federalists—demanding states' autonomy—in the south. At the same time five other parties, Absolutist, Moderate, Conservative, Republican, Radical, subdivided into warring factions each pledged to a different leader, were clamoring, plotting—often as not, rioting—for control of the administration. And Cuba, if it were not to be taken over by the despised Creoles (native-born Spaniards) at the head of their hybrid hordes of peons and black slaves, urgently demanded a powerful army of repression. And, what was more important at the moment, chronic civil war, Isabella's extravagant rule, the staggering peculations of the also exiled Queen Mother, Maria Christina, and her gang of courtiers, and the almost universal malfeasance practiced in public office, had bereft the Treasury of its last real and reduced Spanish credit into a wry jest on the Bourse and in Threadneedle Street. Prim thus faced a crisis as desperate financially as it was politically. That Spain, with her monarchial tradition, feudal psychology, stubborn regionalism, and vast illiteracy, was not ripe for the republican institutions demanded by her more progressive elements, he well knew. Feverishly he was seeking—as a rallying point for the national consciousness—a new occupant for the throne. But first, he realized, he must have some semblance of solvency, public order. For that he needed, above all, a handsomely replenished exchequer. And it was precisely on this well-understood point that Sickles staked his high hope of a successful deal for Cuba. A high hope it was—and large! To adorn the administration of his admired Grant, the prestige of the restored Union, his own diplomatic career, with "the Pearl of the Antilles," bought and paid for, seemed to him an accomplishment lustrous enough to compensate him even for the loss of that other once high hope, the presidency.

Grant, an innocent on most matters not immediately pertaining to his trade of war, had viewed Sickles's project with high favor. Not so the better-informed Hamilton Fish. Cautious to the point of timidity, the new Secretary of State had been at much pains to bring up for inspection the various dangers involved in reviving memories of Ostend—

Louis Napoleon—still smarting from Seward's curt ultimatum to remove his troops from Mexican soil—was no friend to the United States; and he was likely enough to welcome any pretext for a vengeful salvage of the prestige he had lost in the Maximilian fiasco. And Great Britain almost certainly would view with disfavor the extension of American influence into her West Indian sphere. Both powers might protest even the most peaceful hoisting of the Stars and Stripes over Cuba. And should a premature disclosure of the proposed negotiations alarm Spain, and a new party, riding into power on a wave of nationalism, proceed to spurn the gold and draw the sword, both powers well might come to her support. In that event there was the further dark probability that the South, still recalcitrant, would seize the opportunity to cry havoc in aid of the enemy. . . . Yes, there was much to be considered.

So Fish had argued, inculcating Grant with some of his own hesitation. In the upshot, however, Sickles, warmly seconded by Secretary of War Rawlins, had won both to his project and had been given a free hand in its accomplishment subject only to the stipulation that he conduct the negotiations in absolute secrecy, with General Prim alone, and under the guise of an offer of friendly mediation between revolutionary Cuba and the Spanish administration.

Once settled at the Legation, Sickles set out to cultivate such amicable relations with Prim as presently might enable him to broach his proposal in a tentative, off-the-record chat. This was not an altogether easy matter. The Cuban authorities, hounding after the many and various filibustering expeditions surreptitiously dispatched from American ports to the aid of the rebels, had resorted to flagrant interference with even the most legitimate American shipping. And Congress, in retort, was debating a proposal to grant the insurgent party the rights of belligerency—and thus open assistance. Under the circumstances cordial relations between the new master of Spain and the new American minister hardly could be expected. But Prim was large-minded, concerned only with essentials. In his view the strained situation between the two countries was the fault of the regime he just had overthrown and was something to be regretted—and remedied; that was all. And it was not long before Sickles, with his crutches, his prestige as a soldier, his frank and magnetic charm, had become a welcome visitor at the Ministry of War.

In those last months of '69 Prim, Serrano, and the faction-riven Cortes had agreed at last upon constitutional monarchy as the future form of the Spanish government. The three claimants to the throne—Don Carlos, the bellicose Pretender; Isabella's eleven-year-old son, Alfonso; and her brother-in-law, the Duc de Montpensier—were, by the logic of events, barred from consideration. The choice of candidates lay among that honest "elder statesman," Espartero, Duc de Vittoria, who had risen from the ranks to become Regent of the Realm during Isabella's minority; Ferdinand, the former King Regent of Portugal; Amadeo, Prince of Aosta, second son of Victor Emmanuel, King of Savoy; and Prince Leopold of Hohenzollern Sigmaringen, grandnephew of the King of Prussia. The first wisely had refused to serve, pleading age. The second, as wisely, preferred private life and the society of his American bride. The third, as heir presumptive to the throne of Savoy, could not accept a foreign throne until such time as his elder brother might produce an heir. The choice thus narrowed—fatefully—to Leopold. But the trouble there was France. Louis Napoleon, well aware of Bismarck's ambition to transform the loose federation of German principalities into a solidly unified empire under the aegis of the Hohenzollerns, wanted no Hohenzollern on the throne of Spain as well! The Spanish Cabinet knew it, pondered, hesitated. And in any case, how could they invite the scion of a proud house to assume the throne of a country so pauperized that it could not even pay its scattering of schoolteachers, much less the wretched dole allotted the conscripts in the national forces? Money—money—where to turn for money? So went the all-night conferences.

It was at this point that Sickles approached General Prim with his carefully rehearsed suggestion for the solution of Spain's financial problem. What arguments he used in its favor are not known, but are not too difficult to guess! . . . Cuba had become, and was likely to remain, a serious liability. Its present insurrection, apparently supported by the vast majority of the native population, could be suppressed only by large-scale and costly military measures. Should the insurgents triumph, Cuba would become a dead loss to Spain. Should they be crushed, they assuredly would rise again. Therefore, presuming that Cuba could find the funds to purchase her own independence, would it not be the course of practical wisdom to cooperate with her and thus convert a ponderous liability into a most helpful asset in time of need? The transaction, of course, would arouse a certain amount of popular uproar, but if it were presented to the public as the only means of avoiding further crushing taxation, it soon would be accepted. In any case, how else could Spain swiftly stabilize her finances, restore her credit, and pave a tranquil path for the entry of the new monarch? Spain's pride might well be touched were Cuba wrenched from her by force of arms. But surely that could not be the case were Cuba to ransom herself for such a handsome consideration as would mean peace and prosperity for the motherland! This then was the proposition: the United States, acting as friendly intermediary in the matter, stood ready to loan Cuba the funds required to purchase her freedom; and would underwrite the bonds, taking in return a long-term mortgage at nominal interest on the island as a whole.

Prim listened in grim silence. As a Spaniard everything in him recoiled from such a proposal. But as an administrator confronting a financial crisis that, unsolved, might precipitate national anarchy and disintegration, he dared not thrust it aside—not for the present. Reluctantly, at last, he agreed to give it careful consideration, insisting, however, that since the slightest hint of it bruited abroad would cost him his office, his reputation, and—almost certainly—his life, the discussions must be kept in complete confidence, and that in any code dispatches regarding them they must be ascribed, on the part of Spain, to unspecified sources.

In the meantime the search for a king continued. Under Prim's urgings the Cabinet and Cortes had secured Leopold's acceptance of the throne. But, eight days later, warned by the fury of the French press, the prospective monarch had withdrawn his assent. Elated by such easy victory, Benedetti, the French ambassador to Prussia, then proceeded to demand of King William his solemn assurance that the House of Hohenzollern would not again countenance the candidacy of a German prince for the Spanish throne.

Snubbed, he insolently repeated his demand—only to be refused further audience. Bismarck did the rest. Adroitly editing the King's dispassionate report of the affair in such fashion as to give it the ring of deliberate challenge to the "Gallic cock," he shot over the international wires his famous "Ems dispatch." The next morning Paris was aflame. The half-invalid Louis Napoleon climbed into his saddle, brandished his sword. The war he wanted—and thought he could win—was on. Bismarck and Moltke grinned at each other, shook hands. Three months later, at Sedan, Louis Napoleon, chastised and chastened, was climbing limply out of his saddle and offering his sword to King William. He much preferred de luxe captivity to facing the Parisian mob! But if the craven Emperor had capitulated, the French people had not. Ahead lay the grim siege of Paris, Gambetta's escape from its walls by balloon that he might raise new armies in the provinces, a year of hopeless struggle culminating in the fratricide of the Commune, before, by the Treaty of Frankfort, humiliated France, reconverted to a republic, could resume her troubled way among the nations minus Alsace-Lorraine and five milliards of francs!

In the interval the Duke of Naples, Victor Emmanuel's eldest son, had taken his first-born to the font. Amadeo, the second son, was now a free agent. Eagerly the Spanish Cabinet seized upon him. A cultivated liberal, of meticulous honor, wide sympathies, and the coldest courage, he was that rare royal phenomenon—a natural king. But he had no yearnings for a foreign throne. Only Prim's urgent plea and his father's shrewd challenge to his courage at last made him attempt an adventure he seems to have felt foredoomed. But when he set foot on Spanish soil, the man who most anxiously had awaited his coming was not there to greet him. The previous midnight General Prim, driving from a stormy session of the Cortes to the Ministry of War, had been shattered by a fusillade from the dark—by whom, for what, never has appeared. To his tomb went Sickles's high hopes for the acquisition of Cuba. . . . Had the secret leaked?

Upon his accession to the throne it was customary for a Spanish monarch to review the Army and receive its oath of allegiance, regiment by regiment. In the case of Amadeo the day appointed for this ceremony of *La Jura* turned out to be one of the most inclement in the history of Madrid. Nevertheless a sullen, curious crowd jammed the narrow streets to watch the parade pass and to jeer rather than cheer the new sovereign. Anticipating disturbance, Marshal Serrano had lined the route with infantry and provided the closed royal coach for the King—surrounding it with a screen of dragoons. Amadeo, however, bored with the implication that he dared not show himself to his people, waved the carriage aside, mounted his horse, ordered his escort to fall back, and boldly rode alone at the head of the procession. The howling blizzard had driven the disgruntled diplomatic corps into closed carriages. But not Sickles. In his major general's uniform and wearing for once his despised knee-action metal leg, he rode with Serrano close to the King. Bowed to the blast, greeted with ironical cheers and yells of *"Fueran los extranjeros! Viva el Rey Macaroni!* [Away with the foreigners! Long live King Macaroni!]," the royal procession proceeded on its tortuous march from the Plaza del Oriente to the Presidio on the city's outskirts. Suddenly Serrano, intensely on the alert, noted a suspicious movement in the crowd, a glint of pistol barrels, and a bearded Catalan with upraised arm apparently giving a signal to his fellows. Whirling his horse and drawing his saber, he plunged into the group, cut down the leader, slashed the others into terrified flight, and returned to his place in the march as though nothing had happened. To Sickles he remarked calmly, "With us, the leader is everything —deal with him, and the trouble is over." Under a driving sleet the Army performed its maneuvers, lined up for review, plodded drearily through the Ceremony of the Oath. Drenched and shivering, it returned to its barracks, and Amadeo to his gloomy palace. Sickles noted in his diary, "The unhappy inauguration of what I fear will be a brief, unhappy reign."

There was now no one with whom Sickles dared discuss his cherished project. Prim had been virtually an honest dictator in search of a king and a treasure chest, and his personal power had been paramount. But Serrano, the Premier; and Sagasta, the Minister of State, were essentially politicians—and, as such, beyond reach in a matter pregnant with political suicide. Moreover, Sickles's relations with both had become severely strained by recent events.

Early in the same year the American steamer, *Colonel Lloyd Aspinwall*, with legitimate cargo, perfect clearance papers, and bearing important government dispatches for Admiral Poor, commanding the North Atlantic Squadron stationed at Havana, had been stopped on the high seas by the Spanish cruiser *Hernán Cortes* and taken first to Nuevitas, and thence to Havana, over the indignant protests of her skipper, Captain McCarty. For three months, under one pretext or another, captain and crew had been confined aboard the impounded ship in dilatory defiance of the repeated, and increasingly angry, protests lodged by Secretary Fish with the Spanish minister to the United States, Lopez Roberts, and by General Sickles with the Spanish minister of State, Sagasta. Driven from one excuse to another, the Cuban authorities, in a last evasion, had declared the vessel "sub judice," promising that it would be restored to its lawful owners if and when the prize court adjudicating its status should decree that it had been engaged in legitimate commerce. This had given Sickles his opening. In an incisive interview with Sagasta, he had replied that, according to international law, prize-court proceedings in a case of this kind could be recognized only in the event that a "state of war" existed between the parties concerned, bluntly adding that while the Spanish authorities had made no formal declaration of war against the United States, their present action constituted such, and could be construed by his government in no other way. This had brought results!

And after some fourteen days of further procrastination by the Cuban authorities, the vessel had been released—but even so, only under the guns of the North Atlantic Squadron, dispatched to protect her from threatened last-minute destruction by the upper-class Spanish mob known as "The Volunteers." So close had it come to war!

The "incident," coupled with the open advocacy of Cuban independence on the part of many members of Congress, was one well calculated to chill the reception of the United States minister in the highly chauvinistic circles of Madrid society. Nevertheless a military reputation, a personal dignity equal to that of the most fastidious don, soon won him something more than a polite acceptance among the grandee families opposed to the *révolté* administration. For his own part, disregarding a tilted nose here and there, he revived, on a more lavish scale, the hospitable traditions of Stockton Mansion; and the Legation dinners, official and unofficial, were appointed with a splendor savoring more of Spanish royalty than of Yankee democracy! In this studiedly handsome entertaining he was greatly helped by his mother. Knowing well her skill in management, he had sent for her soon after his arrival, to come and play Legation hostess for him; and had arranged to have Laura come with her. For the first time in ten years he had hoped to enjoy again some taste of home life. With her gracious old-fashioned competence, his mother, indeed, had proven a great comfort to him. But not so Laura. He had dared to believe that, under the influence of the novel scenes and pleasures of the capital, she might become reconciled to him. But in the intervening years she had developed into a thin nervous creature with a certain wild beauty—and equally wild moods. Hopelessly neurotic, she quickly had shown herself intractable, full of scornful bravado, and openly hostile to him and his world. Within a week of her arrival Sickles had regretted having brought her again under his roof. Almost at once she had become violently enamored of a young Spanish officer. Her reckless conduct of the affair had forced Sickles to intervene. And in an outburst of defiance she had destroyed the last possibility of more than a formal relationship between them.

Curiously, it was with the exclusive and ultraconservative Court clique accustomed to foregather in the massive old mansion presided over by the widowed Marquise Creagh that Sickles formed his more intimate contacts. A charming reactionary, blind to everything but the divinity of Bourbon blood, the Marquise, from girlhood, had been Isabella's devoted friend. Her husband—descendant of an Irish nobleman attached to the Royal Bodyguard of Carlos III—had held various decorative posts at Court, as also had her brothers; while her young daughter, Caroline, at that moment, was playing lady-in-waiting in the exiled regal ménage. The Creaghs, in fact, were the very heart of the "legitimist" reaction in Madrid. But despite his democratic principles Sickles found them particularly *simpático*. A republican as much by the accident of birth as by intellectual conviction, he still retained in his blood the tastes and temper of his feudal forebears. And it, perhaps, was not so surprising that he should find in the royalist atmosphere of the Creaghs no bar to his friendship for them, nor that he should be intrigued, rather than otherwise, by their romantic allegiance to the woman he well remembered as a vivid, tragic young queen. In any case his curiosity was piqued. And when, toward the close of the Franco-Prussian War, diplomatic affairs summoned him to Paris, and the Marquise begged him to stop off en route at Biarritz and deliver certain confidential dispatches to Isabella, he readily agreed to play courier.

The subsequent meeting was as human in its naturalness as it was fateful in its consequences. At the Château Mont D'Or—loaned her by the Duc de Montpensier—Isabella received Sickles alone, and—as was her negligent wont with visitors high and low—in artistic dishabille. Clad in little but a gorgeous tea gown so loosely swathed about her that it half bared her great breasts, her heavy hair showering her to the waist, her bold obsidian eyes a-sparkle with sex, she seemed far more some fat gypsy witch than the Bourbon queen of the most convention-ridden country in Europe. Sickles was not unprepared for such reception, for he had heard much of her idiosyncrasies. Nor had the letters of the Marquise failed to depict this *"americano muy simpático"*—including the crutches. As the door closed behind him, Sickles bowed ceremoniously. But Isabella, appraising him in one swift glance, came forward, smiling welcome. "It is a long time, *mi general*, since I had the pleasure of seeing you"; and lightly patting his crutches, she gave him her hand to kiss, then put her arms about him and kissed him in return. "We both have changed—*cómo no?* But you have become a great general while I——" Sickles bowed again. "You are more adorable than ever, Your Majesty." She laughed. "Ah—I see you are more gallant than ever! But no 'Majesty,' please—you know how I hate all that. I am Ysabel to my friends." Chattering, she led him to a divan, took away his crutches, and pouring two glasses of her favorite white sherry, sat confidentially beside him while she scanned the heavily sealed missive he had brought her.

After a brief silence Isabella looked up, tapping the bulky letter on her knee. "It's good to know that I have friends at least—and some faint hope." Then, voicing the question always uppermost in her mind, "Tell me, my friend, tell me truly, what do *you* think of my son's prospects for the throne?"

Sickles spoke quite honestly—and very much in the terms of his last dispatch to the State Department. "I think that four or five years from now his chances will be very good." Isabella put an impetuous hand on his knee. "Why, my friend—why?" Sickles pondered a moment. "Well—for two reasons. One is Amadeo, the other is Spain. The King is really a very good fellow. He is doing his utmost to win the confidence of his people. But in Spanish eyes nothing can ever overcome the damning fact that he is a foreigner. And he is far too punctilious to remain long where he is not wanted. If he lasts two years I shall be surprised. His abdication would pre- cipitate a Republican reaction. But it would not last long—Spain is too monarch-minded for that. I don't care to play prophet, but I would venture to guess that after a year or two there will be a gen- eral clamor for the restoration of the throne. Spain will never try another foreign king. She never will accept the Pretender, Don Carlos. And what choice will there be but Prince Alfonso?"

Isabella relaxed with a sigh. "That is really the way you see it?"

Sickles smiled wryly. "As a Republican I ought to wish it the other way, I suppose. But that's the way the stream runs, I think— but the canoe may need a little steering here and there."

"And you will help steer?" The urgency in her eyes was hard to resist.

"For your sake." The words came impetuously—their thanks a kiss by no means formal.

So began between these two disparate beings—the nineteenth- century democrat, the sixteenth-century absolutist—a most com- panionable liaison, sensual, merry, mutually understanding, that, laughing at all surface barriers, was to remain for many years the central fact of their lives. In truth, diverse as they might be in tradition, they had certain strong resemblances in temperament. Both were prodigals—in sex and purse; both were egocentric, yet unfailing in hidden acts of graceful kindness;* both had the magnetism of rich vitality, the power of evoking great personal devotion.

At dinner Isabella introduced her guest to a slight, prim young Spanish beauty with the tight mouth and wooden expression so characteristic of the convention-bound but highly sex-conscious señorita of rank. Sickles found himself chatting with Caroline Creagh, daughter of his good friend La Marquise, with the sense that, against Isabella and the rather lush atmosphere of the *émigré* ladies and courtiers surrounding her, she seemed a little like a nun at a masked ball. But when later he happened to catch her glance, he noticed that her cheeks flushed, and she seemed suddenly confused.

*Scores of letters from humble folk thanking the General for services he had rendered them, services sometimes trifling, sometimes critical—such as rescuing a household from eviction, saving a wild lad from court-martial—came to light in his archives. Isabella's winsome kindness to high and low preserved her popularity long after she had rightfully forfeited it by her negligent misrule.

On the sea-front promenade at Biarritz, where, for the next few weeks, they were accustomed to stroll, deep in talk, the two infatuates were the focus of attention. Of Isabella herself Lady Louise Tenison wrote:

She has grown very stout; and with the most good-natured face in the world, has certainly nothing to boast of in elegance of manner or dignity of deportment. She looks what she is—a most thoroughly kindhearted creature, liking to enjoy herself, and hating all form and etiquette; extremely charitable but always acting on the impulse of the moment, obeying her own will in all things instead of being guided by any fixed principle of action. . . . The one point on which she made a firm stand against her Ministers was to insist upon her right to exercise mercy, and she insisted upon the right even in the case of her would-be assassin, the priest, Martin Marino.*

As for the Queen's new lover, grown a little portly and heavy-shouldered from the use of crutches, accoutered *en règle*—frock coat, silk hat, white choker collar, striped gray cravat, peg-top trousers in the French mode—he had brought from the battlefield and his subsequent strenuous experience as envoy and military governor an authoritatively mature air that La Marquise had hit off rather happily when she wrote of him, "*Un americano magnífico y romántico!* He is very gallant; but has great force; and wears his crutches as though they were medals—as he should!"

But Sickles could not dally long at Biarritz. France was in the throes. The siege of Paris just had ended; but Gambetta was still holding the field; and the revolt against the armistice that was to culminate in the Commune was looming up. Thiers had risen from a sickbed to undertake a desperate embassy to the Court of St. James's, St. Petersburg, Vienna, in the hope of obtaining the intervention of the powers on behalf of less drastic terms of peace for France. Returning empty-handed, he had sought the good offices of the United States. But while the State Department had declined to undertake any official representations in a matter so exclusively the concern of the two European sovereignties, it was not averse from permitting its diplomatic agents to use their influence personally and unofficially on behalf of the reborn Republic. As the United States representative in France, and close friend of Thiers, Minister Washburne felt that his own intercession would be discounted from

*The Gentleman's Magazine, London, 1889.

the start. Accordingly, the Comte de Paris, titular head of the Royalist party and Bourbon claimant to the throne, in consultation with Thiers requested Sickles to assume the task of endeavoring to soften the Iron Chancellor. Both trusted the General's persuasive powers, skill in negotiation. And they wisely concluded that a disinterested spokesman who had held high command in a victorious army and who thereafter had administered conquered territory would know how to talk Bismarck's language better than a civilian diplomat.

Thiers was deeply touched by Sickles's hearty acceptance of the adventure, as was Sickles by the shrewd, scholarly old statesman's steadfastness under crushing responsibility. And their conferences proved to be the birth of a lasting friendship between them.

At Brussels, Sickles, provided with a letter of introduction from the Comte de Paris, a prewar intimate of Bismarck's, had no difficulty in securing a hearing. When his appointment came, Bismarck received him unceremoniously, soon warmed to him, but, learning his business, showed a strong preference—then as in subsequent interviews—for discussing the Civil War, hunting, the virtues of Munich lager and Rhenish wine—in fact, anything and everything else. At the same time Jules Favre, the French Minister of State, was struggling heroically at the Green Table to save part of Alsace-Lorraine and reduce what seemed, at the time, the bankrupting indemnity. Sickles, however, soon saw the hopelessness of persuading the Chancellor to make any substantial concessions and shrewdly concentrated his efforts on trying to save, at least, the industrial center and strategic fortress of Belfort. How much his genial diplomatic chumming with Bismarck contributed to the winning of this sole concession, it would be impossible to say. But it may well be that his frank good will, soldierly talk, connoisseurship in Rhenish may have helped more to that end than the strenuous official representations of Thiers and Favre themselves. In any case, when, a few years later, Thiers, as President of the French Republic, had the power to thank Sickles for his services officially, he did not hesitate to confer upon him, at the request of the Comte de Paris, the all but supreme French honor—hitherto never accorded an American— Grand Croix de la Légion d'Honneur.

At the same time Isabella removed to Paris and re-established her court-in-exile in a baroque old mansion on the Avenue Kléber. Hesitantly she sent the eleven-year-old Alfonso to the Lycée, but, dissatisfied, soon transferred him to Vienna for tutoring under Count Morphy. Finally, however, upon the advice of her faithful but liberal-minded former State Councilor, Don Antonio Cánovas del Castillo, she dispatched him to England—there to absorb British constitutional ideas at Eton and Sandhurst.

A bizarre affair—that court on the Avenue Kléber. Even in the Escorial the Queen had boldly ignored the stiff hedge of convention about the throne, had dressed as she pleased, and had chosen her associates purely on the basis of her own predilections—often in the teeth of her ministers. But now, for the first time in her life, she was really free to indulge her very human, if rather indiscriminate, taste for all kinds of people and to surround herself with the companions of her fancy unconcerned with the bugbears of rank and respectability.

A bizarre court in a bizarre time! Paris in '71 was on the loose. With the fall of Sedan, the Empire had vanished almost unnoticed; and with it had vanished much of the old social decorum. After a few weeks of theatrical gestures as Regent, the Empress Eugénie had stolen away to that refuge of royalty, Windsor, there to shelter beneath the ample skirts of Queen Victoria. While the popular sentiment was Republican, the Corps Législatif—no real constituent assembly, but a mere façade for Napoleon's dictatorship—was strongly monarchial and clerical. With the Empire not only dead but damned, the crisis called for the decisive establishment of a new order. But the Chamber, splintered into factions, seemed not to know from day to day what course to pursue. It was an interim of social disorder, political confusion, well typified by the scarred walls, fallen roofs, rubble of brick, disfiguring a city blasted by German, and again by French, guns within six months. From Versailles to the Hôtel de Ville the air was thick with intrigue. Gathering, each clan to its favorite café, the partisans of the Prince de Joinville, of the Comte de Paris, of Thiers and the Republic, of Karl Marx and Borodin, drank and argued around the clock. Clashes and brawls were frequent. And as the lights came on, the street corners were blocked with groups fiercely discussing, in the characteristic fashion of the Parisian *ouvrier*, the last canard.

And Isabella's Court reflected both herself and the *mise en scène*. The thrones of France and Spain were at dice. And the house on the Avenue Kléber was the natural place for the play. And with that kind of play go pawnbroking financiers, gentlemen with schemes to exploit, secret agents, prospective concessionaires, fringe politicians, the genteel riffraff likely to gather about a royal ménage gone astray. All these wended in and out of Isabella's doors. And rubbing disdainful shoulders with them came the *haut noblesse*. Sneer as they might at this "*blancheuse*" and her assorted associates, these gentry of a vanished day could not disregard the fact that she was a Bourbon. And who could tell but that she or her son yet might reign at the Escorial, and a Bourbon be crowned King of France? So the Faubourg called—lending a touch of distinction and decorum to haphazard assemblies basking in Isabella's bohemian bonhomie. More welcome were the writers and artists of prestige—most of whom, however they might rail against royalty in the saddle, found something of allure in royalty unhorsed. Not Victor Hugo, that godly man, but George Sand, Gustav Flaubert, Jean Paul Laurens, several of whose paintings Isabella purchased for her walls, Félicien David, the venerable composer, Louis Vielliemin, the brilliant Swiss historian and intimate of Thiers, were among those who decorated her jumbled but jolly salons. And behind these came also, here and there, a neophyte of Montparnasse—some indigent painter, poet, more akin to the Queen's taste, picked up by chance and, as often as not, liberally helped from her purse.

Into this milieu Sickles, fresh from the Spartan court and diplomatic drudgery of Madrid, stepped with the sense both of a schoolboy on vacation and of a kingmaker in the making! If to him Isabella was Holiday, her plea that he help her further Alfonso's cause had set him thinking also about another cause—that of his old comrade on campaign, the Comte de Paris. When Louis Philippe abdicated, he had named this eldest grandson of his—then only nine years of age—as his successor. And the growing monarchist agitation in the French Chamber made it plain to the General that now, if ever, was the moment for the Comte to strike and assert his historic claim to the throne.

Once started on this road of Royalist intrigue, Sickles suffered no doubts as to the value of its success to the countries involved. So far as Alfonso was concerned, he had good hope that this young Bourbon's unusual intelligence, well nurtured in British liberal traditions, would make him the type of constitutional monarch Spain so urgently needed. And through four brutal campaigns he had come to know the Comte's integrity and breadth of mind, his innate benevolence, high capacity. There was no man he more admired, none that he deemed more competent to lead France out of her present weltering. And if affection and self-interest largely motivated his ambition to see the son of his mistress on the throne of Spain, his friend on the throne of France, the General was well satisfied that his aims, fulfilled, would serve the best interests of both realms.

But in the case of the Comte there was a novel difficulty. The author of *The History of the Civil War* seemed, for the moment, more interested in polishing the proofs of his monumental work than in claiming his ancestral rights. Against this philosophic detachment Sickles brought to bear all his arts of argument, persuasion. . . . Two Republics had failed. Royalist factions preponderated in the Chamber. And the Comte's strong leadership could easily unite them into a force capable of placing him on the throne—if only he would come out of his retirement and take his stand. Delay would be dangerous; and France needed him.

So Sickles presented the case. Nor could he be deterred by his friend's disinterested attitude, frank reluctance to place himself at the head of a clique or accept the throne in response to less than a national mandate.

Thus all summer, almost living on the Paris-Madrid Express, now closeted at the Creaghs' with the Duc de Serbo, Don Antonio Cánovas del Castillo, General Martinez Campos, Isabella's devout supporters, anon in close conference with the Comte and his royal relatives at Chantilly, the General nurtured his projects—not unmindful of the fact that, should time and tide bring them to successful issue, it would redound vastly to his prestige, give him intimate place, unique influence at the courts of Versailles and Madrid, make him an American power in European politics.

Power the General coveted, but that it was the Queen herself he loved, he made no effort to conceal. If, seated beside her, playing genial king to her motley court, driving with her on the Bois, escorting her to the Opéra Comique, or on bankrupting shoppings to the Rue de Rivoli or the Rue de la Paix, it ever occurred to him that this was hardly correct diplomatic procedure for an American minister to a rival court, he showed no sign of it, continued unperturbed.

And soon all Paris—ever ready to twinkle at an amour, especially one in high places—was dubbing him, "*Le Roi Américain de l'Espagne*"—the Yankee King of Spain.

Meanwhile he was too much occupied to notice more than momentarily—and then with irritation—that Caroline Creagh seemed pointedly to avoid him, and yet was always swishing her skirts across his path.

Suddenly to this bold dreaming came a rude, realistic shock. The Duc de Serbo, Cánovas, and General Campos appeared at the house on Avenue Kléber in a state of dour dudgeon. Angrily, if respectfully, they reported that Bourbon circles in Spain were dismayed that the Queen of their allegiance, the mother of the prince they strove to make king, should be openly flaunting herself in Paris as the mistress of the American minister. Isabella must choose between her lover and her son's chance of the throne. She could not have both. Unless the scandal were stopped immediately, the strong and growing support for Alfonso's claim would melt and be lost.

Isabella was a creature of many passions, but one dominated them all—her desire to see Alfonso on the throne. Rudely confronted with the possible results of her laxity, she broke down in one of her characteristic fits of violent contrition and promised to make amends. But a half-hour later, in the midst of sadly bidding the astounded Sickles adieu, she, as characteristically, dried her tears and began plotting how to circumvent fate and her promise, pacify outraged convention, and still keep her lover.

As they stood at the window in low talk, the solution appeared in the garden below. Watching Caroline Creagh moodily pacing about the lawn, Isabella only half caught Sickles's angry and stubborn "If that's the trouble—why, then, shouldn't we be married?"

Without turning, Isabella shrugged. "You forget that to these people you are what they like to call a commoner. No. That is impossible. In their eyes I should no longer be queen, Alfonso no longer heir apparent." Then, suddenly pointing, "*There* is your marriage. The child is going sick and insane for love of you. But she won't give you a smile because she will not cross me." Sickles stood completely baffled. Isabella became urgent, imploring, "Don't you see? It's the only way out—unless we part for good right now! I know you Americanos don't understand our Latin *mariage de convenance;* but you know as well as I that most of our marriages are affairs of that kind and are perfectly respected. And in your position you need a wife, a wife of wealth, rank—*and complete loyalty to me.* Don't you understand that, married to my lady-in-waiting, you could always be with me as much as you pleased, and no one would question it? With us Spaniards, so long as the outward conventions are preserved, we are not concerned with other people's private affairs. . . . And then, allied with my Court, what influence you could wield for Alfonso in Madrid!"

Against the torrent of her tongue Sickles could only blurt out an expostulating "But—my God! She doesn't interest me. She knows we're together day and night! Has she no pride?"

Isabella, intent upon her idea, caught his hand, swept on eagerly. "You won't be doing her an injustice. She will have what the Spanish woman wants most—established position, security, a distinguished husband. She won't expect love!"

But the General would have none of it. For days Isabella, amid fits of weeping and hysterical appeals to the Virgin, exhausted herself in dramatic efforts to overcome his scruples, his American distaste for such a "Continental" solution of their problem. But her insistence only stiffened him. Suddenly, with woman wile, she switched her tactics, bade him go.

Gloomily the General went to his room, ordered his bags packed. Only then did he realize how much Isabella—with her impulsive warmth and whimsy, her careless bravado, everflowing laughter, quick understanding—had released and refreshed him, how necessary she had become to him.

Impatiently he dismissed his valet, paced the room, brooding. . . . Why was he finding it so hard to take Isabella at her word? He remembered how he had written his friend Seaver, the year before, "Somehow, without any effort on my part, I find myself provided with a new sweetheart every month." So it always had been with him. Beguiled and beguiling, he had amused himself with innumerable mistresses—darlings of a day. They had cost him plentifully in perfume and jewelry—but scarcely a pang in parting. In no one of them had he found a *companion.* . . . That was the trouble now. Isabella was mistress and companion in one—the first in his life. It meant nothing to him, fastidious connoisseur of the feminine as he knew himself to be, that she was plain, fat, and forty.

It mattered less that she was a disgraced and discarded queen perverted by a foul marriage and her own rebellion into a reckless courtesan. Nothing mattered but that, at long last, he had met a woman whose nature and need meshed with his own.

Staring out of the window, he noticed a slim figure restlessly sauntering about the garden. From the room adjoining came the sound of sobbing. He hesitated. "Here I am, making two women wretched and tormenting myself, simply because——"

At the same moment Isabella was weeping tears of strange taste. She had seen this man of fierce energy, restless ambition, abandon himself like a boy in her presence. For the first time she had realized her need of being needed, had tasted the joy of being the joy, instead of the sport or pawn, of a lover. Coming from another world, another century, he had no reserves with her, no scheme behind his kiss, no eye upon her purse or power of appointment. There was nothing she could give him, nothing he wanted, but herself. For the first time she, too, had found a lover who was also a companion. . . . Why was he so stubborn? Such an American provincial in his notions! So *bête!* . . . Disheveled, tear-smeared, she ran to his room. His half-packed bags stood about. He was gone. She glanced into the garden. There in an arbor he sat, talking earnestly to Caroline, her hand in his. In an outburst of the childish religious fervor that swept her at moments Isabella threw herself before the niched Madonna in the corner pouring out passionate, if incongruous, thanks.

CHAPTER XXX

Le Mariage de Convenance

FROM THE FIRST, Caroline had been a misfit at Court. Even in childhood her meticulous propriety had excited the Queen's fond amusement; and the fact that she was a Creagh was sufficient to make her a favorite. But while reared in the Royalist credo, "The King can do no wrong," she had been trained at a fashionable convent school in the strict doctrines of the Church and had grown up as devout a religionist as she was a monarchist. Thus when, on Caroline's eighteenth birthday, the Queen—to the delight of the worldly Marquise—had put a string of pearls around her neck and announced her a lady-in-waiting, she had been more fearful than flattered. And only her mother's urging, her own sense of duty, had induced her to follow the Court into exile. If, with her strict ideas of marriage dignity, she often was shocked by Isabella's disorderly soul, ephemeral infatuations, she was too mindful of the etiquette of her position to permit a hint of her feelings to appear. So she had lived—in a kind of stupor, cultivating the art of discreet blindness, convenient deafness, distracting herself by painstaking attention to her manifold petty duties. But when the General had appeared, she had waked—suddenly had become an impassioned, unpredictable woman. Aloof, straitlaced, disdaining the young fashionables frequenting the Court, she had succumbed at a glance to this crippled Americano, with his mature masculinity, richly informed talk, his air of domination over circumstance—and women. And since that moment, realizing that he had eyes for none but the Queen, she had been twisted between a wild desire to flee and an equally wild need to stay. That the General was studiedly courteous to her, and sometimes would be at great pains to be entertaining, only maddened her. And her behavior—if it perplexed him, amused the Queen—often bewildered herself. But when at last, obviously agitated, the General had sought her in the garden and stammered out something about his need of home and stability and what they might do together on behalf of the Queen and Alfonso, and then, after a few awkward compliments, had blurted out his formal proposal of marriage, she had been too raptly surprised to taunt and test him—too glad that her moment of triumph had come so soon. That, as he had added, he was speaking with the Queen's full approval, had filled her cup—for the royal blessing was needful. And that blessing had been given with disarming ingenuousness. Kissing her maternally, Isabella had murmured, "My child, the General has told me that he wished to marry you. I would not dream of standing between you two. I only regret that I cannot be present at the wedding."

In an hour Caroline had been transformed from forlorn fury to radiant self-confidence. And any doubt as to the sincerity of the General's sudden *volte-face* had instantly been dissipated by his impetuous demand for an early marriage.

Once he had decided upon his course, the General, in fact, had pursued it with whirlwind energy and dispatch. Within the next few weeks he had swept compliantly through the necessary formality of conversion to Catholicism, made a flying trip to Madrid, secured the delighted consent of La Marquise, her brothers, aunts, uncles, all duly assembled in family conclave, had published the banns and had made all the necessary arrangements for the wedding. . . .

Meanwhile the usual property settlement dragged annoyingly. Finally it transpired that until certain of her father's properties could be freed from litigation, Caroline's dowry would be negligible. The discovery—and the excuse—struck the General with sharp misgiving. He knew that many of the grandee families suffered from the general impoverishment of the country and were hard put to it to maintain appearances; but he had always understood that the Marquis Creagh had inherited a vast fortune, and naturally had assumed that Caroline's dowry would be of appropriately handsome proportions. And what made the matter worse was the fact that, deprived of his lucrative law practice, compelled to spend far more than his official salary of $12,000 a year, he had been dipping dangerously into his reserves. At the same time recent advices from his New York brokers had apprised him that his heavy holdings in the Erie Railroad were rapidly becoming worthless under Jay Gould's vicious maladministration. But it was too late to draw back.

Amid a cathedral pomp and pageantry little less than that accorded a royal wedding, watched by a vast congregation dominated by the grandee families pledged to Isabella, and so barred with rows, and splotched with clots, of gaudy uniforms, military, diplomatic, as to give it the air of some exotic ballet ensemble, the General and his bride knelt before the Archbishop of the Indies and made their vows—the one with a grim, the other with a glowing, heart.

In the front pew, beside the Marquise, the bridegroom's mother, proud and perplexed, looked on; but his daughter was not present. Laura was abed. Nor had she feigned indisposition. Disgust at the marriage, amounting to fury as the ceremony approached, had thrown her into a high fever.

Sickles already had decided to make his wedding trip an excuse for an immediate return to New York. In need of money, he had urgent business there. If his holdings in Erie stock were to be salvaged, Jay Gould and his gang had to be ousted from their control of the road, a new directorate appointed. The project had an air of phantasy.

Dark, slight, malicious, with eyes of a ferret, snout of a fox, Jay Gould was by far the most conscienceless criminal in American finance. His "Black Friday" foray on the gold market had precipitated a disastrous panic throughout the whole country. Subsequently filching his way into control of the Erie Railroad, he had paid no attention to it as a business, but used it simply as a base for his elaborately crooked stockjobbing operations. Vigorously resisted in his efforts to gulp a subsidiary road, the Albany & Susquehanna, and finding purchased orders from the bench insufficient for the purpose, he had hired an army of some eight hundred thugs and endeavored to cow his opponents with a slugging, train-wrecking campaign known as "The Erie War." His domination of the courts and the press was complete. Judges hastened to write his dictated decisions and injunctions with hands that trembled—or itched. Such newspapers as did not trumpet him dared not attack him, nor deal with him less than politely. To jolt such a buccaneer from his quarter-deck was no light undertaking. And Sickles knew it.

Getting in touch with the British group of Erie bondholders—gentlemen unaccustomed to the antics of American finance, and now perturbed over Gould's strange conduct of their affairs—he secured their power of attorney; and with this by way of a club—handy if by no means heavy—he set sail for New York, immersed in plotting the strategy of his projected ouster. Caroline, confined to her cabin by severe *mal de mer*, was too wretched to notice his absorption. Few on board suspected that they sailed with a distinguished bride and bridegroom.

By the time he reached New York, indeed, Sickles already seriously regretted his marriage. And realizing that, as a Spanish Catholic and Royalist, Caroline's reception scarcely could be enthusiastic in his New York circle, he contented himself with introducing her to his father and more intimate friends, carefully evading social commitments. Nevertheless he endeavored to preserve the gestures of a happy bridegroom at such dinners, theater and opera parties as were plainly unavoidable. For the rest, his days and no few of his nights were spent at his old office at 74 Nassau Street or on frequent unobtrusive visits to Tammany Hall, Wall Street, certain mansions on Park Avenue.

Never had the General been more absorbed, tight-lipped, remote. To his friends, puzzled at this sudden lapse of his old sociability, he pleaded "pressing diplomatic business." Pressing it was, and highly diplomatic—this secret and thorough organization of an insurrection in Erie.

Three months passed. Then suddenly New York papers blazed with banner headlines. Shouted the *Times:*

GENERAL SICKLES SPRINGS COUP D'ETAT IN ERIE

EXCITING SCENES IN THE GRAND OPERA HOUSE

JAY GOULD DEPOSED FROM THE PRESIDENCY—REORGANIZATION OF THE BOARD OF DIRECTORS

A most extraordinary series of events occurred yesterday at the Erie Railway offices in the Grand Opera House, the result being the final displacement of Jay Gould from the Presidency of the Company and a partial reorganization of the Board of Directors. General John A. Dix was elected and installed as President, and Mr. W. W. Sherman, of the firm of Duncan, Sherman and Company, was appointed Treasurer, Mr. O. H. P. Archer being retained as Vice-President. The details of this remarkable movement are herewith presented in regular order, affording a most exciting narrative.

It appears that the movement really commenced weeks ago, though the proceedings were kept a profound secret in order to take the Gould party utterly by surprise.

General Sickles and S. L. M. Barlow seem to have been the prime movers in the matter, assisted in a great measure by George Crouch, formerly in the pay of Gould and Fisk, but now devoted to the interests of a portion of the English stockholders. The hour was apparently well chosen, for Gould and his adherents seem to have been completely dumbfounded by the strategy of his opponents.

That Sickles, in an hour, could seize possession of the Erie offices and force a quorum of directors to resign in favor of men pledged to oust Gould and appoint a new and trustworthy president and board, indicates the crushing pressure he must have brought to bear, the military thoroughness of his preparation and organization! Caught completely off guard, Gould had only time to rush out a purchased injunction countering the proceedings and fill the corridors of the buildings with his plug-uglies. The first was ignored; and the second—confronted with squads of police and Tammany boys mobilized by Sickles against just such an emergency—evidently preferred playing cards to wielding clubs. Before the sun went down that day, Jay Gould was on the curb, Erie was in good hands, and its stock was already rocketing on the Street.

But the play was not quite over. Gould, outguessed and overpowered, still remained cool and cagey. He had known temporary setbacks before, but he had always known how to make a friend of an enemy—on the right terms! This Sickles was smart—he could use a man like that. And the next afternoon he casually dropped in at 23 Fifth Avenue, the solid, stone-front residence recently leased by his enemy. Ushered into the library where, seated behind a massive desk, Sickles was winding up his affairs preparatory to his departure for Spain, Gould came forward with a knowing, ingratiating air. "General, the man that can outsmart me is my friend. Maybe I've done some pretty neat things in my time, but nothing quite as neat as that trick of yours. What I say is, you're not the kind of man I want for an enemy. Let's get together——"

While Gould was speaking, the General was rising, slowly gathering his crutches under him. Without a word he was oaring himself around the desk, his face a knotted fist. Gould, catching his expression, backed uneasily away. The unfinished sentence ended in a yelp as a crutch, slung at him, caught him square in the face. Bloody-nosed, he stumbled backward toward the great Tudor window, its twin panes thrust open against the unseasonable April heat. Still without a word the General bore down on him, grabbed him by the collar and the seat of his pants, and with only one leg to aid, hoisted him and hurled him through the open window. Fortunately for Gould—and perhaps for his assailant!—the library was on the ground floor. And, from the ledge to the soft flower bed below, it was only a six-foot drop. Terrified but unhurt, Gould scrambled to his feet and fled. At that moment Moseley, the Negro houseman, alarmed by the noise, came running in—to find his master fuming at the window, muttering as he gazed down at the trampled plot, "The damned scoundrel! My poor violets—my poor violets!"

That evening the New York papers ran extras with flaring head-lines—"Sickles Tries to Kill Jay Gould! . . . Sickles Attempts His Second Murder!"

Once back in Madrid, the General, in view of his bride's ardent if irritating devotion and his own official position, set himself to live up to his obligations with such grace as he could. But with Caroline—caste-ridden, inflexible—he could make no easy relation-ship, while at the same time her femininity was in arms against his rather labored attentiveness. The result was that before long both turned instinctively from the poverty of their emotional life to seek distraction together in the only common sphere left to them— *Alfonsista* society.

Fortunately Sickles was now once more in good financial cir-cumstance. He had been awarded a handsome honorarium by the British bondholders in Erie—including the gift of his rented New York home, 23 Fifth Avenue, and had been voted a large block of stock by the subsequently elected directors of the reorganized company. Also he had culled a fine profit from the sale of some of his New Jersey real estate. This renewed affluence, coupled with the enriched social nexus brought to him by marriage, enabled him to give his Legation dinners and balls on a larger scale and in an atmosphere of increased distinction. When, in fact, these two part-ners in a counterfeit marriage were not entertaining in the prodigal style he demanded and she adored, they were being entertained in one or other of the fortresslike grandee mansions where the first toast after dinner was always, "His Royal Highness—soon may he reign!" And it was only upon these occasions that Caroline—the perfect thing in dress and manner, queening it over her *Alfonsista* admirers, parading her husband, sipping the nectar of envy—found passing joy in being the wife of His Excellency; and that His Excel-lency, well wined, found himself admitting that if his marriage was a private trial, it decidedly was a social triumph.

Laura was no longer present. Refusing to live with this strange stepmother, she had broken completely with her father and returned to New York. There the effects of her broken childhood still pur-sued her. After a reckless marriage, followed soon by separation, she lived on the allowance Sickles punctiliously paid her—a disillusioned, devil-may-care existence until her death at the age of thirty-eight.

In the second year of her marriage Caroline bore a girl. She named her Eda. A year later came a boy. And Sickles, combining the name of his father, and the friend who had defended his life, called him George Stanton.

Meanwhile, on the always convenient excuse of diplomatic business, the General found time for frequent trips to Paris—and the house on Avenue Kléber. But now he was more discreet. And, possibly as a gesture of atonement, he presently was taking Caroline on a long, leisurely tour through Germany and Italy. . . .

Early in '73 Amadeo, after a conscientious effort to overcome the prejudice of the masses against his foreign birth, had abdicated; and once again, under the virtual dictatorship of Serrano and Sagasta, the Republic had been re-established. But if the American minister, in a speech widely quoted and acclaimed, officially congratulated the leaders of the new regime, he had no illusions as to the difficulties before them. Soon again, indeed, those Spanish fatalities, factionalism and regionalism, splitting the Cortes into impotent fragments, precipitated a new era of political feuding and national confusion. Staggering from crisis to crisis, the Republic accomplished nothing of importance save the completion of a project fostered by Amadeo and supported by Sickles with all the influence of his office—the abolition of slavery in Puerto Rico. And scarcely had the mint ceased melting down the coinage stamped with "King Macaroni's" handsome head when once more rose a general clamor for the restoration of the monarchy while the supporters of Alfonso, perfecting their organization among the military element, quietly prepared for a *coup d'état*. Events, in fact, were following the repetitious pattern long ago predicted in the General's first chat with Isabella at Biarritz and in his prescient dispatches to the State Department.

CHAPTER XXXI

"An Everlasting Stain"

————◆◆————

IN THE FALL OF '73—the Republic tottering—Spain and the United States again clashed to the verge of war. And it was this episode, marked by lurid provocation on the part of the Spanish authorities, pitiful pusillanimity on the part of Hamilton Fish, that drove Sickles, in protest, to resign his post at Madrid.

On October 31 the speedy blockade runner *Virginius*, owned by an American citizen, John F. Patterson, and *flying the American flag* in accordance with her registration, was chased, fired upon, brought to, and taken as a prize to Santiago de Cuba by the Spanish warship *Tornado*. For three years past she had been engaged in secretly purveying arms and supplies to the Cuban insurrectos. And on this occasion she was bearing a number of insurgent leaders and American volunteers to a rendezvous on the Cuban coast. When sighted, however, she was on the *high seas*, far from Spanish territorial waters, and thus, by international law, immune from Spanish seizure even though loaded to the scuppers with rebels and contraband. But the Cuban authorities, long aware of her activities, promptly confiscated her. And delighted at the capture of such patriot generals as Bernabe Verona, Pedro Céspedes, Jesus de Sol, and the doughty American filibusterer, Brigadier General Washington Ryan, they proceeded to court-martial captain, crew, and passengers, Cuban and American alike, and stand them in batches before the firing squad. This—while an armed guard prevented the United States consul from cabling a report of the seizure and executions to Washington! And, in the course of the next few weeks, fifty-three of the prisoners were put to death before a British man-of-war, steaming under forced draft to the rescue of the one British sailor aboard, peremptorily put a belated stop to the massacre!

Upon receiving news of the outrage from the consul general at Havana, Hamilton Fish, instead of demanding and enforcing the immediate release of the ship, her passengers and crew, pending complete investigation of the seizure, merely cabled Sickles:

The capture on the high seas of the vessel bearing the American flag presents a very grave question which will need investigation. The summary proceedings resulting in the punishment of death, with such rapid haste, will attract attention as inhuman and in violation of the civilization of the age. And if it prove that an American citizen has been wrongfully executed, this Government will require most ample reparation.

Notified of the incident and of the United States Government's protest, the liberal and honest-minded Spanish premier, Castelar, immediately cabled orders to Santiago to suspend the executions and called personally at the American Legation to express his official regrets. From this point, however, Carvajal, the Secretary of State, a man of quite different caliber, assumed the conduct of the case. Spain's control over her officials in Cuba was far less effective than the local pressure of the bloodthirsty "Volunteers." As a result— with Carvajal's tacit consent—Castelar's orders were disregarded, and the executions continued. Again Sickles vigorously protested— demanding that the United States consul at Santiago be permitted cable communications to his government, and sharply reminding the Secretary that, under the Treaty of 1793, Americans accused of unlawful acts against Spain could be tried in Spanish courts only after due notification of the United States Government, with the full protection of the law and in the presence of competent American officials. Carvajal's answer was a cool provocation of war: "The affair is purely a municipal concern of Spain, and one in which the interference of the United States Government cannot be tolerated." At the same time the Madrid press broke into inflammatory editorials; while the American Legation was so beset by howling mobs that Sickles threatened to close his doors and leave the city unless assured proper respect.

At this moment the daily fusillades on board the *Virginius* had only just begun. But although informed by the United States consul general in Havana that they were continuing, Secretary Fish allowed a week to pass before, aroused by a cable from General Sickles reporting the execution of Captain Fry* and thirty-six of the crew—

*Among the immortal letters is his farewell to his wife.

mostly Americans—he proceeded to lodge a second protest. It was, unfortunately, simply a vapid repetition of the first!

With an eagerness that quickly changed to disgust, the General scanned the new instructions. Vain verbalisms, they still gave him no authority to demand the instant cessation of the butchering.

Two weeks—and still the executions continued!

Wishing furiously that he could change places with Fish for a moment, Sickles did all that his instructions permitted him. And while incisively defining the international law in the case, his written protest to Carvajal burned with the horror and rage then sweeping the United States. Carvajal's reply was a masterpiece of studied insolence. Rejecting the protest with "serene energy," he referred in *tu quoque* style to the "sanguinary acts" committed by the United States, and closed with the pompous rebuke:

I have to fix my attention upon the harshness of style and upon the heated and improper words you use to qualify the conduct of the Spanish authorities. If the document subscribed by you lacks the solemnity which might be lent to it by the right to address it to me, the temperance of its form ought at least to have demonstrated that it was not dictated by passion.

Sickles, in a mordant reply, closed on a note clearly reflecting his conviction that the liberation of Cuba by American arms would be acclaimed by the whole western world:

And if at last, under the good auspices of Mr. Carvajal, with the aid of that *serenity* that is unmoved by slaughter, and that *energy* that rejects the voice of humanity, this Government should prove successful in restoring order and peace and liberty where hitherto, and now, all is tumult and conflict and despotism, the fame of this achievement will reach the continents beyond the seas and gladden the hearts of millions who believe that the New World is the home of free men and not of slaves.

And even while he was coding a message notifying Fish of Carvajal's defiant attitude, came the official report that forty-nine of the prisoners aboard the *Virginius* already had been shot the previous week. The two facts, coupled in one dispatch, moved Fish, at last and too late, to cable the instructions the situation had demanded, and that his minister had craved, from the first:

You will demand the restoration of the *Virginius* and the release and delivery to the United States of the persons captured on her who have not been already massacred, and that the flag of the United States be saluted in the port of Santiago, and the signal punishment of the officials concerned in the capture of the vessel and the execution of the passengers and crew. In case of the refusal of satisfactory reparation within twelve days of this date, you will, at the expiration of that time, close your Legation and will, together with your secretary, leave Madrid, bringing with you the archives of the Legation.

Still Carvajal paltered—while devising a counterplay in hour-to-hour cable correspondence with Admiral Polo, the Spanish minister in Washington. First he proposed an arbitration of the dispute. This Fish refused. Then, at the last moment, half an hour after Sickles had asked for his passports, Carvajal played his last trick. Through the Spanish secret service in New York, acting under the direction of Admiral Polo, he had discovered that the registration of the *Virginius* as an American vessel was technically faulty, and had found persons prepared to swear that the money for her purchase had been supplied to Patterson by agents of the Cuban insurrectos. Armed with this information, he wrote Sickles a note stating that his government was prepared to comply with all the demands of the United States Government *"if it appear that the* Virginius *rightfully carried the American flag, and that her documents were regular."*

It was, of course, a brazen begging of the whole question. The issue was not whether the *Virginius* was registered correctly or incorrectly, whether she carried the American flag legally or illegally, or where Mr. Patterson obtained the funds for her purchase. The issue was whether a ship, any ship, carrying the American flag and with American papers in proper order could be seized on the high seas by the gunboat of a friendly power, and her American captain and crew done to death without even the opportunity of appeal to their government.

But patent as was this old courtroom trick of switching the premises of a dispute and proceeding to prosecute the complainant, it completely befuddled Fish. Nonplussed, flustered, apparently panic-stricken at his recent audacity, he reversed his whole attitude; and now, strictly on the defensive, hastened to draw up with Admiral Polo a protocol that, based exclusively on Carvajal's wily contention, undertook to prosecute the *Virginius* and its owner, instead of the Cuban authorities, as the criminals at the bar!

A sweeping diplomatic victory for Carvajal, and a virtual apology to Spain, it provided:

That the *Virginius* should be released—with such of the passengers and crew as happened still to be alive.

"*That if it appear upon investigation that the* Virginius *did not rightfully carry the American flag, the United States would arraign and punish the owners.*"

That the question of damages be submitted to arbitration.

Requested for an opinion as to whether the *Virginius* was entitled to American registry, Attorney General Williams—on the purely technical point that the registration had not been accompanied by the filing of the usual bond—rendered a verdict in the negative. And except for the subsequent payment of comparatively trifling damages, assessed by arbitration, the case was closed.

In vain Patterson, in a most able letter to the press, tore the Attorney General's verdict to pieces; and pointing out that neither as witness nor defendant had he been allowed to participate in the proceedings condemning him, demanded a public investigation as to his ownership of the *Virginius*, its registration, its claim to protection under the flag. His plea was disregarded. And the *Virginius* —her remaining passengers and crew transferred to another vessel —sank while being towed to New York by a government tug. Never did vessel sink more conveniently!

In the matter of the protocol Sickles had been completely ignored. Finding him disposed to brook neither insolence nor chicanery, Carvajal had gone over his head, convinced by the reports received from Polo that Fish would prove much more amenable. In conniving at this breach of diplomatic etiquette Fish, of course, was guilty of no less a breach. And in slighting his minister and taking negotiations into his own hands, he had permitted himself to be betrayed into a hapless mishandling of the whole imbroglio. Not by the General ever could have been signed a protocol that aroused Spanish jeers, British scorn, and a just damnation throughout the United States as—to quote the New York *Tribune*—"an everlasting stain upon the American escutcheon . . . a burning humiliation to American diplomacy."

In complete disgust, the General resigned, closed his desk—and his diplomatic career. Two weeks later, with his wife and small children, he departed for Paris.

CHAPTER XXXII

Holiday

———◆◆———

For the general the move to Paris meant—above all—Isabella. And establishing Caroline and the children in a charming small estate he had leased at Chantilly, and also reserving private quarters for himself at the Crillon, he soon was spending the larger part of his time at the baroque old mansion on Avenue Kléber. As a private citizen allied to court circles, he was at last free to enjoy the society of the Queen without involving her, as formerly, in Spanish strictures and political difficulties. In any case there no longer was the danger of beclouding Alfonso's accession to the throne. That already seemed assured within the year. And having won a clear field for themselves at last—at the cost of a marital subterfuge—the General and Isabella proceeded to discard the last modicum of discretion. Once more at the Opéra, the theater, at the races, on the Bois, the "Yankee King of Spain" and his Queen made their appearance together—jocular, middle-aged inseparables.

For Caroline—hitherto tenacious in her confidence that she could win her husband away from the Queen—the situation was both a social humiliation and the extinguishment of her hopes. Out of loyalty to Isabella she endured it with proud stoicism for a year. But on the day that the news of Alfonso's summons to the throne flashed over the wires she made her decision. In Madrid now an honored position at court awaited her. Here in Paris she saw nothing before her but the lot of a discarded wife. Abruptly she faced the General with the demand that he return with her to Spain and once and forever forswear his intrigue with the Queen.

It was a hopeless demand. The past year had seen the two become completely estranged. Sickles himself was enamored of Isabella more deeply than ever. And, to a man accustomed as he to place and power, the idea of living in Madrid as a private citizen, merely the husband of a Court lady, was wholly unthinkable. In a scene full of torture for both, he refused. The stark *"adiós"* that ended the discussion was the last word these two were to exchange for nearly forty years. A few days later Caroline, taking little Eda and George with her, returned to her mother's home in Madrid.

But beside Isabella, Paris held for Sickles another persistent lure. Recently the Duc de Broglie, leading a Royalist coalition in the Chamber, had forced the resignation of the aged Thiers as the head of the Provisional Administration, and maneuvered the election of the Maréchal MacMahon, Duc de Magenta, as President of France. This sudden political backwash, indicating an imminent restoration of the monarchy, had swept the Comte de Paris to the very foot of the throne. By the Pact of Bordeaux—a political truce entered into by all parties pending the release of France from the German army of occupation—the final form of the new government had been held in abeyance, and no general election had been held. But this state of affairs could not long continue. And should an election come, the influence of Thiers, the reassuring effect of his able interim leadership, almost certainly would tend to return a Corps Législatif strongly Republican. The moment, therefore, was one to be seized without an instant's delay. And again Sickles—now through Isabella brought into intimate contact with the Royalist noblesse—set himself to aid Maréchal MacMahon, the Duc de Broglie, and their allies in their efforts to unite the other members of the House of Bourbon in support of the Comte de Paris, on the basis that only a monarch of liberal views and soldierly prestige could hope to counter the Republican opposition. But as far as the three rival claimants were concerned, the effort proved superfluous. The Prince de Joinville, the Comte's uncle, by resuming his seat in the Chamber against his public pledge, had brought himself into popular disrepute; while the Comte de Chambord, grandson of Charles X, and, as such, the head of the House of Bourbon, had proceeded to commit monarchial suicide by declaring, in manifesto after manifesto, that never would he consent to be "the King of the French Revolution"! At the same time Prince Napoleon, son of Napoleon III, had disappeared from the scene in search of a life of adventure that presently ended on the barbs of Matabele spears. Thus, in opposition to the Comte de Paris—the clearly legitimate heir—there remained only three possible and secondary claimants to the throne: the Duc de Nemours and the Duc de Montpensier, his other uncles, and his younger brother, the Duc d'Orléans. And Sickles, with his usual keen grasp of situation, and knowing well that he served Isabella's wish, Bismarck's preference, used his favorable position as the friend of all parties to reconcile their differences and obtain from them a pledge of agreement to support the Comte de Paris as the head of the House of Orleans.

At this moment the issue whether France would become a monarchy or a republic quivered on a knife edge. The Royalists were in control of the Chamber. And even Thiers, once the buttress of the Bourbons but now convinced that their day was done, had little heart to oppose the enthronement of a prince he so profoundly trusted and admired. Meanwhile MacMahon, counting on his own military prestige and popularity, stood prepared to break the Pact of Bordeaux and force upon the country a new constitution prescribing a limited monarchy as the future form of government— accompanied by a proclamation announcing Louis Philippe Albert, Comte de Paris, the King of France.

But there the whole carefully prepared scheme crashed on a ridiculous quibble. At the last moment, the Duc d'Orléans, aware that his support was imperative, demanded that the arms of his House—the Fleur de Lys on a White Shield, borne by Jeanne d'Arc on her triumphant campaign—be made the national emblem in place of the Tricolor. In view of the profound sentiment of the French masses for the flag encarnadined by Napoleon and forever associated with the cry, "*Liberté! Egalité! Fraternité!*" the Comte stoutly opposed the change. And MacMahon, in a phrase to become famous, roared, "*Si le drapeau blanc était dévelopé en face du drapeau tricolore, les chassepots partiraient d'eux mêmes!* [Were the White Flag unfurled in place of the Tricolor, the guns would fire of themselves!]" Bitterly chagrined, the Duc d'Orléans, repudiating his pledge to support his brother, stalked out of the conference. With him went—followed by a muttered "The damned fool!" from Sickles, a sigh of sudden relief from the quite unambitious Comte— the last hope of monarchy in France. Out of such a cracked eggshell was the Third Republic born!

Born it might be; but no one at the time could be sure of it. And when finally MacMahon was compelled to call a national election, he still had good hope of a Royalist majority. By the same token Thiers, despite the obviously growing Republican sentiment in the provinces, was deeply concerned as to the result. Just then it happened that President Grant and his wife, having arrived in London on a vacation tour of Europe, were about to leave for Paris. Thiers, aware that MacMahon, by an ostentatious official reception and banquet, was planning to make the utmost political capital out of this first visit of a President of the American Republic to a President of the French Republic, urged Minister Washburne to advise Grant of the situation and suggest that he postpone his arrival until after the election. But Grant, a little obtuse in matters of diplomacy, could see no good reason for this change of plan; and Thiers, in despair, turned for aid to Sickles—now disgusted with the monarchists and keen to serve the Republic. Followed an amusing episode. Within the hour Sickles had caught the boat train for London and in two days was back with Grant's promise to place France last in his itinerary. Crutching it hastily up the steps of the ex-President's home on La Place de St. Georges, he was ushered into the library by Madame Thiers herself. At first he could see no one. Then by the dim light of a single reading lamp he discerned Thiers enjoying an after-dinner nap on a divan before the fire. Madame Thiers stepped forward to wake her husband; but Sickles interposed with a whispered "Let him sleep." While the two were chatting together softly, the ex-President's celebrated sister-in-law, Madame Doche, entered. And conversing with her, Sickles presently noticed that Madame Thiers also had dozed. In a few moments Thiers's private secretary, Barthélemy St. Hilaire—later a prominent figure in French politics—came in, eager to learn the results of the mission. Scarcely had Sickles answered his questions before he observed that Madame Doche, too, had dozed off! For years, it seemed, it had been the habit of the three old people to snatch an after-dinner siesta before their guests of the evening arrived—a habit, apparently, hard to break! And Sickles, arriving hotfoot, found his anxiously awaited news greeted with a little chorus of sedate snores!

The subsequent elections turned thumbs down on a monarchy; and the Third Republic was established—to endure sixty-eight years . . . and perchance longer!

But if one of his pet schemes had perished, the General had good reason to be cheered by the fruition of the other. When, on the last day of December 1874—as the result of a bloodless *coup d'état* led by Cánovas, the Duke de Serbo, and General Campos—Alfonso, then seventeen, had been called to the throne, he immediately had given promise of fulfilling the hopes of a people wearied by political chaos. Under the tutelage of the wise old Cánovas, his first speech from the throne had begun with the pronouncement, "Señores, I would wish to be known as Spain's first Republican." And his first action after the coronation had been to entrain for the front. There, in a stiff engagement with the still-recalcitrant Carlos rebels, he had missed death by the bullet that killed the aide at his side. Thereafter he had shown himself a good listener in council, a quick student of affairs. Seriously bent to acquit himself constitutionally and well— after the patient British fashion of "progress by compromise"—he provided Spain, until his early death eleven years later, with precisely the national focus she needed.

In the interval between Alfonso's coronation, Caroline's departure early in '75, and the final establishment of the Republic in '77, the General and Isabella had enjoyed to the full, and always together, the vivid and varied life of contemporary Paris. There was the Opéra on Mondays, the Comédie Française on Tuesdays, the races and hunts at Chantilly; and in the famous salons—such as those held by Madame Alphonse Daudet, the Comtesse Brissac, Princess Mathilde, Madame Aubernon, and Judith Gautier—they met most of the eminent of the day in politics, art, and letters. It was a period rich with striking personalities. And at one salon or another might be found—among many later to achieve fame—Gambetta, the fiery leader of the Commune, and last to admit French defeat; Louis Blanc, the economist of the Revolution; Ivan Turgenyev, the exiled Russian novelist; Louis Ernest Meissonier, painter of French battle scenes; Ernest Renan whose *Life of Christ* had scandalized the pious; Guy de Maupassant, twenty-seven and already famous; Charles François Gounod, whose *Faust* had long since proclaimed him a composer of the first rank; Echegaray, the brilliant Spanish dramatist; Pierre Puvis de Chavannes, limning his *spirituelle* figures auraed in light; Rosa Bonheur, patient anatomist, and supreme painter of nobly muscled horses; not to forget Alphonse Daudet and the apostolic Victor Hugo. For Sickles, with his aptitude for quick, discerning friendship, his keen feeling for the world of culture born in Da Ponte days, it was a rich interlude—soon ended.

Suddenly the Cortes, at the urgent request of Alfonso, passed an act repealing the decree of exile against the Queen and permitting her return to Spain as a private citizen. For Isabella it mean reunion— and farewell. Tumultuous joy and deep sadness. But knowing well her passionate desire to be with her monarch son, the General had not the heart to withhold her. Nor could he return to Madrid. The hour for parting had struck.

At the same time the General's mother, long invalided and under special care at a Parisian sanitarium, died—perplexed to the last by her strange but always devoted son.

At a stroke Paris, for the "Yankee King of Spain," had become gray and empty—empty as his purse looted by four years of lavish expenditure. New York called. Soberly he packed his bags. Holiday was done.

CHAPTER XXXIII

"Tenting Tonight"

———◆———

Few men of action have enjoyed so prolonged and useful a sundown as the General. When he returned to New York—to all appearance a man in his prime—he was nearly sixty years of age. One life—the bold, varied, dramatic, strenuously expended for state and country—lay behind him. But now a new life lay ahead. Again it was one of public service. But whereas the first had been official, rewarded, motivated by personal ambition, the second—wholly different in its even quietude—was to be honorary, unrequited, motivated only by patriotism and broad benevolence. The change was abrupt. Scarcely had he installed himself in his substantial old mansion and resumed his practice of law when, aroused by the sight of be-medaled beggars on the streets, he was organizing a campaign for the establishment of a commodious State Soldiers' Home. The completion of that project proved the birth of his new career. Himself a crippled, if by no means disabled, veteran, his eyes were lifted to the peak he had reached—where the cannon thundered and the cavalry threshed by and, the decision made, the command belched from his guts meant life or death to thousands of men and the fate of the Union. That absent leg would not let him forget it or the men who had fought and fallen at his side. Gradually, and with increasing urgency, those men, living or dead, absorbed his thought. And to aid the one, commemorate the other, became the new goal of his life.

Thenceforth he threw himself into every enterprise in behalf of the forgotten wounded. Irked by the meager pensions allotted them, he turned pertinacious lobbyist for more liberal allowances. And while waiting for legislative action, his house and pocketbook stood open to every needy son of battle that sought his help. Upon his father's death a handsome inheritance freed him to expand his activities from succoring the neglected living to honoring the neglected dead. As a result of his efforts the New York legislature in 1886 passed an act creating the New York Monuments Commission for the Battlefield of Gettysburg, appointing him its honorary chairman assisted by Generals Slocum, Carr, Richardson, and Porter as fellow commissioners. This marked the beginning of the task that was to engross him for the next quarter of a century—that of raising appropriate and correctly placed monuments to all the New York regiments, batteries, and ranking commanders who had shared with him his own Great Moment. It was an undertaking arduous and complex. And, as its inspiration and director, the greater part of the work involved in it fell, with ready acceptance, upon his own shoulders. His first step was to plan an all-inclusive monument dominating the cemetery where lay the sons of the Empire State—one third of those who fell in the battle!—beneath their drab markers. His next was to seek and secure a term in Congress that he might rescue the field of Gettysburg from vandals and souvenir hunters and convert it into a national Memorial Park under federal care and supervision. Meanwhile there were annual appropriations to be secured from the legislature; an elaborate detailed map of the three-day battle to be charted; surveyors, engineers, sculptors, foundrymen to be selected, and their work vigilantly supervised and co-ordinated to the end that each path and plot and monument might contribute to a longrange artistic whole. And as the statues, monoliths, and cupolas sprouted upon the field—recording in bronze and granite hieroglyphs the otherwise unstoried dead—there followed their dedication on each Fourth of July. No mere glorification of Union victory, these. From the first the Confederate survivors of the battle were invited to participate in them as honored guests. Thus began the historic Gettysburg reunions of Blue and Gray, signalizing, as could nothing else, the healing of old animosities, the closing of the Chasm. And again on the chairman fell the burden of organization required for transporting, feeding, tenting scores of thousands of veterans.

Creative planning, constant conference, endless detail—daily, unremittingly, the General gave them all his energies. To those untouched by the national pulse it may have seemed an activity pale beside the drama of politics, diplomacy, war. But to him it glowed—as the worthy completion of his life's ambit. Soon, one might say, he came to live from one dedicatory reunion to the next, watching his work grow. On these, his great days, his speeches, recapturing the spirit and significance of the struggle, always deeply stirred his ever thinning audience of aging men. Nor did the old eloquent clarity, intuitive touch fail with the years. His last speech, delivered at the age of ninety, able as any, closed with the most memorable peroration of his career:

It is sometimes said that it is not wise to perpetuate the memories of civil war—and such was the Roman maxim. But our Civil War was not a mere conspiracy against a ruler; it was not the plot of some militarist to oust a rival from power; it was no *pronunciamento*. The conflict that raged from 1861 to 1865 was a war of institutions and systems and politics. It was a revolution ranking in importance with the French Revolution of the eighteenth century, and with the English Revolution of the seventeenth century, and universal in its beneficent influence upon the destinies of this country, and ineffaceable in the footprints it left upon the path of our national progress. *For all of us, the Blue and the Gray, it was our heroic age.* The memories of such a war are as indestructible as our civilization. The names of Lincoln and Lee and Grant and Jackson never can be blotted from our annals. The valor and fortitude and achievements of both armies, never surpassed in any age, demand a record in American history. And now that time and thought, common sense and common interests have softened all the animosities of war, we may bury them forever, *while we cherish and perpetuate as Americans the immortal heritage of honor belonging to a Republic that became imperishable when it became free.*

Throughout these years, the General moved among a cloud of friends. Upon his departure for Spain a large group of the outstanding men of New York had given him a farewell rally—no political or merely courtesy affair, but a spontaneous expression of regard for the man himself. Many of these old friends were still around him, and as one by one they dropped away, unable to compete with his own tenacity of life, their places in his circle were filled by the new generation of leadership. President McKinley delighted in him, sought his counsel—especially during the crisis of the Spanish-American

War—and, at his request, appointed his son, young Stanton, attaché to the United States Legation at Brussels. Theodore Roosevelt held him a man after his own heart. Sulzer fought unsuccessfully to gain him promotion to the rank of lieutenant general. Mark Twain, his neighbor for a while, often came to sit by his fire, twitch quizzical eyebrows at him—to note later in his diary, "It is my guess that if the General had to lose a leg, he'd rather lose the one he has than the one he hasn't!" Elihu Root, Mark Hanna were his political cronies. With George Francis Train and Charles D. Warner he loved to sit sunning himself on a bench in Washington Square, arguing the case of classic English against the vogue for American folk speech. Roland Hinton Perry—later to be ranked an Old Master—painted his portrait. The Vanderbilts, from year to year, reserved a chair for him in their box at the opera. Even the reactionary press, the former Copperheads, renegade Democrats, Plunderbund Republicans who once virulently attacked him at every disputed point in his career—his efforts to raise United States Volunteers, his saving change of front at Gettysburg, his welfare measures for the poor whites and Negroes during his military governorship of the Carolinas, his vigorous diplomacy as minister to Spain—forgot their past asperity toward him. His daily late afternoon walk up the Fifth Avenue he loved was a promenade of greetings as courteously exchanged with newsy and bootblack as with the passing financier, lady of fashion. And in course of time he who had been known to Paris as the "Yankee King of Spain" came to be known to all New York simply as "the General"—an institution, the living reminder of a past few remembered save as children.

But amid all this—true to his favorite quotation (from "The Lady of Lyons"), "It is astonishing how I like a man after I've fought with him!"—the friend he counted dearest was the man he once had battled most fiercely—that mystical, magnanimous, scientific man of war, Longstreet. Nothing at the time could have so symbolized the reunion of North and South, the spirit of chivalry pervading the conflict itself, as the virtual adoration of these two old opposing commanders for each other. It was to Sickles that Longstreet, impoverished and broken in health, owed his timely appointment as commissioner of railroads. And if anything could exceed the grace of Longstreet's defense of Sickles's action at Gettysburg, it was Sickles's defense of Longstreet's action on the same occasion. Invited to attend the dedication of General Slocum's monument, the venerable Confederate wrote:

MY DEAR GENERAL SICKLES:

My plan and desire was to meet you at Gettysburg. . . . But today I find myself in no condition to keep the promise made you—for I am unable to stand more than a minute or two at a time. Please express my sincere regrets to the noble Army of the Potomac, and accept them especially for yourself.

On that field you made a mark that will place you prominently before the world as one of the leading figures of the most important battle of the Civil War. As a Northern veteran once remarked to me, "General Sickles can well afford to leave a leg on that field."

I believe that it is now conceded that the advanced position at the Peach Orchard, taken by your corps and under your orders, saved that battlefield to the Union cause. It was the sorest and saddest reflection of my life for many years; but today I can say with sincerest emotion that it was and is the best that could have come to us all, North and South, and I hope that the Nation, reunited, may always enjoy the honor and glory brought to it by that grand action.

Always yours sincerely,
JAMES LONGSTREET*

One likes to think of these two in their sturdy, gnarled seventies—as contemporaries reported them—the guests of honor at a banquet in Charleston, the deaf Longstreet leaning on the shoulder of the crippled Sickles the better to hear his after-dinner speech, and then himself singing—in good voice too!—"The Star-Spangled Banner" . . . or after a St. Patrick's Day celebration at Atlanta, both somewhat mellowed, alternately seeing each other home, Longstreet insisting at the door of his hotel, "Sickles, you're a cripple, and I can't let you be on these dark streets alone. I'll go back with you!" and Sickles insisting at the door of his hotel, "Old fellow, you're deaf, and you might get run over by a hack. I'll go back with you!" and, with nips of Irish at each end to sustain them, weaving arm in arm their gossiping way along rickety board sidewalks . . . or climbing Round Top together, the less active Longstreet dependent on his friend's one-legged aid, chuckling, "Yes suh—you ought to help me up now, seeing the way you kept me from getting up here in '63!"

And when in 1904, just after Longstreet died, Helen, his young

*Published in *Lee and Longstreet at High Tide*, by Helen D. Longstreet.

wife—a vivacious southern schoolgirl when she married him in 1897—completed her *Lee and Longstreet at High Tide* in answer to the belated attacks leveled against him on the score of dilatory response to Lee's orders at Gettysburg, Sickles came to her aid; and in a masterful introduction, written as one "with personal knowledge of the battle," completely annihilated the critics. In the course of it he paid noble tribute to the friend who "in folding up forever the Confederate flag he had followed with such supreme devotion, and thenceforth saluting the Stars and Stripes with unfaltering homage, had set an example that was the rainbow of reconciliation between the North and South." Never before in military history had the vanquished so defended the victor, the victor the vanquished.

Surrounded by friends, yet lonely for his family, the General in 1900 was greatly heartened by the visit of his son and daughter—last seen only as tiny children. Taking a suite for them at the Waldorf, and placing a carriage at their disposal, he lavished upon them a fatherly if belated affection. His pride in them was as obvious as it was poignant. In the quarter century past, Stanton, a tall, disdainful fellow, and the youngest attaché in diplomacy, had married the Comtesse Ysabel Napoleon Magne, daughter of the prominent French banker, Leonard Brocheton, and godchild of Queen Isabella. And Eda, engaging as she was lovely, with much of the Van Sicklen energy of spirit—that later was to bring her death as a nurse at the front during World War I—had become the wife of the British diplomat, the Hon. Dayrell Crackanthorpe. For the aging builder of monuments, it was the last taste of family joys.

It had happened that, soon after his return to New York, the General had found in Miss Eleanor Earle Wilmerding—a middle-aged spinster of respectable family—a highly competent housekeeper. Appreciating her fully, he had paid her liberally, treated her with marked consideration. And as, with the passing decades, he became more and more dependent upon her, she in turn had become—with an ever increasing jealous possessiveness—more and more devoted to him. That the General was a great trial to his feminine manager there can be no doubt. If the emphasis of his life had changed, his old amorousness had not! But while his many, varied—and sometimes scandalous—affairs chagrined and shocked her, she tartly resented any criticism of him on the part of others. Her chief concern for him, as the years went by, was on the score of his finances. As gradually she was compelled to assume some supervision of his accounts, her thrifty good sense was horrified by his mounting extravagance. Yet she had not the heart to rebuke or deny him.

Generous, of course, the General always had been; but in his last years generosity turned to wild largesse. Needy sycophants panhandled him unmercifully. To his door every Sunday gathered a throng of veterans to receive his bounty—usually a five-dollar gold piece to each! And as his lifelong orderliness and acumen in financial matters began to desert him, and his investments turned awry, his always abundant liberality toward his mistresses took on an oriental tinge. Nothing they could ask of him was refused. His bills for the feminine were enormous—the florists', the vintners', the couturiers'. And the great bureau in his bedroom was stuffed with exotic perfumes, intriguing jewelry culled here and there reckless of cost—even imported silk hosiery, embroidered Parisian lingerie—that he never might find himself, at a critical moment, lacking some graceful gift of allure for the coy, or of gallantry to the willingly seduced. And the Princess Parlaghy—the painter of his last portrait, and his own last infatuation—had but whimsically to express a passing wish for a lion cub, to find herself promptly presented—at a cost of some thousand dollars—with a litter of six!

Inevitably came the crash. At the age of ninety-two, almost blind, mentally failing, confined to a wheel chair, he was charged with defalcation in the funds of his own cherished Monument Commission and arrested by his successor in the office he once briefly had held—the sheriff of New York!

Miss Wilmerding fought the officers, screamed, "It's a lie!" The sheriff apologized. Friends followed him to jail, instantly bailed him out. On every corner the newsies were shouting, "The General arrested! General Sickles goes to jail!" And overnight from North and South alike came a burst of protest, a shower of wires, bales of letters, sizzling with indignation, proffering assistance. Helen Longstreet followed a telegram of passionate concern with an eloquent letter to the press appealing for suspended judgment, public generosity to him who had been so unfailingly generous. An unknown admirer, a Mr. William Dodge, of Ohio, wrote offering to take the General's note for the entire deficit—some twenty-five thousand dollars. Contributions from posts, Blue and Gray, poured in. And what gave a touch of pathetic drama to the incident—Caroline, after thirty-seven years of absence, silence, hearing of her husband's difficulties, arrived by the earliest boat in New York, bringing her rich heirloom jewelry to offer in pawn for the payment of the default. Somehow, from a hundred sources, in a torrent of public sympathy and endorsement, the General's confused misplacement of funds was made good. Bewildered, he could only understand that once more he was vindicated —and by a world of friends!

CHAPTER XXXIV

Taps—Muted

———————◆———————

SHRUNKEN, wearing an eyeshade, the General came to his last reunion in a wheel chair pushed by Frazier Moseley, his old Negro valet, and attended by the ever faithful Miss Wilmerding. He made no speech, but from the porch of the Rogers house, not pistol shot from the spot where shrapnel had shattered his leg exactly fifty years before, he watched the events of the three-day celebration. The proprietor of the Gettysburg Hotel had reserved quarters for him and had installed a special elevator for his convenience. But stubbornly the old General insisted on "bunking with the boys," and spent his nights on a cot in a tent occupied by "Joe" Twichell, formerly the chaplain of the Excelsior Brigade, and now the Reverend Joseph Twichell—the most popular spiritual parent Yale had ever had. A man of great love, much beloved, "Joe"—as everyone, even the undergrads, called him—had been close beside the General in every engagement, had held him in his arms when wounded, had given him, through fifty-two years, an adoration fervent and unfailing. For both it was the last reunion; and, even in their waning strength, they talked, rather than slept, the nights away.

At the end of the third day—when Woodrow Wilson had spoken and departed, and the survivors of Pickett's Brigade, tottering, stum-

GENERAL SICKLES AT THE AGE OF NINETY

GENERAL SICKLES WITH HIS STAFF
AT GETTYSBURG IN 1909

bling, but determined still, had made a ghostly rehearsal of their historic charge across the upland to embrace the waiting Blues at the wall, and the ceremonies had closed—a troop of white-bearded Grays stormed the steps of the Rogers house and, lifting the General on their shoulders, carried him out to receive the last salutes of the Confederate detachments trooping homeward. As they redeposited him, with farewell handshakes all around, he whispered to Helen Longstreet—then a correspondent for the Southern press, hovering near all day, "How Jim would have loved all this!" Then, turning away to the sundown, "Never mind, old fellow, soon I'll be with you—where conflicts cease and friendship is eternal!"

And when, at length, the field was empty, the General had himself wheeled about awhile, wistful for a last look at his beloved monuments—the lordly Empire State monolith with its surmounting figure of Victory; the cupola of the Excelsior Brigade memorial, the bold statues of Greene and Slocum, Hancock and Reynolds, and, circling about them, the memorials of the eighty-five New York regiments and batteries, many of them under his own command, that had served and suffered with him that day—could it be half a century ago? Suddenly Twichell, walking beside him, exclaimed, "Dan, I never realized it before, but in all this there's no monument to you, only that plaque on the pediment of the state shaft!" With the fleeting sweetness that was as much a part of him as his crusty dynamism and determination, the General smiled up at him. "Never mind, Joe— all this is monument enough, isn't it?"

Six months later, fatally stricken, Miss Wilmerding ceased from shepherding her fiercely loved but unruly charge. In the interval she had been the cause of a new breach between the General and his wife. Dismayed and disgusted at finding her husband apparently in the clutches of his housekeeper, Caroline had endeavored to assume command of the household. But the woman who had served the General with all devotion for thirty years was in no mind to stand aside before this deathbed appearance of a haughty absentee wife much concerned, apparently, with matters of inheritance. Imperiously Caroline had demanded Miss Wilmerding's dismissal. With a last flash of his old gusty anger, the General had refused. And Caroline, barred from the house, had withdrawn to her suite at the St. Regis Hotel—there to await the obviously imminent end. Stanton, bitterly critical of his father, had hastened overseas to reinforce his mother's claims. And with one stroke of the old paw, the General had laid him out—dismissing him with battlefield peremptoriness and cutting his share in a mythical inheritance to one dollar!

But now, at last, the doors were unbarred. Silently Caroline assumed charge of the house and its patient. The General's heroic vitality was ebbing fast. In his vast loneliness often he called for his young grandson and namesake, Daniel Edgar. Only once, for a few days, had he met him—when in 1910 Stanton had brought him on a brief visit to New York. And the old General, finding this young Daniel a slender, breedy boy full of high spirits, spontaneous affection, had loved him on sight. Now he wrote him a note of remembrance, tinged alike with pathos and prophecy:

My dear Dan, your old grandpa is very ill; he would like to see you once more. I see big clouds in Europe. The Emperor Wilhelm II is a little Bismarck. I predict war, a big war in the near future, but I will not see it. Please ask your mother to send you over to see me.

It was April 1914. Prescient to the end!

Burglars long ago had rifled his safe, stolen his medals, and—more important—his memoirs. Apart from that little grandson overseas, nothing was left to him now but this foreclosed house, this stranger-wife, stranger-son—cold pity in the eyes of the one, cold scorn in the eyes of the other. Ghosts surrounded him . . . the fainting cloud of friends . . . the lost comrades of the battlefield . . . the streaming covey of women he had kissed and never known . . . Isabella's jolly face grown oddly dim . . . the sudden vivid image of her whose name had not crossed his lips since that night of mortal pain fifty-five years ago. . . .

A vast sense of emptiness seized him. He who had never lost—had he lost everything? Had he fought a bootless fight? But had he? A trembling hand sought the sheaf of embossed parchments he now kept close at his side. He could not read them, but he knew what they said—"Colonel . . . Brigadier General . . . Major General . . . Envoy and Minister Plenipotentiary . . . Congressional Medal of Honor . . . Grand Croix de la Légion d'Honneur."

The old hand gripped the parchments convulsively, went rigid. The General, unanswered, had ceased to care.

BIBLIOGRAPHY

Adams, James Truslow, EPIC OF AMERICA. (Little, Brown & Co., 1931)

Ames, Mary Clemmer, TEN YEARS IN WASHINGTON. (Queen City Co., 1873)

Bache, R. M., LIFE OF GENERAL GEORGE GORDON MEADE. (Henry T. Coates & Co., 1897)

BATTLES AND LEADERS OF THE CIVIL WAR, 3 vols.

Beard, Charles A. and Mary R., THE RISE OF AMERICAN CIVILIZATION. (MacMillan, 1937)

Bigelow, Major John, Jr., THE CAMPAIGN OF CHANCELLORSVILLE. (N. Y.)

Bismarck, BISMARCK'S AUTOBIOGRAPHY, 2 vols. (Harper & Bros., 1899)

Blake, E. Vale, THE HISTORY OF THE TAMMANY SOCIETY. (Souvenir Publishing Co., 1901)

Blake, William, THE COPPERHEADS. (Dial Press, 1941)

Bradford, Gamaliel, DAMAGED SOULS. (Houghton Mifflin, 1923)

Clay, Mrs. Clement, A BELLE OF THE FIFTIES. (Doubleday, Page, 1928)

Coles, Arthur Charles, THE IRREPRESSIBLE CONFLICT. (Macmillan, 1934)

Curtis, George T., THE LIFE OF JAMES BUCHANAN. (Harper, 1883)

Dark, Sidney, PARIS. (Macmillan, 1926)

Daudet, Alphonse, TRENTE ANS DE PARIS. (Paris, 1872)

DeWitt, SPECIAL REPORT ON HON. DANIEL E. SICKLES TRIAL. (1859)

Dictionary of American Biography.

Dictionary of National Biography.

Doubleday, Abner, CHANCELLORSVILLE AND GETTYSBURG. (Scribner, 1890)

Dudley, Dean, OFFICERS OF THE UNION ARMY AND NAVY. (L. Prang, 1862)

Earland, Ada, JOHN OPIE AND HIS CIRCLE. (Hutchinson & Co., 1911)

Emerson, Edwin, THE HISTORY OF THE NINETEENTH CENTURY, 4 vols. (P. F. Collier's Son, 1901)

Fiske, Stephen, OFF-HAND PORTRAITS OF PROMINENT NEW YORKERS. (George R. Lockwood & Son, 1884)

Flower, Frank A., EDWIN McMASTERS STANTON. (Saalfield Publishing Co., 1905)

Goodrich, S. G., A PICTORIAL GEOGRAPHY OF THE WORLD. (University Press, Cambridge, 1840)

Graham, John, OPENING SPEECH TO THE JURY, SICKLES' TRIAL, 1859

Grant, Ulysses S., PERSONAL MEMOIRS. (Charles L. Webster, 1894)

Hale, Edward Everett, JAMES RUSSELL AND HIS FRIENDS. (Houghton Mifflin & Co., 1899)

Halevy, Ludovic, L'INVASION. (Paris, 1887)

Hertz, Emanuel, THE HIDDEN LINCOLN. (N. Y., 1938)

Higgin, L., SPANISH LIFE. (G. P. Putnam's Sons, 1904)

Hone, Philip, THE DIARY OF PHILIP HONE. (Dodd, Mead & Co., 1889)

Huddleston, Sisley, PARIS SALONS, CAFES, STUDIOS. (Lippincott, 1928)

Hutton, E., CITIES OF SPAIN. (Methuen & Co., 1906)

Jackson, Mary Anna, MEMOIRS OF STONEWALL JACKSON. (The Prentice Press, 1895)

Johnson, Rossiter, CAMPFIRE AND BATTLEFIELD, 3 vols. (Knight and Brown, 1867)

Junkin, D. X., THE LIFE OF W. S. HANCOCK. (D. Appleton & Co., 1880)

Keim, DeB. Randolph, SHERMAN. (1904)

Lansdale, Maria Horner, PARIS. (Paris, 1901)

Latimer, Elizabeth W., SPAIN IN THE NINETEENTH CENTURY. (A. C. McClurg, 1897)

Leech, Margaret, REVEILLE IN WASHINGTON. (Harper, 1941)

Leiding, Harriette Kershaw, CHARLESTON HISTORICAL AND ROMANTIC. (Lippincott, 1931)

LeGoff, François, LOUIS ADOLPHE THIERS. (G. P. Putnam's Sons, 1879)

Longstreet, Helen D., LEE AND LONGSTREET AT HIGH TIDE. (1905)

Lossing, Benson J., OUR COUNTRY. (Jones and Stanley)

Lowe, Charles, PRINCE BISMARCK, 2 vols. (Cassell & Co., 1887. London)

McCabe, James D., THE LIFE AND CAMPAIGNS OF GENERAL ROBERT E. LEE. (National Publishers, 1868)

McCLELLAN'S REPORT AND CAMPAIGNS. (Sheldon & Co., 1868)

McCLELLAN'S OWN STORY. (Charles L. Webster & Co., 1887)

MEN OF AFFAIRS IN NEW YORK. (L. R. Hamersly & Co., 1906)

"Miles," CAMPAIGN OF GETTYSBURG. (Small, Maynard & Co., 1912)

Minnigerode, Meade, FABULOUS FORTIES. (G. P. Putnam's Sons, 1924)

Muzzey, D. S., THE AMERICAN PEOPLE. (Ginn & Co., 1933)

Myers, Gustavus, TAMMANY HALL. (Boni & Liveright, 1917)

Nicolay, John G., and John Hay, ABRAHAM LINCOLN: A HISTORY. (Century, 1890)

Official Publications:

Adjutant General's Report, State of New York, 3 vols.

Bulletin Third Army Corps Society

Fiftieth Celebration New York, Veterans Gettysburg. (J. B. Lyon, 1902)

Gettysburg National Military Parks Commissions, 1893–1904

Greene and His New York Troops at Gettysburg. (J. B. Lyon, 1909)

Lincoln Fellowship, address of Major-General Dan Sickles, 1900

New York at Gettysburg, 3 vols., Report
Slocum and His Men, N. Y. Monuments Commission. (J. B. Lyon, 1904)
Soldiers National Cemetery Gettysburg. (Singerly & Myers, 1864)
Trinity Church Report

Paris, Comte de, HISTORY OF THE CIVIL WAR, 3 vols. (Porter & Coates, 1888)
Partridge, Bellamy, COUNTRY DOCTOR. (McGraw-Hill Book Co., 1939)
Partridge, Bellamy, BIG FAMILY. (McGraw-Hill Book Co., 1941)
Poore, Ben: Perley, PERLEY'S REMINISCENCES, 2 vols. (Hubbard Bros., Philadelphia, 1886)
Proctor, Lucien B., LIVES OF EMINENT LAWYERS OF NEW YORK, 2 vols. (S. S. Peloulet & Co., 1882)
Reynolds, John S., RECONSTRUCTION IN SOUTH CAROLINA, 1865–1877. (Columbia, S. C., 1905)
Rusling, James Fowler, LINCOLN AND SICKLES. (Third Army Corps Reunion, 1910)
Sandburg, Carl, ABRAHAM LINCOLN, 4 vols. (Harcourt Brace, 1939)
Sandburg, Carl, MARY LINCOLN, WIFE AND WIDOW. (Harcourt Brace, 1932)
Seymour, A. B., SEYMOUR'S REMINISCENCES. (A. B. Seymour, c. 1893)
Sprenger, George F., HISTORY OF THE 122ND REGIMENT, vol. 1. (New Era Steam Boat Printers, 1885)
Stine, J. H., THE HISTORY OF THE ARMY OF THE POTOMAC. (J. B. Rodgers Printing Co., 1892)
Stoltz, Charles, THE TRAGIC CAREER OF MARY TODD LINCOLN. (Round Table, 1931)
Taine, H., NOTES ON PARIS. (John F. Trow & Sons, 1875)
Tarbell, Ida M., LIFE OF LINCOLN, 2 vols. (McClure, Philips, 1900)
Taylor, E. G., GOUVERNEUR KEMBLE WARREN. (Houghton Mifflin, 1932)
Twain, Mark, WORKS OF MARK TWAIN, AUTOBIOGRAPHY, 2 vols. (Gabriel Wells, 1925)
Vanderslice, J. M., GETTYSBURG THEN AND NOW. (G. W. Dillingham, 1897)
Washington, John E., THEY KNEW LINCOLN. (E. P. Dutton & Co., 1942)
Werner, M. R., TAMMANY HALL. (Doubleday, Doran & Co., 1928)
Whitehouse, H. Remsen, THE SACRIFICE OF A THRONE. (Bonnell, Silver, 1897)
Woodward, W. E., A NEW AMERICAN HISTORY. (Garden City, 1938)
Young, Jesse Bowman, THE BATTLE OF GETTYSBURG. (Harper, 1913)

Periodicals and Newspapers

Godey's Lady's Book, 1850–54
Harper's Magazine, 1859
Harper's Pictorial History of the Great Rebellion, Nos. 16, 18, 20, 22, 35
New York Herald, 1859, 1861–64, 1867, 1887
New York Times, 1859, 1900, 1914

New York Tribune, 1867, 1890, 1904, 1910
Washington Daily Globe, 1859–63
Washington Star, 1865–67

Manuscripts

"Leaves from My Diary," Daniel E. Sickles in The Journal of the Military
    Service Institution of the U.S., 1885, Vol. VI
Daniel E. Sickles Papers, Manuscripts in N.Y. Public Library
Diary and Archives of Daniel E. Sickles—PRIVATE SOURCE

Index

Index